THE CHANNEL ISLANDS IN THE GREAT WAR

About the Author

Stephen is a retired Police officer having served with Essex Police as a constable for thirty years between 1983 and 2013. He is married to Tanya who is also his writing partner.

Stephen's sons, Luke and Ross, were members of the armed forces, collectively serving five tours of Afghanistan between 2008 and 2013. Both were injured on their first tour which led to his first book, *Two Sons in a Warzone – Afghanistan: The True Story of a Father's Conflict*, which was published in October 2010.

Both of Stephen's grandfathers served during, and survived, the First World War, one with the Royal Irish Rifles, the other in the Mercantile Marine, whilst his father was a member of the Royal Army Ordnance Corps during the Second World War.

Stephen collaborated with one of his writing partners, Ken Porter, on a book published in August 2012, *German POW Camp 266 – Langdon Hills* which spent six weeks as the number one best-selling book in Waterstones, Basildon between March and April 2013. They have also collaborated on four books in the Towns and Cities in the Great War series by Pen and Sword. Stephen has also written other titles for the same series of books and in February 2017, *The Surrender of Singapore – Three Years of Hell 1942-45*, was published. In addition he has written three crime thrillers, published between 2010 and 2012, which centre around a fictional detective named Terry Danvers.

When they are not writing, Stephen and Tanya enjoy walking their four German Shepherd dogs early each morning when most sensible people are still asleep.

THE CHANNEL ISLANDS IN THE GREAT WAR

STEPHEN WYNN

Pen & Sword
MILITARY

First published in Great Britain in 2019 by
Pen & Sword Military
An imprint of
Pen & Sword Books Limited
Yorkshire - Philadelphia

ISBN 978 1 78346 3 305

A CIP catalogue record for this book is available from the British Library

Printed and bound in the UK
by TJ International, Padstow, Cornwall

Pen & Sword Books Limited incorporates the imprints of Atlas,
Archaeology, Aviation, Discovery, Family History, Fiction, History, Maritime,
Military, Military Classics, Politics, Select, Transport, True Crime, Air World,
Frontline Publishing, Leo Cooper, Remember When, Seaforth Publishing,
The Praetorian Press, Wharncliffe Local History, Wharncliffe Transport,
Wharncliffe True Crime and White Owl.

For a complete list of Pen & Sword titles please contact
PEN & SWORD BOOKS LIMITED
47 Church Street, Barnsley, South Yorkshire S70 2AS, United Kingdom
E-mail: enquiries@pen-and-sword.co.uk
Website: www.pen-and-sword.co.uk

Or
PEN AND SWORD BOOKS
1950 Lawrence Rd, Havertown, PA 19083, USA
E-mail: Uspen-and-sword@casematepublishers.com
Website: www.penandswordbooks.com

Contents

Introduction

The Channel Islands are made up of a total of twenty separate islands or islets, of which only seven are permanently inhabited. The main two, which also have the largest populations, are Jersey, with a population of 100,000, followed by Guernsey, which has 63,000 residents. Then comes Alderney, with 2,000, and Sark with just 600. The three other islands are Herm, Jethou and Brecqhou.

Geographically the islands are much closer to mainland France than they are to England and they have not always been under British sovereignty. The remnants of the ancient Duchy of Normandy, they are not part of the United Kingdom but Crown Dependencies, self-governing possessions of the British Crown. As such the people of the islands are British citizens by right but British Acts of Parliament do not automatically extend to the islands as law. This can only take place by what is known as an Order of Council, and then only after consultation with the individual islands' primary legislature, known as the States which governs each of the islands.

When the United Kingdom chose to join the European Economic Community on 1 January 1973, the Channel Islands did not follow suit, choosing instead to remain outside.

It is well documented that the Channel Islands were occupied during the Second World War by some 10,000 invading German soldiers, but what is not so widely known is that there were also German soldiers in the Channel Islands during the First World War as hundreds of prisoners of war. The camp which housed these men was situated at Les Blanches Banques on the island of Jersey.

During the First World War, many men from the islands left for England and served with numerous regiments of the British Army, whilst others enlisted closer to home with local units such as the Royal Guernsey Light Infantry and the Royal Guernsey Artillery. Men from Sark and Alderney are also included in this equation. The sacrifice made by the Channel Islands in the First World War, wasn't just down to the men from the bigger and possibly better-known islands of Guernsey and Jersey.

Approximately 3,000 men from Guernsey served in the military during the First World War, with an estimated 1,500, or 50 per cent of them, not returning home after the war. Some 1,000 of the Guernsey men who served, did so with the Royal Guernsey Light Infantry.

Regardless of which regiment or corps men enlisted in, approximately 6,000 of them left the Island of Jersey during the First World War to join the military, and of those, an estimated 862, or 14.5 per cent of them, never returned. So many families lost loved ones that they would never see again, sons, husbands, uncles, cousins, nephews, brothers and fathers. For many, all they had left to remember their loved ones by, was a faded photograph or a name on a roll of honour or war memorial. For those who died on the battlefields of Europe, most were buried close to where they had been killed or died of wounds, there to lie for evermore. Those whose bodies were never found had no grave, only their name on one of the many memorials that adorn the French and Belgian countryside. If a man was wounded and sent back to the UK and then subsequently died of his wounds, there was no guarantee that his body would be sent back to his home. It was usual practice that he would be buried in a cemetery or churchyard near to the medical facility where he died.

None of the Channel Islands were occupied by the Germans during the First World War, although it was thought a possibility during the earlier stages of the fighting, but thankfully that did not happen.

The Royal Militia of the Island of Jersey was officially formed in 1337, although a militia force had been in existence on the island prior to this, as a result of an order issued on 24 July 1203, by King John of England, who reigned between 6 April 1199 and his death on 19 October 1216. The order instructed the local authorities to provide a *sufficiency of men and money to defend the island from the enemy.*

In 1905 the militia in Jersey was reorganised to create an artillery regiment of two field companies and a further two garrison companies, along with an engineering company, a medical company and three infantry battalions.

In 1915 one of the companies of the Jersey Militia was sent off to become part of the 7th (Service) Battalion, Royal Irish Rifles, although the militia itself remained as an organisation in Jersey throughout the years of the war.

CHAPTER ONE

1914 – Starting Out

The outbreak of hostilities of the First World War was one of the world's worst kept secrets, as it had been brewing throughout the early years of the twentieth century. Initially there was shock, surprise and disruption. People were worried, those who had savings in particular. There was panic buying in the shops and men quickly started to leave the islands in large numbers, some to France but most to England to enlist.

With the islands being the closest part of Great Britain to the French coast and easily accessible from the English Channel, they faced the most realistic threat of a German attack or invasion, especially in the early stages of the war. Thankfully such worries and concerns were short lived and normality, or what passed for normality in such times, quickly returned.

Once the fighting had begun in earnest, the Channel Islands certainly did their bit for the British Empire. According to figures compiled from the Commonwealth War Graves website, British and Commonwealth losses during the first five months of the war, August to December 1914, totalled 42,219. Of these, at least twenty-six were from Guernsey, forty-six from Jersey, and two were from Alderney. These figures are derived from the above website, and are therefore only as good, and accurate as the information that was originally entered for each man.

It is interesting to see the different regiments, corps and units, with which men from the Channel Islands served during those first five months of the war:

Royal Navy, Mercantile Marine, Bedfordshire Regiment, South Wales Borderers, Manchester Regiment, Dorsetshire Regiment, Coldstream Guards, East Surrey Regiment, Devonshire Regiment, Royal Marine Light Infantry, Northamptonshire Regiment, Highland Light Infantry, The Buffs (East Kent Regiment), 4th Dragoon Guards, Gloucestershire Regiment, Royal Marine Artillery, King's Own (Royal Lancaster Regiment), Irish Guards, 59th Scinde Rifles (Frontier Force), South Staffordshire Regiment, Norfolk Regiment, Royal Irish Regiment, Welsh Regiment, Royal Garrison Artillery, Queen's Own (Royal West Kent Regiment), Leinster Regiment, Leicestershire Regiment, Royal Sussex Regiment, East African Mounted Rifles, Royal Munster Fusiliers.

A theme of the First World War, throughout towns and villages of Great Britain, were civilian Volunteer Corps. The problem with this in the early stages of the war, was a lack of co-ordination. Although well intentioned in their formation, often led by retired Army officers, there was a concern from Government that some men would see joining one of these unofficial corps, as a way of attempting to avoid taking up military service and did not initially support their introduction. Despite their initial trepidation, there was an overwhelming desire by men up and down the country who were either too old, or not fit enough for wartime military service, to do their bit in their country's time of need. Add to this the real worry and concern in both Great Britain and the Channel Islands of an invasion and it was easy to see how and why these corps sprung up.

Such was the combined enthusiasm for these Volunteer Corps, that in September 1914 a central committee was formed to oversee their running, and on 19 November 1914 it was renamed the Central Association of Volunteer Training Corps and recognised by the War Office. Guernsey was on board with the idea and had her own Volunteer Corps up and running in the early months of the war. Their overall intention was to be able to assist the military authorities should the occasion arise, so to this end they were trained in military duties. Men of the corps had to purchase their own uniforms, which could not be khaki green in colour, and they had to wear a red coloured arm band, with the letters GR (*Georgius Rex*) emblazoned on it.

With the introduction of conscription, brought in by the British Government in March 1916, came Military Service Tribunals, bodies that were formed to listen to men who had applied for exemption from having to undergo military service. One of the outcomes these bodies could find, was to make an order that an applicant would join their local Voluntary Training Corps (VTC) in lieu of undertaking military service. By the end of the war, 110,000 men had ended up in the VTC via this particular route.

In the first month of the war, August, there were fifteen major battles, only two of which saw British involvement. The Battle of Mons which took place on 23 August 1914, was the first major action that the men of the British Expeditionary Force had seen, when they attempted to hold back forces of the German First Army, at the Mons-Condé Canal. Despite being in relatively strong defensive positions, which were greatly assisted by a canal separating them from their attackers, a spirited defence of their position, and inflicting heavy casualties on their German attackers with rifle and machine-gun fire, they eventually had to retreat due to overwhelming enemy numbers, and the sudden exposure of their right flank, when troops of the French Fifth Army, inexplicably retreated.

The battle saw the death of Guernseyman Private (4834) Patrick John **Ryan** of the 2nd Battalion, Royal Irish Regiment. A married man, he lived with his wife at 1 Cliff Terrace, St Peter Port, Guernsey. He has no known grave, but his name is commemorated on the La Ferté-Sous-Jouarre Memorial, in the Seine-et-Marne region of France.

Soldiers resting up after Battle of Mons.

Three days later, on 26 August 1914, during the Allied retreat from Mons, came the Battle of Le Cateau. But this was totally different from the Battle of Mons. The real damage here wasn't so much down to rifles and machine guns, but artillery.

By the end of the day the battle was over, and the British and French forces, under the command of General Sir Horace Smith-Dorrien, had suffered nearly 8,000 casualties which included 2,600 men who were captured and a further 700 who had been killed. Of these, 36-year-old Company Serjeant-Major (5811) William Sharp, a Scotsman by birth, who was serving with C Company, 1st Battalion, King's Own (Royal Lancaster Regiment), lived in Jersey. He had initially been reported as missing in action, with the hope that he had been captured by the Germans and taken as a prisoner of war, but sadly, it was not to be.

He had enlisted in the army for twelve years, on 14 October 1898, and served in the Second Boer War, arriving in Natal, South Africa, on 30 December 1899. He had been stationed at Fort Regent in Jersey and is recorded as being there in the 1911 Channel Island Census. William Sharp married Lydia Maud Jolin on 1 June 1911 at St James Parish Church, Jersey. Their witnesses were Mr Albert Allen and Miss Doris Orment. At the time of his death, the family home was at 6 Roseville Street, St Helier, although Lydia, would later move to 2 Torque Villas, Lewis Street, St Helier. The 1911 Channel Island Census, showed Lydia, living with her 72-year-old widowed mother, Martha, at the unusually numbered, thirty-one-and-a-half,

Green Street, Jersey. Lydia, later married Laurence George Rowe, and they went on to live at 18 New St John's Road in St Helier.

September saw no respite from the fighting with a further seven major battles taking place. The first to involve British forces was the Battle of the Marne, between September 6 and 12, which was a counter-attack by French and British forces as the Germans approached the eastern outskirts of Paris at the River Marne near Brasles. It was predominantly a French – German affair with the French pitting thirty-nine of their divisions against twenty-seven German ones. Britain's support came in the shape of just six divisions. This was reflected in the number of casualties each side sustained. France suffered an estimated 85,000, killed, wounded and missing, whilst Germany suffered 67,700 and Britain, 1,701.

This was immediately followed by the First Battle of the Aisne which took place between 13 and 28 September 1914 and left the British with 13,541 men killed or wounded.

Corporal (8877) William Edward Walsh, of the 2nd Battalion, Welsh Regiment, first arrived in France on 13 August 1914, as part of one of the earliest units of the British Expeditionary Force. Sadly, his war was not destined to last long, as he was killed in action on 14 September 1914. He has no known grave, but his name is commemorated on the La Ferté-Sous-Jouarre Memorial in the Seine-et-Marne region of France.

His father Martin William Walsh, at one time lived at 1 Lower Cottages, Delaney Hill, St Sampson, Guernsey, but when that was is not clear.

In October 1914, there were a further five major battles, which included British involvement.

10 October – 2 November 1914 Battle of La Bassee
12 October – 2 November 1914 Battle of Messines
13 October – 2 November 1914 Battle of Armentières
16 – 31 October 1914 Battle of Yser (Naval support only)
19 October – 22 November 1914 1st Battle of Ypres

During the overall time frame of these battles, twelve men either from, or with, Jersey connections were killed, along with seven from Guernsey. But it wasn't just on the battlefields of France and Belgium where men from the Channel Islands were dying for king and country. A number of men met the same fate thousands of miles away from their homes and loved ones, off the coast of central Chile, close to the city of Coronel.

On 1 November 1914, the sea Battle of Coronel took place between the East Asia Squadron of the Imperial German Navy, under the command of Vice Admiral Maximilian Graf von Spee, and the British West Indies Squadron, under the command of Rear Admiral Sir Christopher Cradock.

What led to the Allied and German navies being in that part of the world at a time when most of the fighting was taking place on land throughout Europe, especially across France and Belgium? Early in the war, Allied warships had gained control of the previously held German colonies of, Kaiser-Wilhelmsland, Yap, Nauru and Samoa, islands that were dotted throughout different parts of the Pacific Ocean. With the imminent expectation of war with Japan, the German East Asia Squadron, had also abandoned their base at Tsingtao, China.

Rather than return to Germany, Spee took the decision to stay in the area and attack Allied merchant shipping, plying their trade along the west coast routes of South America. It had been guessed by those at the British Admiralty that this might be the course of action Spee had in mind, so the Fourth Cruiser Squadron under the command of Cradock was sent to the area of the Western Pacific Ocean to seek and destroy the German vessels. When the two squadrons did eventually meet, it was more likely down to chance rather than anything else, but once they came into contact with each other there was no avoiding what had to be done.

By the end of the battle Germany had secured a noted victory. All of their ships were intact and their total casualties, were just three wounded men. As for Cradock, he had lost two of his cruisers, HMS *Good Hope* and HMS *Monmouth*, along with the lives of 1,570 of his men.

Of those who lost their lives on board HMS *Good Hope* and HMS *Monmouth*, the following men were from the Channel Islands:

Leading Telegraphist (J/8529) Bertie Charles **Hockey**, (21) of HMS *Monmouth* was born in St Helier, Jersey. His name is commemorated on the Plymouth Naval Memorial.

Leading Seaman (208615) Clarence Gordon **Underhill**, was on board HMS *Good Hope*. He was the son of Henry and Esther Underhill, who lived at 10 Val Plaisant, St Helier, Jersey. His name is commemorated on the Portsmouth Naval Memorial.

Petty Officer 1st Class (155565) Alfred **Smith** (40) was serving on HMS *Good Hope*. He was a married man who lived with his wife, Edith, at Leap Cottage, Gorey Pier, Jersey. His name is commemorated on the Portsmouth Naval Memorial.

Bombardier (RMA/8476) Charles William **Poling**, (32) of the Royal Marine Artillery, with which he had served for a number of years, was part of the crew of HMS *Good Hope*. His name is recorded on both the 1901 and 1911 Census as a member of the Royal Marine Artillery. At the time of his death, and in the 1911 Census, he is shown as a married man, who lived with his wife, Emily, in Southsea, Portsmouth, but who was actually born in Colombo, Ceylon. His connection to the Channel Islands came from his parents who lived in Jersey. His name is commemorated on the Portsmouth Naval Memorial.

Stoker 2nd Class (K/21979) William Francis **Journeaux** (21) was on board HMS *Good Hope*. Before enlisting, he lived at 3 St Luke's Cottages,

Plaisance Road, Jersey, with his parents, Richard and Mary Journeaux, although the 1911 Census, shows William living with just his father, Richard, at Belverdere View, Bagot, Jersey. The 1901 Census, shows the family living at 6 L'Auvergne Lane, St Luke's, Jersey, and William as the youngest of six children, the five other siblings all being his sisters.

Shipwright 2nd Class (342455) Taussaint Marys **Marquer**, was born on 28 May 1879 in St Helier, Jersey, the youngest of three children born to Pierre and Marie Marquer. On 28 December 1899, when he was 20 years of age, he enlisted in the Royal Navy and joined the crew of HMS *Good Hope*. Before he enlisted he had earned his living as a carpenter, but by the time war broke out, he had been in the navy for nearly fifteen years. At the time of his death, he was living at 21 Union Street, Southsea, Portsmouth with his wife, Caroline. His mother, Marie, still lived in St Helens, Jersey. His name is commemorated on the Portsmouth Naval Memorial.

Able Seaman (203886) Harry Thomas **Wright** served on board HMS *Good Hope*. His wife, Mabel Annie Wright, lived at Columbus Street, St Helier, Jersey. He is also commemorated on the Portsmouth Naval Memorial.

Lance Serjeant (PO/11383) Stanley Roland **Saunders**, was in the Royal Marine Light Infantry serving on board HMS *Good Hope*. He was a married man, and after the war his widow, Ethel, was living in Fareham, Hampshire, whilst his mother, Mary, was living at St Helier, Jersey. He is also commemorated on the Portsmouth Naval Memorial.

Able Seaman (SS/1351) Edmund John **Le Page**, aged 26, was serving on board HMS *Good Hope*. His parents, Alfred and Maryann Le Page, lived at Cantraine, Catel, Guernsey, whilst after the war, his widow Elsie was living at Les Dunes, Catel, Guernsey. His name is commemorated on the Portsmouth Naval Memorial.

Stoker 1st Class (K/20426) Alfred John George **Solley**, aged 19, was lost with the sinking of HMS *Good Hope*. Prior to the outbreak of war, Arthur Solley, had lived with his mother, Nancy Solley, his elder sister, Annie, his younger brother, Cecil, and a cousin, Lilian, at 42 Pedvin Street, St Peter Port, Guernsey. The 1911 Census, records the family as living at 29 Pedvin Street. Alfred's name is commemorated on the Portsmouth Naval Memorial.

The *Good Hope* was engaged by the German armoured cruiser, *Scharnhorst* at 1904 hours, which quickly found her range, causing the *Good Hope* to lose her forward 9.2-inch turret, immediately putting her at a massive disadvantage. Undeterred, and with no thought of leaving the battle, she sped as fast as she could towards the German ships, knowing that her only chance of survival was to close the range between them, so that her own 6-inch guns could become effective. She was struck repeatedly by the shells from her German adversaries and, with fires breaking out all over the ship, she finally came to a halt, having been hit an estimated thirty-five times.

HMS Good Hope.

At 1950 hours a large explosion rocked the *Good Hope* as her forward magazine exploded with such force, that it ripped off the bow, causing her to sink with the loss of her entire crew, some 919 officers and crew.

Stoker 2nd Class Thomas **Long** at 18 years of age, was the youngest of the Channel Islanders to die that day on board HMS *Monmouth*. Born in Guernsey, his parents, were living at 2 Catherine Street, Plymouth, after the war. His name is commemorated on the Plymouth Naval Memorial.

The *Monmouth* was engaged at 1904 hours by the German armoured cruiser, *Gneisenau*, her accurate fire from 12,300 yards striking the *Monmouth* early on. This put the British ship at an immediate disadvantage only having 6.2-inch guns, which meant the *Gneisenau* was out of range of any fire power she could return. Despite fires raging on board *Monmouth* she bravely continued towards the *Gneisenau*, so as to reduce the distance between them so that she could return fire. At 1923 hours, another accurately fired shell from *Gneisenau*, struck the *Monmouth*, blowing the roof off her forward turret, causing yet another fire, which in turn led to an explosion of some of her ammunition.

By 2035 hours HMS *Monmouth* was showing a ten-degree list to port, but still refused to give up the fight. The list quickly worsened, rendering her

HMS Monmouth *at anchor.*

port side guns unusable as they were now partly under the water line, but still she would not yield. By now, the German light cruiser, *Nurnberg* had *Monmouth* in her sights, and was at a distance of just 600 yards, but rather than open fire on the clearly stricken vessel, she awaited her surrender. None was forthcoming, so she fired a warning shot, then a torpedo which thankfully for the *Monmouth* and her crew, missed. Rather than removing herself from the battle her captain, who must have known the potential danger he was placing himself, his crew and his ship in, increased her speed and made after the *Nurnberg*, leaving her with no option but to defend herself. Once again, her firing was accurate, striking the *Monmouth* at will. In the turbulent waters of the Pacific Ocean rescuing sailors from the sea was impossible. In Force 7 winds and high sea, HMS *Monmouth* capsized and sank at 2158 hours. Not one of her 735 officers or crew survived.

In that one battle, eleven men from the Channel Islands were killed in the space of just two hours. Eleven families had lost loved ones, never to be seen again with not even a grave where they could pay their respects.

The *Leeds Mercury* dated Monday, 3 August 1914, carried a photograph and an article, showing remnants of the 2nd Battalion, West Yorkshire Regiment leaving the Island of Guernsey where they had been stationed, on 2 August 1914, on board the British War Department Steamer *Sir Redvers Buller*. Their places were taken by men of the Guernsey Militia who had been fully mobilized.

Yet an article about the 2nd Battalion, West Yorkshire Regiment, which appears on the website www.wartimememoriesproject.com, states that when the war broke out in August 1914, 2nd Battalion, West Yorkshire Regiment was stationed in Malta, and that they arrived back in Southampton on

25 September 1914, where they became part of 23 Brigade, 8th Division, at Hursley Park, near Winchester.

On the morning of Friday, 14 August 1914, a soldier's body was discovered floating in St Peter Port Harbour, Guernsey. It was of a Private Tinsley, a reservist in the Yorkshire Regiment, who was from Huddersfield in West Yorkshire. The inquest into his death took place the following day, where it was heard that he had visited a cabaret on Thursday evening where he had drunk a pint of beer mixed with rum. On leaving the establishment he was heard to comment that he was now returning to his barracks. His body was discovered at first light with a wound to the head and his regimental cap was found on the steps of the pier. After all the available evidence had been heard, an open verdict was returned.

A check on the Commonwealth War Graves website found no record of anybody with the name Tinsley having died on the date in question. I carried out a similar check on the British Army's Medal Rolls index cards, for soldiers having served during the First World War, but found no record of anybody with the name of Tinsley having died on that date.

On 24 August 1914 a letter was sent out to newspaper groups by the Government Office in Guernsey, it read as follows.

> *To the Editor,*
> *Dear Sir,*
> *My attention has been called to a paragraph which has appeared in some newspapers, in which it is stated that something approaching a panic exists in Guernsey, and that there is only a fortnight's supply of food. As these statements are apt to be misleading, I shall be much obliged if you will contradict the same. There is no panic in Guernsey. Thanks to the system of compulsory service in the Militia, the island is amply provided for in the matter of defence, and as practically the whole manhood population is trained in arms, the force at present embodied can be trebled in a few hours.*
> *There is no scarcity of food or supplies. Communication with the mainland is open, and supplies are received daily. These are ample in the island to last for a considerable time and there is no danger of shortage. As to Herm, as the island is occupied by British troops, it cannot be cause for concern.*
> *Your obedient servant*
> *John Macartney*
> *Government Office, Guernsey.*

On Wednesday, 26 August 1914 the States Legislator of Guernsey voted to spend an additional £10,000 on the island's militia. The island's Lieutenant Governor stated that they had been mobilised on 30 July at full war strength, had been inspected and presented themselves as professionally as would be expected of such a fine body of men.

Conscription

The First World War was predominantly fought with millions of conscripted soldiers, men who were not full-time professional soldiers and who before the war had been living ordinary lives. The origins of conscription had been born of the French Revolution at the end of the eighteenth century and was simply the mass mobilisation of all male citizens. The premise of the day from a French perspective, was that all men had a duty to bear arms in defence of their nation when called upon to do so.

The 1911 Guernsey Census records that 1,005 French-born men were resident in Guernsey, many of whom were students studying at schools on the island, who would have been old enough to have been conscripted for war-time military service in the French Army.

In December 1914 a photograph appeared in some British newspapers of a group of men from the Royal Guernsey Light Infantry practising a bayonet charge across open ground. Although it was possibly quite romantic in its intention, it was also naïve, the reality of such a blatant act, possibly head first towards a German machine-gun position, would have meant certain annihilation. There was also a photograph of men of the Royal Guernsey Artillery practising as well, although their role was seen more as a defensive one in the event of a German invasion.

The final major battle of 1914 was the Battle of the Falkland Islands, fought between the Royal Navy and the Imperial German Navy on 8 December, which ended in a resounding British victory. In retribution for the sinking of Admiral Cradock's ships HMS *Good Hope* and HMS *Monmouth* at the Battle of Coronel, Vice Admiral Sir Frederick Doveton Sturdee's squadron sank six German ships including SMS *Scharnhorst* and *Gneisnau* with the loss of 1,871 of men against British losses of just ten killed and no ships lost.

December 1914 saw the loss of at least eleven men from the Channel Islands. Able Seaman (205253) Walter Henry **Lock**, aged 31, served aboard HM Submarine *D2* was, according to the Commonwealth War Graves Commission website, killed in action on 1 December 1914, when it was sunk by being rammed by a German patrol boat off Borkum in north-west Germany. All twenty-five of the crew, including Walter Lock, were killed and none of their bodies were recovered. Walter's parents, Edwin and Louisa Lock, lived in Jersey. He is commemorated on the Portsmouth Naval Memorial.

An article concerning the same incident, which appears on Wikipedia, has the date of the sinking as 25 November 1914, a week before.

The *D2*'s commanding officer, Lieutenant Commander Jameson, died two days before the submarine was sunk when he was washed overboard.

Private (935) George Edward **Male** was born in Guernsey in 1889, but in his late teens he joined the army and served in the 1st Battalion, Manchester Regiment. According to the 1911 Census he was still in the

HM Submarine D2.

Manchester Regiment and stationed in India. Like many of the regular soldiers of the BEF he was killed in action early in the war on 21 December 1914. He was buried in Béthune Town Cemetery, in the Pas de Calais region of France. His parents, Charles and Mathilda Male, lived at 2 Allendale Villas, Gibauderie, Guernsey.

Private (9209) F. **Bovin** of the 2nd Battalion, Devonshire Regiment, was killed in action on 17 December 1914, and is buried at the Aubers Ridge British Cemetery, Aubers, in the Nord Region of France.

Private (6662) Reginald Clifford **Le Vasseur** was born in St Peter Port, Guernsey in 1884. He was in the 1st Battalion, Leicester Regiment, and arrived in France on 9 September 1914. Sadly, his war wasn't to last long, as he died of his wounds on 15 December 1914. He was buried at the Ration Farm Military Cemetery, at La Chapelle-d'Armentières, in the Nord region of France.

Lieutenant Harold Augustus Rupert **Tooley,** aged 35, was born in Leighton Buzzard, Bedfordshire. When the war broke out he became an officer in the 1st Battalion, Royal Guernsey Light Infantry, attached to the 2nd Battalion, Leicestershire Regiment. He was killed in action on 20 December 1914. He has no known grave, but his name is commemorated at the Le Touret Memorial, in the Pas de Calais. A married man, before the war had lived with his wife, Zelie Laine Tooley, at 1 George Place, Guernsey.

Captain Francis William **Durand,** aged 39, was serving in the 3rd Battalion, attached to the 2nd Battalion, Royal Munster Fusiliers, when he was killed in action near Givenchy on 22 December 1914. He has no known grave, but his name is also commemorated on the Le Touret Memorial. In the years before the war he had served in Matabeleland in 1896, which is today part of Zimbabwe, and in 1897 in Mashonaland, then known as Rhodesia but today part of Zimbabwe, when there was a revolt against the British South Africa Company, led by priests of the Mwari religion.

Francis Durand was seconded by the Foreign Office to the Government of Zanzibar, where he remained for ten years between 1903 and 1913, before returning to the UK. For his efforts he was awarded the Brilliant Star of Zanzibar 3rd Class, and the Order of El Aliyeh 4th Class. He was quite possibly the only Englishman, ever to have been presented with these awards. His mother was still living in Guernsey after the end of the First World War.

Deck Hand W. **Gallicham**, aged 52, was on board the steam trawler *Cygnus* sailing out of Grimsby, when it was sunk after striking a mine on 12 December 1914. The vessel, under the captaincy of Frank Allenby, was on its way from its home port of Grimsby to its intended fishing grounds in the North Sea when the explosion occurred. All nine members of the crew were lost, none of their bodies were ever recovered. Mr Gallicham was born in Jersey and his name is commemorated on the Tower Hill Memorial for those merchant seaman who were lost at sea and have no known grave.

Serjeant (9310) William John **Nolais**, aged 24, was born in Jersey in 1890. At the outbreak of the war, he enlisted in the 1st Battalion, Bedfordshire Regiment. Having first arrived in France on 16 August 1914, he was wounded in action and admitted to the No.2 British Red Cross Hospital at Rouen, where he died of his wounds on 8 December 1914. He was buried at the St Sever Cemetery, Rouen, in the Seine-Maritime region of France. Before the war he had lived with his wife, Gertrude Eileen Nolais, at 20 Wellesley Terrace, St Helier, Jersey. Despite being married, the Army Register of Soldiers Effects, that covers the period 1901–1929, recorded the fact that William's sister Margaret was his principal heir.

Private (6410) John Francis **Collins,** aged 34, served in the 2nd Battalion, Devonshire Regiment. He first arrived in France on 6 November 1914 and was killed in action on 18 December 1914. He has no known grave, but his name is commemorated on the Le Touret Memorial, in the Pas de Calais. His father Richard Collins, lived at 30 Pier Road, St Helier, Jersey.

Donkeyman Walter George **Mauger** was born in Jersey in 1872. At the start of the First World War he was serving with the Mercantile Marine on board SS *Therese Heymann,* when he was killed on 25 December 1914 when his ship was sunk. He was a married man, who lived with his wife Jessie at 31 Seymour Street, Dunston-on-Tyne.

Private (4922) Edward **Dudley**, aged 36, was serving with the 2nd Battalion, Gloucestershire Regiment, when he died of pneumonia on 8 December 1914. He is buried at the Arnos Vale Cemetery in Bristol. He had previously served in the South African War. His parents, George and Emma Dudley, lived at 5 Bond Street, St Helier, Jersey.

Victoria College VCs

Victoria College, Jersey has a long tradition of military service. During the First World War 631 members of the OTC joined up of whom 126 were killed and many others wounded.

William Arthur McCrae Bruce, VC.

Lieutenant William Arthur McCrae **Bruce** VC, aged 24, of the 59th Scinde Rifles (Frontier Force) Indian Army was born in Edinburgh on 15 June 1890 and educated at Victoria College in Jersey. From there he attended the Royal Military College, Sandhurst, where he was a King's Indian Cadet and, after passing out in the autumn of 1909, he was gazetted as a second lieutenant on the unattached list for the Indian Army on 29 January 1910.

He sailed for India on 11 February 1911 aboard HM Troop Ship, *Plassy*, from Southampton. On arrival in India he was attached to the 5th Northumberland Fusiliers, before transferring to the 59th Scinde Rifles, Frontier Force, at Kohat in the Punjab on 8 March 1911.

In 1914 he was granted eight months leave to return to England, where he arrived on 10 April. At the beginning of the war he was ordered to return to India and re-join his regiment, but en route he was told to disembark his ship in Egypt and make his way to Cairo and await his regiment's arrival. He eventually arrived in Marseille, France on 17 September and was killed on 19 December near Givenchy.

He was a well-liked individual. In June 1914, his commanding officer, Colonel Fenner, wrote of Bruce:

> *A big, fine and promising young officer of excellent ability. As Transport and Signalling Officer, has performed his duties with marked success. Personally popular, good at games and a fine rider. He is good tempered, has tact, judgement, self-reliance, reliability and common sense. His influence with officers and men is good, he is active and temperate.*

On 20 December 1914, the day after his death, Major I.L. Leede, the commanding officer of the 59th Scinde Rifles, wrote a letter to Bruce's father. It included the following comments:

> *I am deeply grieved to have to write and tell you that your son Lieut. Bruce was killed yesterday during a night attack. He met his death in a German trench which he had taken, he was shot through the chest and died instantly.*

Until Colonel Fenner was killed, your son was my company officer, and I was very fond of him indeed, and I am more grieved than I can say to have to tell you of his death. I consider him to have been a young officer of most exceptional promise, and I have seen him under fire off and on for two months. Will you please accept the very sincere sympathy and condolence of the whole regiment.

At least three other officers wrote letters about Bruce and his exploits on the day of his death, pointing out, how well-liked he was by both officers and men alike.

The citation for the award of his Victoria Cross reads as follows:

For most conspicuous bravery and devotion to duty. On 19 December 1914, near Givenchy during a night attack, Lieutenant Bruce was in command of a small party which captured one of the enemy's trenches. In spite of being severely wounded in the neck, he walked up and down the trench, encouraging his men to hold on against several counter-attacks for some hours until killed. The fire from the rifles and bombs was very heavy all day, and it was due to the skilful disposition made, and the example and encouragement shown by Lieutenant Bruce that his men were able to hold out until dusk, when the trench was finally captured by the enemy.

Captain Allastair Malcom Cluny McReady Diarmid, VC. (Formerly Arthur Malcolm McReady-Drew)

Sadly, he has no known grave as his body was never recovered. The name of William Bruce is commemorated on the Neuve-Chapelle Memorial, in the Pas de Calais region of France. It is also engraved on a plaque inside St Clement's Church, Jersey, as well as on a memorial at the Jersey Militia Museum at Elizabeth Castle.

Victoria College, Jersey, subsequently purchased Bruce's Victoria Cross, and loaned it to the Jersey Museum.

His parents, Colonel Andrew McCrae Bruce CB and Margaret Hay Bruce, lived at La Fontaine Pontac, Jersey and had another property at La Roche d'Or, Samares.

Captain Allastair Malcolm Cluny McReady **Diarmid** (1888-1917) of the 17th Middlesex Regiment, was awarded his VC for his actions on 30 November/1 December 1917 for leading successful attacks during the Battle of Cambrai.

He was the son of Mr H. Leslie McReady-Drew. His mother being a native of Jersey, he attended Vistoria College in 1904. Letters from brother officers show that in a soldier's life he had found his real career; he was described as 'cheery and full of humour, he was always keeping our spirits up'. In 1915 he was wounded by a shell and spent four months in hospital. Because of serious internal injuries he was told that he must never again throw a bomb – advice which his VC citation shows he did not adhere to:

> In the Moeuvres Sector, France, when the enemy penetrated into our position, and the situation was extremely critical, Captain McReady Diarmid led his company through a heavy barrage and immediately engaged the enemy and drove them back at least 300 yards, causing numerous casualties and taking 27 prisoners. The following day the enemy again attacked and drove back another company which had lost all its officers. The captain called for volunteers, and leading the attack, again drove them back. It was entirely due to his throwing of bombs that the ground was regained, but he was eventually killed by a bomb.

Sir Arthur Conan Doyle, describing the fighting at Cambrai, said:

> There was no more wonderful individual record in the battle than that of Captain McReady-Diarmid, of the 17th Middlesex, who fought like a d'Artagnan of romance and is said to have killed eighty of the enemy in two days of fighting before he himself at last met that fate from which he never shrank.

Women of the Channel Islands and their part in the war

The work that women from the Channel Islands undertook went on throughout the five years of the war and this is where it began in 1914. Elsewhere in this book there are stories about the women from Alderney, Guernsey, Jersey and Sark, who worked for the British Red Cross, Voluntary Aid Detachments and the St John Ambulance, throughout the Channel Islands, the United Kingdom and in overseas theatres of war both Europe and further afield such as Gallipoli.

Nearly all communities throughout the United Kingdom had to deal with the loss of a high number of their men folk during the war. The numbers of those who were conscripted was almost matched by those who volunteered to join the armed forces. This all added up to a dwindling work force, which at the time was predominantly male, especially when it came to roles such as labourers, drivers, factory workers and mechanics, to name but a few. But these were all roles that still needed to be filled; somebody had to do the work, and if it couldn't be men, because so many of them were in the armed forces, then it would have to be done by women.

For many women this literally turned their worlds upside down. Prior to the war they had been wives and mothers, which meant looking after their husbands, children and the family home. Anything other than a basic education wasn't seen as essential for the majority of women, as the expectation for most was marriage and children, and what they had been taught would have had connections with these aspects of their future lives.

For those who did work, it was usually in such roles as shop assistants, infant school teachers, domestic service, bar maids, dressmaking and nursing. This meant working long hours for little pay and once they had finished their 'day jobs' the married ones, still had to go home, feed their husbands and children and keep house. Society placed many unwritten rules on women and what was expected of them. How they were supposed to dress for example, but once the war broke out these expectations almost disappeared. It became quite common to see a woman wearing trousers or overalls in her place of work, or on her way to and from her home.

Few women were financially independent during the years of the First World War, and for those who were, many were in that position due to inheritance, as very few women owned properties or ran businesses.

	Guernsey	Jersey	Alderney	Sark
Barmaid	3	1	0	0
Waitress	8	26	0	2
Shop Assistant	164	220	1	1
Servant	1,444	2,167	51	25
Teacher	200	252	7	0
Headteacher	1	0	0	0
Dressmaker	115	194	19	7
Seamstress	6	26	0	1
Nurse	169	283	10	1
Worker	38	49	1	0
Lodging House Keeper	19	3	0	0
Private means	740	1,484	13	17
Widowed	1,695	3,064	77	35
Student	2,157	2,818	124	39
Wife	7,224	8,366	378	110
Female population	**13,983**	**18,953**	**680**	**238**

The effort that was put in on the home front, mainly by women, undoubtedly played a major part in the nation's war effort and the eventual overall victory by Britain and her Allies. It is useful to look at some facts and figures in more detail, to see the different jobs and roles that women undertook, across the four islands of Guernsey, Jersey, Alderney and Sark. To do this I looked at the 1911 Channel Islands Census, the nearest available census to the war years.

This is not to suggest that the above list is fully inclusive, and that there were not other jobs that women undertook. It was more about providing the reader with a flavour of the numerous different roles which women in the Channel Islands would have undertaken during the First World War.

As more and more men were needed to go off and fight in the war, the island's women took on a more prominent role in the workforce. Suddenly they found the demand for their services had greatly increased. What had previously been a job seen to have been the sole domain of a man, was now a job that simply needed somebody to do it, no matter who or what they were. In many respects, the Channel Islands were no different from anywhere else in the UK. Farmers needed labourers to toil the land, look after their animals and tend to their crops. If they weren't collected they would simply rot in the fields, and for an island nation the ability to grow and harvest much needed crops, was an absolute necessity. This was an extremely important factor on the home front, because if people suddenly found themselves without food, their morale would be affected, which then greatly affected their ability to produce the required munitions and equipment that the different branches of British military required to be able to continue the fight.

Women were also used as bus conductors, mechanics, post women delivering the mail door to door – although that had been the situation in Guernsey for many years and was not a wartime innovation as it was in other towns and villages throughout the UK.

Many travelled to the UK to work in the extremely dangerous environment of munitions factories. Such women became affectionately referred to as 'munitionettes', or 'canaries' because, some had their skin turn yellow because of the effect of the materials they had to work with.

In March 1916 a Guernsey woman, Miss Dorothy Nicolls, travelled to the UK, in response to a national appeal for Shell Filling Factory Welfare Supervisors. Having been accepted for one of these positions, she was sent to work at National Shell Filling Factory No.6, in Chilwell, Nottingham. Hers was an important role, firstly, to look after the health and safety of the work force, which at Chilwell, numbered some 10,000 workers, many of whom were women. The possibility of workers contracting TNT poisoning was a real and present danger from the material's dust, and secondly, the very real risk of an explosion, because of the volatility of the chemicals and other materials that were used in the manufacture of the munitions. The shell casings were

Chilwell Munitions Factory.

made elsewhere and brought to the Chilwell factory by train where they were filled with their explosive contents.

This possibility sadly became a reality on 1 July 1918 when the factory was badly damaged and some parts destroyed, by a massive explosion of eight tons of TNT, which killed 134 workers and injured another 250. Only 32 of those who were killed were identifiable, such was the devastation caused. Most of those who were unidentifiable were buried in a mass grave at St Mary's Churchyard, Attenborough.

Although the incident wasn't exactly covered up, not much was reported about the incident at the time. What information was released under the restrictions of the Defence of the Realm Act, greatly played down the numbers of those injured and killed.

In January 1919 at Buckingham Palace, Miss Dorothy Nicoll, was awarded the Medal of the Order of the British Empire, for her courage and devotion to duty on two occasions when explosions occurred at the Chilwell factory. In 2014 a commemorative set of six stamps were issued by the Guernsey Post to commemorate the island's contribution to the First World War. One of these stamps depicted Dorothy Nicolls, whilst another was to commemorate Ada Le Poidevin, who was a member of the Salvation Army, and who worked in respite huts for soldiers in France, at such places as Arras and Boulogne.

The numbers of women undertaking nursing and factory work dramatically increased during the war years. Apart from munitions work factory workers were needed to produce items for the war effort, such as gas masks, tin helmets, boots and uniforms.

Those women who turned to nursing to do their bit, did so in a variety of ways. Many of the women from Jersey tended to be more home based, than their counterparts on Guernsey, who not only worked at the island's Victoria Military Hospital, the one at Fort George or the Convalescent Hospital at Les Touillets, but also at numerous hospitals throughout the UK as well as across the English Channel in France and Belgium. Although not exclusively so, trained and qualified nurses generally worked in military hospitals, whilst unqualified volunteers, usually undertook work for the Voluntary Aid Detachments in convalescent hospitals, where wounded soldiers were sent to recover after their initial treatment.

Volunteering for the common cause throughout the years of the First World War, became a popular pastime, especially for women from the middle classes. There were many different reasons for this. For some, it was as straight forward as there was a war on and they wanted to do their bit. For others, it was a chance to break away from the shackles and restrictions of living at home with their parents. For those who had lost loved ones to the war, there was a mixture of guilt and the strong desire to do something so that the loss of their loved one had not been totally in vain.

Some joined the Women's Legion; a group of nineteen of them from Guernsey, travelled out to work in France on 5 May 1917. One of those who went was 22-year-old Miss Beatrice Hamblen. Later that same year the Women's Legion amalgamated with other organisations to form the Women's Auxiliary Army Corps. The Corps women carried out such work as cooking hot meals for the troops.

It wasn't just for the military that women volunteered to help. They also helped ordinary people, members of the community, who were struggling to make ends meet because of the war. Families whose main bread winner had gone off to war, which had resulted in a family business having to close.

Mr Edward Ozanne was the Bailiff of Guernsey as well as an experienced and well-respected barrister. His wife, Mrs Frances Ozanne, was extremely active as a wartime volunteer and was a person who had a knack of getting things done. In the early part of the war she had crossed the English Channel and worked as a nurse in a military hospital in St Malo. Once back in England she didn't rest on her laurels, but targeted her enthusiasm into helping her own community. Along with other women, including, Mrs W.J. Le Page, Mrs J. Vessey, Mrs W.R. French, Mrs E.V. Gibson, Mrs J. Vivian Thomas, Mrs E.C. Ozanne, Miss Violet Carey, Mrs S. Cooper, Miss Clothier and Miss Christie, she helped set up and carry out the work of communal kitchens, to provide food and drink, to those who were in urgent need of it.

There are so many stories about women and the deeds which they carried out during the war, that it could fill an entire book on its own merits and I have had to be selective. But it would be remiss of me not to finish this piece by highlighting the collective, and possibly the most difficult task that women had to contend with and that is the grieving process they had to endure for the loved ones lost as a result of the war. That is not to say that the men folk didn't grieve for a lost father, son, or other male relative, but as men they were expected to display the old fashioned stiff upper lip approach. Women, on the other hand, were expected to be emotional, shed tears and grieve, but that's not to say that it was an easy process to deal with.

A particularly sad example of this, and one which emphasises the emotional trauma which many women experienced, were the Sarre family. The 1911 Census records that John, who worked for the States of Guernsey on the building and maintenance of public roads, and Nancy Sarre, lived at Roc Poisson, St Peter in the Wood, Guernsey with their four sons, Wilfred, Nicholas, William and Peter, and their daughter and youngest child, Mabel.

In 1881 Nancy had been married to Abraham De La Mare, also written in the form of 'Delamare', who was a fisherman. They lived at 32 La Rocque Road, St Peter in the Wood, Guernsey, along with their four sons, Abraham, Edmund, Alfred, and John. They also had a lodger living with them, John Sarre, an agricultural labourer, who would become Nancy's second husband. By 1891 Nancy and John Sarre were married, and had four children of their own, Louise, John, Angela, and Nicholas. With Louise being 7 years of age at the time, my assumption is that Nancy and John had been together as a couple, for about 8 years, so since about 1893. By 1901 Nancy and John, had a further four children, William, Pricilla, Peter and Mabel.

By the time of the First World War Nancy Sarre had to deal with the heartache and worry of having nearly all of her sons serving in the army. Would they be killed or would they survive? That was the daily dilemma she had to wrestle with. The premise that no news was good news, must have helped her keep her sanity in check.

November and December 1917 saw the Battle of Cambrai take place in France. One of the units that took part in the fighting, was the 1st Battalion, Royal Guernsey Light Infantry. Two of her sons who were serving with them, were both killed on the same day. Private (894) Nicholas Sarre (27) and Private (936) Wilfred Sarre (29) were both killed in action on 1 December 1917. Nicholas was buried at the Point-du-Jour Military Cemetery at Athies in the Pas de Calais. Wilfred's body was not recovered so he has no known final resting place, but his name is commemorated on the Cambrai Memorial at Louverval in Northern France.

On the same day that Nicholas and Wilfred were killed, Private (1452) John James Sarre, (21) and Private (1008) Peter Sarre (19) were captured and taken prisoner. They were held as prisoners of war at Minden, Westphalia in Germany and did not return home to Guernsey until December 1918.

The *Guernsey Weekly Press* carried a report about Private (135) William Sarre, who was wounded in action whilst serving in France, on 22 January 1918, and treated at an unnamed base hospital 'somewhere in France'. The seriousness of the wound was not mentioned in the article, but William had been sufficiently well enough to write a post card to his mother.

By the end of the war, Nancy Sarre had experienced so many different emotions, it is surprising she survived the war herself. How she felt on hearing the news that two of her sons had been killed on the same day, can only be guessed at. To then discover that two of her other sons had been taken prisoner on that day, must have been a massive relief, but how does the human brain cope with both of those pieces of information at the same time.

Nancy's story is just one of many, as sadly there are numerous other accounts of families from the Channel Islands, experiencing multiple deaths as a result of the war.

CHAPTER TWO

1915 – The Deepening Conflict

The New Year had been ushered in, 1915 had begun and sadly for all concerned the fighting showed no signs of coming to an end, quite the opposite in fact. Germany had been building up the size of her military strength for years, and in August 1914 they were finally ready to go to war in the belief that it was a war that they would win. When the fighting hadn't come to an end at Christmas, as had been suggested at the start of the conflict, the question now on everybody's lips, was when would it come to an end? Once the large numbers of men who had been killed and wounded became known, any uncertainty around what was at stake, quickly became abundantly clear.

There were hundreds of hospitals throughout the United Kingdom, working at full capacity, nearly all the time. There were hospitals for officers, for Indian soldiers, Australians, Canadians and New Zealanders. There were hospitals where wounded men would be sent for operations, and auxiliary hospitals where they could recover from their wounds. The sight of badly wounded British, Dominion and other Allied troops, arriving in England by ship, to then be transported on to hospitals all over the United Kingdom by special trains, made the public sit up and take stock of the situation that the nation was in. For most people, even though they knew there was a war going on, to see the reality of it that close for the first time would have been a massive shock.

There were battles and events that took place nearly every day of the year throughout 1915, some more momentous than others. This was the year that saw the first Zeppelin raid on England. The German submarine blockade of Great Britain began, in an attempt to stop much needed supplies reaching the British public in an effort to starve the nation into submission and surrender.

One of the biggest 'own goals' of the entire war, the sinking of the Cunard ocean liner, RMS *Lusitania* off the coast of Ireland by the German submarine, *U-20* took place on 7 May 1915. Of the 1,959 passengers on board, 1,198, were killed and of these 128 were Americans. This act of aggression by a German military vessel against an un-armed, passenger liner was widely condemned by all concerned, initially even being denied by the Germans themselves. This one act was seen as one of the major contributing factors to the United States' eventual entry into the First World War on the side of the Allies. This had not been a forgone conclusion as America had a very high German population at the time. Between 1881 and 1920, official figures for the immigration of Germans into America, shows that nearly 2,500,000 made the journey across the Atlantic in search of a better life. As recently as 2016 there were 44,754,050 Germans or people with German ancestry, living in America, which made up 14.4 per cent of the country's population.

Future research into the sinking of the *Lusitania*, would show that the incident was perhaps not as barbaric as was first suggested and, as Germany had maintained soon after the event, she was in fact a legitimate military target. As well as the 1,266 passengers and 696 members of her crew, she was carrying, four million rounds of .303 calibre ammunition, nearly 5,000 shrapnel shell casings, as well as 3,240 brass percussion fuses. These had been sent by America to Britain, to help with the Allied war effort.

On 17 February 1915 British and French naval vessels and ground forces, attacked the Ottoman Empire in the Dardanelles in what would become known as the Gallipoli campaign. After nearly eleven months of fighting, the remaining Allied troops were withdrawn from the island.

The British nurse, Edith Cavell, was executed on 12 October 1915 in Brussels after a German court martial found her guilty of assisting British soldiers to escape from Belgium.

The Commonwealth War Graves Commission website records that during 1915 Britain and her allies, from all parts of her Empire, suffered the deaths of 151,982 of its military personnel, a staggering number of men by anybody's standards. This included three men who had connections with Alderney, fifty-seven with Guernsey, and eighty-two with Jersey, remembering of course that the Royal Guernsey Light Infantry, wouldn't be formed for another year and most of those serving in the militias were needed on the home front.

Guernsey Volunteers 1915.

Some of the men serving with the Guernsey Militia had volunteered for overseas service and became part of already established regiments of the British Army. A company of infantrymen, which consisted of seven officers and 239 men, left Guernsey on 4 March 1915 to join the 16th Irish Division in Ireland, becoming D Company, 6th Battalion of the Royal Irish Regiment. Subsequent drafts of Guernsey men would become part of the 7th Battalion, Royal Irish Fusiliers and the 7th Battalion, Royal Irish Rifles.

This is a story of good fortune and bad luck all rolled in to one. The day in question was Saturday, 9 October 1915, and it resulted in the tragic death of Private (6/3312) Leonard Edwin **Pasquire** of B Company, 6th (Service) Battalion, Royal Irish Regiment, who died as a result of a training accident at Aldershot, when he suffered a fatal gunshot wound to the chest. Incredibly Leonard wasn't in the room where the fatal shot was fired, but in an adjoining one. The bullet initially struck another soldier in the hip, passed through him, continued on through a wooden partition which separated the two rooms, struck Private Pasquire, penetrating his body, and went through another partition on the other side of the room. The soldier who was initially struck by the bullet, Corporal (3525) Daniel O'Brien, survived, but unfortunately Private Pasquire died of a haemorrhage that day after being admitted to Connaught Hospital in Aldershot. The coroner's verdict was 'accidental death from gunshot wound in the chest'. The only point that was not covered in the relevant paperwork on Leonard's Army Service Record, was who fired the fatal shot. It did not clarify whether he accidentally shot himself or was shot by one of his colleagues. He was buried at the nearby Aldershot Military Cemetery in Hampshire.

The other man injured was Corporal O'Brien who had enlisted in the Army when he was 34 years of age in Limerick, Ireland, on 19 April 1915, when he became a private in the 6th Battalion, Royal Irish Regiment. His home was in Clare Abbey, County Clare, where he was a farmer.

One of the forms in his Army Service Record signed by his commanding officer states that he was injured 'on 9 October 1915 at a lecture on the Lewis Machine Gun, in a barracks room at Blackdown camp, Canterbury. The soldier was in no way to blame.' The form also noted that the injury which he sustained, would not interfere with his future efficiency as a soldier. By 22 February 1916, he had been transferred from the 6th Battalion, Royal Irish Regiment, to their Depot Command.

Private Pasquire was 30 years of age, born in St Peter Port, Guernsey, and a married man with three children, although he had been legally separated from his wife by a court order since 20 November 1911. She had subsequently become a patient and inmate of the Guernsey Lunatic Asylum at St Peter Port. He had enlisted at Guernsey on 8 February 1915 and, after having initially been sent to Ireland, he continued his training in Aldershot.

On 17 April Leonard's widow was awarded a pension of 20 shillings and 6d a week, for her and her three children, which was made up of 10s for her, and 10s 6d for the three children. The value of that today is £112.51. Prior to the award of the pension there had been a number of letters written on the matter, the first of which appears to have been sent on 6 January 1915, by Lieutenant Colonel Fitzroy-Curzon, Officer Commanding, 6th Battalion, Royal Irish Regiment, British Expeditionary Force, in relation to the monies due to be paid to Mrs Pasquire. Copies of two of these letters are attached to Leonard's Army Service Record.

SUBJECT – Pension to Dependants of No. 3312, Pte L Pasquire, 6th R.Ir. Regt. (deceased).
Infantry Record Office
No. 12 District, Cork,
14th January 1916

Lieut. Colonel Fitzroy-Curzon,
Officer Commanding,
6th R. I. Regt.
B. E. F

I am in receipt of your communication of the 6th instance as to pension awarded to the widow and three children of the deceased soldier. In reply, I beg to inform you that prior to his death, separation allowance of 15/- per week was paid to Mrs Poole (soldier's mother) in favour of the children, but at your request the Regimental paymaster transferred payment to the President, Poor Law Board, Guernsey, as the children had been placed in that Institution. The pension forms were rendered to the War Office on the 6th November, 1915 in favour of the three children, the name of the widow was not included, as she is an inmate of a Lunatic Asylum.

Captain for Colonel
In command Infantry Records, No.12 District.

The Poor Law Board was a 'committee' that was in charge of and ran the Workhouse on Guernsey. The following letter would appear to be in direct response to the one above that is dated 14 January 1916. The President of the Guernsey Poor Law Board, was Mr H.D. Oliver.

SUBJECT – Pension to Dependants of No. 3312, Pte L. Pasquire, 6th R.Ir. Regt. (deceased).
Infantry Record Office
No. 12 District, Cork,
31st January 1916.
With reference to attached correspondence, the pension forms were rendered to the War Office on the 6th November 1915, in favour of the three

children. The name of the widow was not included, as she is an inmate of a Lunatic Asylum. I am writing to the War Office to ascertain what pension (if any) has been granted, the result of which will be communicated to you.

Captain for Colonel
In command Infantry Records, No.12 District.

The letter was sent to the Hon. Secretary of the S & S F A, in Guernsey.

On being enlisted in the army, a separation allowance of 15s was, it would appear, paid to his mother, Mrs Poole, who for a period, had looked after the three children, Mildred Eileen, Leonard Edwin and Hilda May. But, at some point Private Pasquire's children, had been placed in the care of the President of the Poor Law Board, for Guernsey, Mr H.D. Oliver. On 5 October, just four days before he died, he had informed his commanding officer, that he wished his future pay to be paid direct to Mr Oliver, the President of the Poor Law Board, where his children were resident.

Two months after Leonard's tragic death, his colleagues from the 6th Battalion, Royal Irish Regiment, had finally finished their training in England and were ready to go off to war. They arrived in France at Le Havre on 19 December 1915, and began their preparations for battle readiness.

The Guernsey volunteers from the Royal Guernsey Artillery became part of the 9th Scottish Division, but were utilised as a Divisional Ammunition

Men of the Royal Irish Regiment.

Column, rather than an artillery unit. They also left for training in France in March 1915.

It was potentially a very dangerous role as they were almost constantly under threat of German artillery bombardments as they went about their work. Their job was to supply and resupply front-line infantry and artillery units, with their required ammunition, whether that was bullets or artillery shells. To remain effective, these front-line units required a constant supply of ammunition. There was always a fine balance between having too little or too much. If an infantry unit had too much ammunition and their position was subsequently overrun by a German ground attack, all of that ammunition would be taken. In the case of artillery units if they had an excess of shells stored in their location, they became vulnerable during a German bombardment of their position. When those units moved on to other locations, it was down to the Divisional Ammunition Column to sweep up behind them, and collect the empty shell and cartridge cases, along with any unused munitions.

In 1915 there were three major battles which involved British troops. The first was the Battle of Neuve Chapelle, a British offensive in the Artois region of France, which lasted for nearly four days between 10 and 13 March. During this time, 3,416 soldiers from Britain and other Commonwealth countries were killed and one of these had connections to the Channel Islands.

Divisional Ammunition Column.

Private (3/8615) James Henry Roach, of the 2nd Battalion, Bedfordshire Regiment, had first arrived in France on 11 November 1914. He was killed in action on 12 March 1915. He has no known grave, but his name is commemorated on the Le Touret Memorial in the Pas de Calais.

His elder brother John Francis Peter Roach, lived in Bel Royal, St Lawrence Valley, Jersey, with his wife, Mary, and their four children, where he was a gardener. The 1901 Census records that James was living with his brother John and his family and was also a gardener. According to the British Army's Medal Rolls Index Cards, John was James's next of kin, and the person to whom his wartime service medals were sent.

The next was the Second Battle of Ypres, which took place between 22 April and 25 May 1915, and consisted of six smaller battles with the final prize being the strategic Belgium town of Ypres. It saw the might of the German Empire pitted against the mass ranks of the Allied armies, including troops from India, Canada, South Africa, Australia, New Zealand, Newfoundland, United Kingdom, France, Algeria, Morocco and Belgium.

The month-long fighting saw more than 59,000 Allied casualties, of whom nearly 15,000 were killed. One of these was Second Lieutenant Robert William McLernon of the Royal Field Artillery, who was killed in action on 8 May 1915 and was buried at the Larchwood, Railway Cutting Cemetery, in the West-Vlaanderen region of Belgium. He was the son of Robert and Harriet McLernon, of Oliver Street, Alderney, although by the time of the 1911 Census he was already in the army, a bombardier in the Royal Field Artillery, stationed at the Royal Artillery Barracks in St Matthew, Ipswich, Suffolk.

During the same time frame, ten men who had connections with the island of Jersey were killed, of these nine had no known graves, but their names were commemorated on the Menin Gate Memorial in Ypres. Seven men who had Guernsey connections were also killed, of these, four are also commemorated on the Menin Gate Memorial.

The third major battle of 1915 involving British troops was the Battle of Loos, which lasted for thirteen days between 25 September and 8 October. It was the biggest attack by the British throughout the whole of 1915 and was the first time that they used poison gas, but despite this, it was a German victory. The British casualties at nearly 60,000, were more than twice as many as those sustained by the Germans.

Ten of the British soldiers who were killed, had Guernsey connections, six of whom had no known graves and are commemorated on the Loos Memorial in the Pas de Calais region of France. A further five men who were killed during the fighting had connections to Jersey.

According to the Commonwealth War Graves Commission website, there were a total of 151,982 British and Empire military personnel, who during the course of 1915 were killed or died during the fighting. This equates to 12,665 men each month, 2,714 per week, or 416 men, each and every day of the year. For the Channel Islands this roughly equated to 82 men from Jersey, 57 from Guernsey and 3 who were from Alderney.

It is a widely known historical fact that during the Second World War the Channel Islands were the only part of the British Isles that were invaded and occupied by Nazi Germany. A prize that, although it was handed to them on a plate by the British Government, they held on to for five years between 30 June 1940 and 9 May 1945. It was a strange situation, because the British Government, decided that the islands held no strategic importance and would therefore not be defended, a decision with which Winston Churchill, the British Prime Minister, strongly disagreed. As for the Germans, the occupation of the islands served absolutely no military purpose whatsoever. All they gained was the propaganda value of occupying British territory.

From a historic view point, looking back on the events of June 1940, it is quite staggering how readily the British Government, had decided to abandon the islands and their people to what was after all, an unknown fate. This was, however, not the first time that German soldiers and sailors had set foot on the Channel Islands. They had first done that in March 1915 during the early months of the First World War.

There was a German prisoner of war camp on Jersey at Les Blanches Banques, near Le Braye, during the war. Its location, close to the sea and situated on a flat basin of land, gave it quite a relaxing atmosphere. The camp consisted of fifty accommodation huts for the prisoners, with thirty men to a hut, each of which measured 60ft in length and 15ft in width. There was also sufficient accommodation for bathing as well as a cookhouse and dining huts, and its own hospital. The camp was extremely modern for its time; it had running water and electric lighting, facilities that many of the nearby residents didn't have. The decision about using electricity for lighting, rather than gas or petrol, was purely for practical reasons. To lay the required pipes for gas or petrol would have meant living with the constant possibility that they would be damaged, whereas the wires needed for the electricity could easily be hung safely overhead.

In April 2017 an article appeared in the *Mail on Line* website which included several rare photographs that had been taken in the camp by Captain Eli Bowers of the Royal Jersey Militia and showed German prisoners of war having a snowball fight, along with some of the camp guards. Two of the photographs are particularly interesting. One of them appears to show the end of a tunnel that came up outside the camp. There were at least two known escape attempts from the camp where prisoners tried to tunnel their way out. The other photograph shows a barbed-wire fence encircling the camp, at least 7ft high, and which appears to be electrified, which was also unusual.

Despite its somewhat isolated location, there were barbed-wire fences, guard towers and armed guards to help prevent any escapes by the camp's detainees. A more scenic and tranquil setting for a prisoner of war camp would have been hard to find, an ideal location to see out the war in peace and comfort, or so you would think. But despite this, there were attempts by some of the prisoners to make good their escape. One determined attempt saw a small group of prisoners dig a tunnel under a nearby road.

Situated just outside of the main camp were the accommodation huts and offices for the camp guards and clerical staff. It opened for business on 20 March 1915 and over the next two days some 1,000 German prisoners of war walked through its main gates. This first batch of captives were followed by a further 500, four months later on 7 July 1915.

The camp finally closed on 6 October 1919 when the last of the prisoners, which by then consisted purely of German non-commissioned officers, left the camp to be repatriated back home to their families in Germany. The terms of The Hague Convention, by which the British War Department strictly adhered, stated that non-commissioned officers could not be forced to carry out manual labour; one can only assume that officers deemed such labour as being beneath their status in life.

Two other locations on the island had been given serious consideration as sites for the proposed camp, one of which was progressed as far as having a camp built on it which was never subsequently used to house prisoners of war. The other location was an existing building on the island.

One of the German prisoners of war who was held captive at the camp, was, Erich, also sometimes referred to as Frederich, Gussek. Little is known about him and his stay at Les Blanches Banques during that time. During the Second World War he returned to the islands as Major Erich Gussek. He was in command of the first German troops who landed on Jersey on 30 June 1940. His second visit to the island was quite possibly a lot shorter than his previous one during the First World War. He left Jersey on 19 September 1940 just over three months after he had first arrived. What his feelings were on returning to Jersey, this time as a victor, are not recorded.

Major Erich Gussek.

Saturday, 10 April 1915 saw the London and South-Western Railways Steam Ship *Guernsey*, which was full of flowers and vegetable produce, en route from Guernsey to Southampton, run aground on rocks off of Cape La Hogue, or so it was initially believed.

The *Guernsey*, which was built in London in 1874, carried a crew of nineteen,

Côte d'Émeraude   3675. SAINT-MALO — Le Départ du Bateau de Jersey G. F.

Collection GERMAIN fils aîné, Saint-Malo

SS Guernsey.

twelve of whom were rescued alive and taken to Southampton by the Steam Ship *Cherbourg*, reaching there on Sunday, 11 April.

The vessel, which made the journey three times each week on Mondays, Wednesdays and Fridays, had left Guernsey at seven o'clock on the evening of Friday, 9 April 1915. Just three hours later at ten o'clock, whilst off the rocks at Cape La Hogue, she was torpedoed by a German submarine. Had the *Guernsey* remained stationary she would have no doubt been saved, but while rescue work was continuing to save both vessel and the crew, she suddenly lurched, rolled over and sank in deep water. Twelve of the crew managed to get into the ship's lifeboat and rowed round in an attempt to pick up their colleagues, sadly to no avail. The situation was made worse by the darkness. Captain Berrow, along with six of the crew were lost, their bodies were never recovered. The captain was actually seen struggling in the water but disappeared under the waves before he could be rescued.

All of those who were lost were married men from the Southampton area. Other than Captain Berrow, some of the other men who lost their lives were, Second Officer Munday, Seaman Etheridge, Fireman McAllen, Fireman Lewis, Trimmer Bisson and Steward Weaver.

Seaman Etheridge had been a survivor of the sinking of the SS *Stella*, another vessel owned by the London and South Western Railway, that was wrecked off of the Casquets Lighthouse on 30 March 1899, during a crossing between Southampton and Guernsey. A combination of heavy fog and the speed at which the *Stella* was travelling, were found to be contributing factors to the vessel's sinking and the subsequent loss of life. Of those who survived,

67 were picked up and taken to St Helier in Jersey, whilst another 37 were taken to St Peter Port, Guernsey. In total 86 passengers and 19 members of the crew were killed.

In relation to SS *Guernsey* survivors, two of those who survived, were the Chief Officer Ellison, who was the last to leave the ship, and Chief Engineer W.T. Penny. All of the twelve survivors managed to reach the coast near Cape La Hogue, where they made contact with the French coastguard and were sent on to Cherbourg.

Wednesday, 21 April 1915, saw the wedding of Miss Annie Burton Hall, the eldest daughter of the Reverend and Mrs Matthew Hall of the Vicarage, Burnley, to 20-year-old, Lieutenant John Leale, who in addition to holding many prominent offices in the Channel Islands, was a Justice of the Guernsey Royal Court.

The ceremony was conducted by the Reverend Bosward of Radcliffe, a friend of the bride's family. Miss Hall looked resplendent, dressed in a blue moiré silk dress, which was complemented by a hat trimmed with ostrich feathers and pale coloured roses. She was given away by her father. The bridegroom was immaculately dressed in his military uniform. There were no bridesmaids, but Miss Hall was accompanied by her sisters, Miss Gladys Hall and Miss Dorothy Hall, along with the bridegroom's sister, Miss Miriam Leale.

A reception was held at the vicarage, after which the newlyweds left for a brief honeymoon in London, before beginning their married life in their new home, Braermer Delancy, St Sampson, Guernsey, where the bridegroom, Mr Leale, had to resume his military duties.

The 1911 Channel Island Census records that the bridegroom's father, John Leale, owned an ironmonger's business, where his son Roy worked; the family, his mother Amelia and an older brother and sister, lived at The Hanchorus, St Sampson, Guernsey.

Sadly, Annie and Roy's marriage was not a long one. According to the Army Register of Soldiers Effects, which covered the period 1901–1929, Roy died on 21 April 1919 whilst serving as a lieutenant in the Royal Guernsey Light Infantry, attached to the 7th Battalion, Royal Fusiliers. There was no explanation as to how he had died, but it could only have been due to an accident, illness, or wounds received during the war. His death, somewhat surprisingly, was not recorded on the Commonwealth War Graves Commission website. In his Will Roy left Annie just over £670, which by today's equivalent is more than £40,000.

It was reported in May 1915 that the Channel Island's much needed potato trade, which had been greatly affected by the outbreak of the war, would once again be up and running to full capacity. With potatoes a part of most people's staple diet, this was excellent news, and would have no doubt been a great morale booster, not just for the local population, but for those living across in mainland Great Britain. Ships left the Channel Islands soon afterwards to deposit their cargos at British ports, with Southampton being the main destination.

The harvesting of the 1915 season's potato crop had been delayed somewhat from the previous year, although in the circumstances, with the beginning of the war and a large reduction in available man power, as men from the islands began enlisting in different units of the British Army, as well as the Royal and merchant navies, it was only to be expected. Along with other everyday foods the price of potatoes had almost doubled in price during the war years. This certainly wasn't in line with how much wages had increased during the same period, but in the circumstances the increase in the food stuffs was only to be expected.

In June 1915 an appeal was received from the Jersey YMCA, by the National Council of the YMCA, for assistance in the erection of a hut for the use by the troops from the Staffordshire Regiment who were stationed on Jersey. The YMCA's National Council recognised the continuous good work that had been carried out by those involved with the Jersey section, for all military personnel who had been stationed on the island since the outbreak of the war and, with this in mind, were more than happy to whole heartedly support the appeal. Besides supporting the building of the requested hut financially, the YMCA's National Council had also received an offer from a Staffordshire building firm to erect such a hut free of charge, on condition that some of the troops serving with the Staffordshire Regiment assisted with the work.

All parties concerned in the matter were pleased with the outcome, especially as having such a facility built for the benefit of the troops on the Island of Jersey, was seen as an urgent need. It was somewhere the visiting troops could call their own, where they could relax and be at ease.

At the beginning of the war, the 4th (Service) South Staffordshire Regiment was based at Lichfield in Staffordshire, but immediately moved to Jersey, where they stayed for the next two years. After being sent to other locations around the British Isles, they finally made their way to France on 10 October 1917. They saw action during the Third Battle of Ypres (Passchendaele), the Battle of Pilckem the fighting on the Somme during 1918 and the Battle of the Lys, which was part of the German Spring offensive, a final attempt to break through the Allied lines. This was where the 4th Battalion, South Staffordshire Regiment sustained very heavy losses. On only the second day of the battle, 10 April 1918, the men of C Company were totally wiped out, by the combination of a heavy artillery bombardment and gas shells.

The Commonwealth War Graves Commission lists the names of fifty-three men of the 4th Battalion, South Staffordshire Regiment who were killed on 10 April 1918, many of whom had been stationed and lived in Jersey for two years between 1914 and 1916. Many had become part of the local community, no doubt some of them even dating local girls.

Private (46666) Neville Oliver John **Attewell**
Private (43717) Robert William **Balls**
Private (42662) John **Blyth**
Private (42660) Carson **Bowmar**
Private (235279) Alfred **Bromley**
Private (36182) Joseph George **Brown**
Private (203690) William Henry **Clapp**
Private (241996) Arthur Charles **Collier**
Private (48076) John Oliver **Cookson**
Private (36069) Bernard **Corbett**
Private (39002) Frank Joseph **Davis**
Private (42696) Arthur Henry **Davies**
Private (43736) John Hastings **Dickenson**
Private (42026) J **Dixon**
Private (42693) H **Dungworth**
Lance Corporal (39330) I S **Fox**
Private (241036) J H **Garfield**
Private (45629) Hubert **Greaves**
Lance Corporal (36920) William Ernest **Grimsley**
Lance Corporal (43038) William Henry **Hayes**
Private (42724) Joseph **Hough**
Private (39083) W **Hodson**
Private (202617) Thomas **Howard**
Private (36913) George **Hughes**
Lance Corporal (46975) G **Hunt**
Private (38385) Joseph **Hunt**
Private (46863) Thomas Graves **Johnson**
Corporal (29868) Harold **Jones**
Private (39219) John **Jones**
Private (45674) George **Jukes**
Private (20356) Robert **Keeton**
Private (42741) William Levi **Longley**
Private (42744) Walter **Lord**
Private (42866) William James **Luckings**
Private (42747) Jones **Marr**
Private (38394) Walter Henry **Morton**
Serjeant (17384) James **Mottram**
Private (203567) Walter **Ogle**
Serjeant (6790) A J **Parkes**
Private (36070) Joseph Allen **Pitt**
Private (39130) Frederick John **Rignall**
Private (46634) William Enoch **Robinson**
Private (35705) William **Sayer**

Private (42797) Frank Gaunt **Stafford**
Private (37021) Arthur Percy **Thaxter**
Private (202747) James **Thompson**
Corporal (35817) Walter **Titley**
Private (42809) Bernard **Truman**
Private (39325) P B **Wale**
Private (203623) Frederick Edgar **Walker**
Private (42834) Sydney George **Watson**
Private (42825) Frank Laurence **West**
Private (38386) Horace J **Woodhall**

A staggering statistic about these fifty-three men of the South Staffordshire Regiment, is that only nine of them have a known grave. The other forty-four men have their names commemorated on the Ploegsteert Memorial in the Hainaut region of Belgium.

On 8 October 1918 the battalion lost one other man: Corporal (39050) Hubert Edward Harold **Hartill**.

In the news in November 1915 was an interesting story about one of the smaller Channel Islands, Herm, which is about 1½ miles in length by about ½ a mile wide, which had for many years before the First World War, been leased to a German company and occupied by a German Prince, that had been taken back into Crown possession.

At the beginning of the war there was, understandably, great concern amongst the other Channel Islands, but in particular Guernsey which was only some 3 miles away from Herm. Whispers led to rumours, which in turn led to total conjecture and a belief by some that the island had in fact been used for secret military preparations and had been fortified. It hadn't but the rumours came about because a large part of the island had been closed and kangaroos and other animals had been allowed to roam there freely. But the main ingredient of the concern and uncertainty was based on the fact that the man who had rented the island was German. A Prince Blücher had rented it from the West Bank Liegnitz Limited. He was in fact a Prussian Count.

The misplaced concerns over the island had reached such fever pitch that the island had twice been searched by British military authorities, who had gone as far as leaving a small garrison of troops stationed there.

In reply to a question asked in the House of Commons on the subject, the Home Secretary, Mr McKenna, had categorically stated that no trace of any foreign military preparations had been found on the island. Not long after the outbreak of the war, the British Government had asked the States of Guernsey to take steps to terminate the lease with the German company concerned, which they did. It was subsequently proposed to split the island into five lots with the proviso that no tender for any or all of the five plots would be considered by any nation considered to be an enemy of Great Britain.

On Monday, 29 November 1915, the States of Jersey adopted a law in relation to the sale of what were then referred to as 'spirituous liquors'. The new law prevented all such relevant licensed venues and premises from serving spirits after six o'clock each weekday evening, for consumption off the premises they were purchased in. On Sundays special licence holders could not sell spirits for consumption off premises. No licence holder was allowed to sell spirits in quantities of less than one and a half pints for consumption off their premises. Under the new law off licence holders were allowed to remain open until 9pm for the sale of goods other than spirits.

The main reason for the introduction of this new law, wasn't to interfere with people's social recreation, or because of a shortage of spirits and beers, but to ensure that vital war production wasn't affected. The fear was that the more alcohol people consumed the more likely they were to get drunk, which in turn meant the possibility of more people potentially not turning up for work, which ultimately would affect the nation's important wartime production in such areas as munitions, ship building and the production of aircraft. After all, if the nation's fighting men had to forgo alcohol for long periods of time, then it was only right and proper that the civilian population played their part as well.

There used to be a newspaper, entitled *The Bystander*. In one edition, dated Wednesday, 8 December 1915, there was an article written by a Major G.W. Redway, concerning the Channel Islands Militia. Major Redway, was a well-known military expert of the day, who had written for the *Daily Mail* as well as *The War Illustrated*. He had also written such books as, *Wellington & Waterloo* (1913) and *The War of Secession – 1861-1862 – Bull Run to Malvern Hill.*

The article he wrote in *The Bystander* read as follows:

> For a month past there has been a commotion in Jersey about the question I raised in THE BYSTANDER on October 20. Is it not a fact that the Channel Islands Militia have been standing by for a twelve month at the expense of the taxpayer? Newspaper discussion has culminated in a meeting of The States at which it was resolved to forward to Mr Asquith a return of Jerseymen who had joined the Army or Navy. So far so good; but this action does not really touch the point of issue.
>
> The fact is that our Army estimates bear an annual charge of £11,600 for the maintenance of five battalions of infantry, besides artillery, engineers and medical units, who are raised in the Channel Islands on the basis of compulsory and gratuitous service, and it does not appear that these troops have yet been invited to proceed overseas, although they are reputed to be of excellent quality. The law enables the authorities to recruit the extra numbers required to repair the wastage of war, and thus a Channel Islands brigade might have been added to the Army in France. Why this has never been attempted, is still to be explained.

So 1915 was a difficult year as it had been a time of acceptance and consolidation. It was the year that the war became real. Men were dying and others were returning home wounded, some with life changing injuries. Loved ones were being killed, women were being widowed and children were losing their fathers, and all the signs were that the war was not going to be over any time soon and certainly not before even more death and destruction had followed.

CHAPTER THREE

1916 – The Realisation

It was the midway part of the war, yet there was still no end in sight. A lot happened in 1916. Although both Guernsey and Jersey had their own militia, these units were for home service only and never left the island – well, not as militia they didn't.

Conscription was introduced for the first time by the British Government in March 1916, although it was not utilised until later in the year in Guernsey, when the Royal Guernsey Light Infantry was formed on 17 December 1916. This ultimately led to most of the men who were from the Channel Islands and who had originally joined the Irish Regiments transferring to the Royal Guernsey Light Infantry.

The first Guernsey man who was killed as a result of enemy action, died in the same month that men of the 6th Battalion, Royal Irish Rifles found themselves standing in the front-line trenches for the first time. Captain George William **Le Page** was 40 years of age and in D Company, 6th Battalion, Royal Irish Regiment, when he was killed in action on 26 January 1916. He was buried at the Noeux-les-Mines Communal Cemetery in the Pas de Calais. He was a married man and before the war he had lived with his wife, Lilian, and their daughter, Marjorie, at Strathmore House, Grange, Guernsey. The 1911 Census showed George and his family living at 2 Amherst, Guernsey, where he was a fruit grower.

What has gone down in history as the most significant battle of the First World War, the Battle of the Somme, began on 1 July 1916. Guernsey men, serving with the 7th Battalion, Royal Irish Rifles took part in the battle and gave a very good account of themselves, but at a cost.

There were men from the Channel Islands serving with D Company, 7th Battalion, Royal Irish Rifles, D Company, 7th Battalion, Royal Irish Fusiliers, and D Company, 6th Battalion, Royal Irish Regiment, during the Battle of the Somme. Of these, 142 men with connections to the Channel Islands were killed or died of their wounds. There were 3 from Alderney, 57 with connections to Guernsey and 82 to Jersey. Sadly, 36 of these men have no known grave. All that marks the part that they played in the war is their names on the Thiepval Memorial in Picardy. It commemorates the names of more than 72,000 men of the British and South African forces, who died in the region before 20 March 1918 and have no known grave. Most of the names are those who died during the Somme Offensive of 1916.

The Three Amigos - unknown soldiers grabbing a quick bite to eat.

The youngest of the Channel Islands' Irish contingent to be killed, was actually too young to have been serving on the Western Front. He was only 17 years of age, when the legal age to serve in the army was 18. Private (21891) Fred Queripel with the 7th Battalion, Princess Victoria's (Royal Irish Fusiliers) died of his wounds on 10 September 1916. He was buried at the Cote 80 French National Cemetery at Etinehem on the Somme. Fred's father, John William Queripel, lived at Grande Rocque, Castel, Guernsey.

The battalion's War Diary for the days leading up to Fred's death, records a few instances where they suffered casualties, but sadly men from the other ranks were not mentioned by name, regardless of whether they were wounded or killed. Only officers had their names included in the diaries, such was the custom of the times.

Like the Isle of Man, the Channel Islands enjoyed Home Rule, but they were not included in the area to which the Compulsion Bill applied. The reason for this was that conscription, albeit solely for Home Defence, had been law in the Channel Islands from time immemorial. The Compulsion Bill, or the Military Service Act 1916, as it was more widely known, imposed conscription on all men who were aged between 18 and 41 years of age. There were exemptions to the rule: men who were medically unfit for wartime military service were exempt, as were widowed men with children, ministers of recognised religious orders, teachers and certain classes of industrial workers. Throughout the war the Bill would go through changes. As more men were lost, so even more men were required to replace them.

In 1916 the Royal Guernsey Militia was embodied as being at full strength, but direct enlistment into regular regiments of the British Army and the drafting of special contingents to Royal Irish Regiments, had greatly thinned the pool of men from which militia men could be drawn. To ensure the militia force was kept up to full strength, it was necessary to look to the men of the army reserves up to the age of 60.

It is interesting to remember that by law, in 1916, the Channel Islands Militia could only be used for two purposes: to defend the islands against foreign invasion and to assist King George V to reconquer England should it be lost to an enemy nation.

On Saturday, 5 February 1916 the Barquentine *Geraldine*, a British-made wooden, three-mast vessel under the command of Captain T.B. Jones from Cardigan, foundered off Sark and east of Herm. She had left Guernsey the previous Sunday on her way to Trinidad with a cargo of ballast, but when the ship reached the Bay of Biscay, the cargo shifted and the ship listed badly. Captain Jones realised the extreme danger he was in and that there was no chance of him reaching his intended destination. Instead he decided to turn around and make his way back to Guernsey. To this end the Channel Islands steamer, *Channel Queen* went out to meet the *Geraldine* and took her in tow, but shortly after hooking her up, the *Geraldine* turned turtle and sank. All of the *Geraldine*'s crew were rescued alive, and taken to St Peter Port, Guernsey where they were cared for.

In February 1916 Eric Marshall Thorne, a water supply contractor, who was living at 11 Sibthorp Street, Lincoln, made an application for his green card to be signed by the local magistrates, to enable him to leave the country. Mr Thorne told the magistrates that he only lived in Lincoln because of his current working commitments, but that his actual home was in the Channel Islands, where he had attested under Lord Derby's scheme and had been called up to report himself for military training on 2 March. In the circumstances, he wished to return home for a week to spend time with his relatives before his military service began, not knowing after this time when the opportunity to do so would arise. The magistrates, having heard Mr Thorne's reasons, agreed to sign his green form.

Eric Marshall Thorne returned to the Channel Islands and his home, Ivy Gates in Guernsey, where he lived with his parents, Francis and Marianne Thorne, and his two elder brothers, Francis and Arthur. Like his father and two brothers, he was also a qualified engineer. In late 1916 he was commissioned as a second lieutenant in the Royal Guernsey Light Infantry. He survived the war and returned to his occupation afterwards.

On Thursday, 6 April 1916 a case appeared before Belper Magistrates in Derbyshire, of two colliers, Charles Ackers and Bernard Twigg. Both men had been charged with using abusive language on 25 March at Belper, an allegation that they denied. Police Constable Adcock told the court that Twigg had claimed to be a light-weight champion boxer of the Midlands. They were 'scrapping', Adcock informed the magistrates, and complaints had been received by concerned residents in the area at the time.

Charles Ackers told the magistrates that he wasn't in Belper on the date in question, having just been discharged from the army and arriving in Belper on 25 March having left the Channel Islands. The case against Ackers, and one assumes the same for Twigg, was dropped, the magistrates taking into account that Ackers had been wounded whilst serving his country and that was the reason he had been discharged from the army.

On the afternoon of Friday, 7 April 1916, a session of the Portsmouth Recruiting Tribunal took place in the mayor's parlour, whereby a conscientious objector was refused an exemption for having to undertake military service.

He had first decided that military service of any kind wasn't for him in about 1903, at which time he lived in Guernsey, and he subsequently left the island to avoid military training. His objections were far reaching; he did not even want to undertake a non-combatant role, on the grounds that it was contributing to military service. For working in a hospital where wounded men were being treated, he offered the same reason.

When asked what religion he belonged to, he was vague, instead entering into a long-winded explanation of his theological views, the purport of which was that he was baptised according to the Baptist denomination. He had studied the social life of the people, especially of the working classes, and believed that Socialism was the menace of the working classes, which could only be met by one class of religious men. In order to study the social life of the poorer classes he had travelled the country and spent two nights in tramp wards. Replying to a member of the tribunal's committee, he said he was not an aristocratic tramp, as he had no money.

Asked what he would do if a German hit him on the nose, the man declared that such an occurrence could not possibly happen. Another member of the tribunal asked him if he held the opinion that nothing could happen to him if he simply continued with the stance that he was taking, the man replied that he did not hold such an opinion, but added that he had a most precarious life although no accident had ever happened to him. Asked what he had to done to help his country in its fight against Germany, he simply replied, 'nothing'.

It was put to him that he was evidently the type of person who comfortably remained at home, happy for others to do the fighting. He did not reply on the assumption on the grounds that he took the words as an observation rather than a direct question.

Although there were plenty of such reports from these Military Tribunals, the one thing that was never included was the name of the person requesting such an exemption, and at the end of the war, the paperwork relating to the tribunals was ordered to be destroyed. Some survived, notably the Middlesex tribunals, but most no longer exist.

If a man did not wish to fight in the war, he could appeal against having to undertake military training and service. His case would be heard by a tribunal, made up of prominent local people, who would ultimately determine whether such an appeal constituted cowardice or conscience. What particular skill these individuals had to be able to make such a decision isn't clear. The man making the appeal had to be able to prove his objection, which wasn't always a strongly held belief, and does not seem tangible from a legal perspective.

Between the beginning of conscription in March 1916 and the end of the war, there were an estimated 750,000 of these cases brought before Military Tribunals. Of these only 16,000 men, or just over 2 per cent were officially registered as legitimate conscientious objectors.

In June 1916 the Channel Islands argued for an extension of the Compulsion Act. The following was written by a native of the islands to a contemporary:

> *Now that compulsory service has become a fait accompli, the English Public may reasonably ask why this Act should not be extended so as to embrace the Channel Islands.*
>
> *These Islands, containing a population of over 100,000, with an available manhood of over 10,000, are obliged to keep up a militia for the defence of the island. This militia is a trained body of men which, with little if any further training, is available for service at the Front. This militia is now mobilised for the defence of these islands, but what its use is for this purpose under present conditions is, to say the least of it questionable.*
>
> *There has been a certain voluntary response on the part of the islands, but in nothing like the numbers available. These islands owe their immunity from attack to the protection afforded them by the mother country, and it would only seem reasonable that their States should be asked to pass a Bill for compulsory service for defence of the Empire.*

The next story is about a Jersey man, who having been 'called up' and attested to serve in the army, then made an application for an absolute exemption from having to undergo military service on the grounds that it would cause serious hardship to his parents should he be called up.

The man in question was Edward Romeril Le Ruez, a 35-year-old man, a Licensed Lay Reader, whose application showed his address as 32 Great Union Road, St Helier, Jersey, although at the time of his application he was living in London. The paperwork included two addresses for him, 42 New Road Hill, Lower Edmonton, and 2 Leopold Road, Ealing Common. The Jersey address is presumably where his parents lived.

He was attested at Hornsey in North London, the area where he was living at the time, on an unknown date after March 1916. On 14 June 1916 he submitted his application for an exemption from having to undergo military service to the Heston and Isleworth Military Tribunal, which heard the case on 5 July 1916. By this time the military representative on the panel, Captain Chapman had read through the reasons given for requesting the exemption. He commented as follows: *'I OBJECT to the application and contend that no serious hardship will ensue if he is called up for Army service.'*

There was also a supporting letter attached to the file from the Reverend W. Barnsley of 5 Ronge Bouilton, St Helier, Jersey, dated 22 June 1916. In it he states:

> *Re the statements made by the applicant, Edward Le Ruez of 42 New Road Hill, Lower Edmonton. I may say that I have every reason to believe that they are strictly accurate. I know the family well, and at the present time, his presence is urgently needed here to attend to affairs. His father is not capable of attending to business, and his mother is ill, and has been so for some time past. On his shoulders rests the whole responsibility for everything. I think this is a case for exemption. It appears to me that the life of the family depends absolutely upon him.*

The man's application having been considered, it was rejected, the Tribunal having noted that this was, 'not a case of serious hardship', a decision which the man in question appealed. The Appeal Tribunal was heard on 30 August 1916 at the County of Middlesex Guildhall in Westminster, London. They in turn having fully considered the appeal, rejected it. The panel having fully endorsed the decision of the original Local Tribunal.

The following information was included in Edward Le Ruez's appeal:

> *My presence is urgently needed in Jersey to look into, and take over the management of affairs, as my father is now (and has been for some time past, without my knowledge) incapable at attending to business, which has been so neglected that I have not the least idea of what is, or how much is involved, but I understand that unless matters are attended to at once, serious consequences may develop(e), both to my people now as well as myself in the future.*
>
> *My mother has been and is now seriously ill and will never again be able to look after herself, leave (let) alone any other matters. Therefore, being the only son the whole responsibility of everything falls on me, and further as far as I am able to judge the position from here, the very life of the family depends on one (me). Under the circumstances I feel that it is my bounden duty to them whilst they are alive, to (do) whta (what) I can for thwm (them) (and) I respectfully suggest that the Local Tribunal did not quite understand my appeal, ther (the) serious consequences it involved to my people, and therefore after placing the above facts*

*before you gentlemen, if total exemption cannot be granted to me, I
pary (pray) that sufficient time may be given to me to return to Jersey
to attend to matters and to do what I can and to make such provision as
circumstances permit for such aged parents.*

*It is very necessary that my wife and I should make up our home in
Jersey and undertake the care of my aged mother and father, owing to
the prolonged serious illness of my mother, as well as to the incapacity
of my father to attend to matters of important business, and being (the)
only son living, I am responsible, and the only one able to do anything
for them.*

Edward was one of nine children, born to Edward Henry aged 60, and Ann
Mary Le Ruez, who was 65. Three of them were sons and six were daughters,
although by the time of the 1911 Channel Islands Census, five of the siblings
were dead. One of them, Ada, was living in Jersey in 1911 married to Albert
Moon.

On Saturday, 15 July 1916, the death was announced in Germany of
Prince Gerhard Blücher von Wahlstatt, who was the great-grandson of
Gerbhard Leberecht von Blücher, who defeated Napoleon at the Battle of the
Nations, at Leipzig, Saxony, 16–19 October 1813. He also played a decisive
role in the final allied victory at the Battle of Waterloo on 18 June 1815 at the
remarkable age of 73.

The prince was very unpopular in Germany because of his marked
friendliness towards Great Britain, in fact he had lived here for many years,
on the Island of Herm in the Channel Islands and only left there because of
pressure from the British Government at the outbreak of the war. This was
at odds with the British Royal Family of the time. On 17 July 1917, King
George V changed the name of the British Royal House from that of Saxe-
Coburg and Gotha to the House of Windsor. The king's cousin, Prince Louis
Battenberg, who earlier in the war had been forced to resign his position as
First Sea Lord of the Royal Navy, because of anti-German feeling, suddenly
became Louis Mountbatten, the 1st Marquess of Milford Haven.

At the outbreak of the war, there was an outcry in a section of the British
newspapers over his continued presence on the island of Herm, which was of
absolutely no military importance. Prince Blücher spent so much time living
in Britain, some factions in Germany often referred to him as 'the English
Prince' and one of his sons was a British subject. A German newspaper of
the time, the *Lokal-Anzeiger* carried an article which stated that 'but for the
war the Prince would not have died on German soil'. In fact the Prince was
actually in Prussia at the outbreak of the war.

On Wednesday, 23 August 1916 the Legislative Assembly at Guernsey,
passed the Compulsory Military Service Bill, which had been drawn up by
the Crown Officers of the Island on the lines of the English Act. There was
however, one striking difference in the clause concerning exemptions, the one

concerning conscientious objectors; in the Guernsey version, none would be allowed. The Act came into force fifty days after it had been registered on the island's Law Book, that is to say, as soon as it was returned by the Lords of the Privy Council with Royal Sanction. It would be another three months before the Jersey States would similarly fall in to line with the same Act.

By Saturday, 26 August 1916 the beautiful islands of Guernsey, Alderney, Sark and Jersey, had more than played their part in the First World War. Besides sending many of their young men off to fight, they had also done a great deal on the home front. Flag days and garden parties helped to swell the fund-raising efforts of numerous local charities, that were supported by different groups throughout the islands, most of which were run by women, thus allowing them to show their compassion and generosity for the local men who were away fighting in the war.

The many wounded British soldiers who had been sent to the Channel Islands to recuperate were grateful for having been sent to such a location. The only complaint from the local residents came in the form of a simple question, why hadn't more wounded military personnel been sent, to experience the knowledge and friendliness of the medical staff, as well as the clean fresh air and the scenery on view from any of the islands.

Many of the local young men enlisted in the Royal Navy or the Mercantile Marine (today's Merchant Navy) because they came from generations of sea-faring families, who had either been fishermen, sailors in the navy, or had worked on ships in one capacity or another. For many families throughout the islands it was a choice between either a life of working on the high seas or farming and labouring on the land. The seafaring men were respected and appreciated for what they did, and the dangers they endured, for the benefit of their local community and their nation.

On Tuesday, 5 September 1916 Second Lieutenant Harold Buchanan **Ryley** of the 4th Battalion, attached to the 1st Battalion, North Staffordshire Regiment was killed in action on the Western Front, during the Battle of the Somme. He was the second son of the Reverend Harold Buchanan Ryley, who was formerly the headmaster of the Emmanuel School, Wandsworth Common.

When war was declared, Harold junior volunteered for service and was given a commission in the North Staffordshire Regiment. He spent a number of months stationed in Guernsey, with the 4th Battalion, before being attached to the 1st Battalion, and sent to France in May 1915, where he remained until he was killed leading a bombing party towards enemy lines. His body was not recovered and he has no known grave, but his name is commemorated on the Thiepval Memorial on the Somme.

On Saturday, 15 December 1917 Lieutenant Harold Buchanan Ryley senior, who was 49 years of age, was killed in action. He served in the 1st/5th Battalion, Suffolk Regiment and was buried at the Ramleh War Cemetery in Israel.

Second Lieutenant Adolphe Barbier **Amy** (33) served with the Jersey Militia, on the island of his birth, before joining the 9th Battalion, Royal Irish Rifles, with whom he went to France on 14 May 1916. It was initially reported that he had been missing in action and wounded. It subsequently transpired that he had not been captured and held as a prisoner of war by the Germans. No body having been found, he was officially reported as having been killed on 19 September 1916, the same day he was reported as missing. His name is commemorated on the Menin Gate Memorial which is situated in Ypres.

A newspaper report dated Friday, 17 November 1916 explained how the Military Service Act was registered at the Guernsey Royal Court, the required official documentation having been received by them from His Majesty's Government in London. The Act suspended all laws appertaining to the island's Militia, and gave thirty days notice from the date of the Act's official registration at the Guernsey Royal Court, that all British subjects in Guernsey, Sark, Herm, and Jethou, who were between 18 and 41 years of age, were, with certain exceptions, liable to be conscripted into the army for the duration of the war.

In enabling the Act throughout the Channel Islands, the British Government recognised that a large number of eligible men were already serving in the Royal Navy or one of the British Army's regiments.

It was sad to think that the Military Services Act 1916, which brought in and legalised conscription, was the first time in British military history that such steps had been taken. All previous British armies had consisted of volunteers, militia and professional soldiers. The Military Services Act 1916 also brought in another issue which had never previously been considered, conscientious objectors; men who did not want to fight, not because they were cowards but because they didn't want to kill other human beings. Some were simply pacifists, whilst others had genuinely held religious beliefs which prevented them from wanting to fight. Some of these men were prepared to act as stretcher bearers, orderlies, ambulance drivers and in Labour Corps.

As an example of just how brave some of these men were take the case of William Harold Coltman (23) who volunteered for Army Service in January 1915 and was posted to the North Staffordshire (Prince of Wales's) Regiment, and sent to the Western Front as a rifleman. The death and destruction he witnessed at first hand convinced him that the killing of other human beings was not what he wanted to do. Bravely he asked to be allowed to serve as a non-combatant soldier, undertaking stretcher bearer duties because of his religious beliefs.

Slightly built physically and only 5ft 4in tall, what he lacked in physical prowess, he more than made up for in courage and a steely determination to save as many of his comrades as possible from a slow, lonely and painful death in no man's land. Whilst acting as a stretcher bearer, and without firing a single shot or killing one single German soldier, William Harold Coltman, became the most highly decorated soldier from the other ranks of the British Army throughout the First World War. He was Mentioned in Despatches and was awarded the French *Croix de Guerre*, the Military Medal twice, the Distinguished Conduct Medal twice, and the Victoria Cross which was presented by King George V at Buckingham Palace, in May 1919.

On Thursday, 23 November 1916, the States of Jersey unanimously amended the Local Military Service Act 1916, bringing it into line with the English version of the Act. By its provisions, all men between 18 and 41 years of age would be liable to be enrolled in the British Army. The conscientious objectors' clause was unanimously thrown out by the States and the Militia Bill was suspended for the duration of the war. Oddly enough they also prohibited the export of all potatoes from the island until further notice.

December 1916 brought with it some much needed, yet totally unintentional humour. A woman from the Channel Islands wrote to the Foreign Office in London to apply for a passport, so that she could pay a visit to England. This was the official reply that she received, signed by a clerk and accompanied by the official rubber stamp of the Foreign Office:

> *Miss,*
>
> *It is my pleasure to inform you that passports are not issued to British Subjects living abroad for the purpose of coming to England. They may however be obtained from the British Consul in the Channel Islands.*

Sad yet funny that an official of whatever position working in the Foreign Office in London, didn't appear to know that the Channel Islands wasn't a foreign country and that there was no British Consul in the Channel Islands in 1916.

As the war approached its third Christmas, it was known to some that peace could have possibly come about, not once but twice during the year, because of a German realisation that this was a war which had turned out to be much more expensive in both financial and human cost than they had ever imagined. There were newspaper reports as early as 8 February 1916 with talk of the German Chancellor Theobald von Bethmann-Hollweg having put forward a peace proposal, but this faltered early on, as its main tenet was a return to pre-war boundaries which if accepted would have meant that the hundreds of thousands of Allied soldiers had died for nothing, with even larger numbers having been wounded, and all for what?

In November 1916 the new British Prime Minister David Lloyd George reiterated that the British and French position on the war was that an acceptable peace could be only be achieved with the total and absolute defeat of Germany. This dismissed the letter which had been circulated by Henry Petty-Fitzmaurice, the 5th Marquess of Lansdowne, who had called for a negotiated peace for the benefit of the world as a whole.

CHAPTER FOUR

1917 – Seeing It Through

The third year of the war saw the formation of the Royal Guernsey Light Infantry, which was an official infantry regiment of the British Army. The men's training, and most of their wartime commitments, took place from 1917 onwards, so rather than split their endeavours into each of the yearly chapters they are included here.

The regiment's origins came from the Royal Guernsey Militia, a group of unpaid volunteers, whose task was to defend the island from foreign invaders. The other Channel Islands of Jersey, Alderney and Sark had similar militias.

Although official documents make mention of an armed body of Guernsey men formed as far back as 1203, by order of King John, it wasn't until more than a hundred years later, in 1337, when Thomas de Ferres had been tasked by King Edward III to form and train local militias, that the militias of Guernsey, Jersey, Alderney and Sark became officially supported fighting units, thus making them the oldest in the British Army. By then the militia had already proved its worth by twice, repelling attempts by the French to invade the islands, the last occasion being in 1336. But the French were not to be deterred from their quest to conquer the islands, because in 1338, they tried again and on this occasion French forces, under the command of their highly respected Admiral Nicolas Béhuchet, landed on the west coast of the island. They were met by men of the Guernsey Militia at Les Hubits. That same year the French navy defeated the English at the Battle of Arnemuiden, where Béhuchet ordered the massacre of the captured English prisoners.

Two years later the English fleet of King Edward III attacked the unsuspecting French fleet of King Philip VI, which was at anchor in the inlet at Sluys, between West Flanders and Zeeland. It resulted in a resounding English victory with King Philip's navy being nearly completely destroyed. Béhuchet was taken prisoner, but his captivity was to be short lived; when once it was realised who he was, he was hanged for his massacre of English sailors at the Battle of Arnemuiden.

The French continued their attempts to occupy the islands and were successful in 1340 when they landed in Guernsey and held out in Castle Cornet, in the east of the island, for five years until August 1345. In 1358 the French returned in force yet again, but this time held out for only a year before they were sent packing back home. There were two further attempts to regain the islands in 1372 and 1461, both of which failed.

Badge of the Royal Guernsey Light Infantry.

In 1783 the militia men of Guernsey showed their worth yet again, when on 27 March of that year, they played a prominent role in quelling a mutiny by some 500 mainly Irish troops who were stationed at Fort George.

A law was passed on Guernsey in 1901 which made service in the militia compulsory for all men up to the age of 45 in peace time and 60 in a time of war. The establishment of this compulsory force stood at 1,000 during peacetime and double that number during a time of war. The Royal Guernsey Militia consisted of three regiments, two of which were infantry units and the other artillery. But they were a home based, defensive force which could only become involved in an armed conflict outside Guernsey to help the monarch regain his throne. On 17 December 1916 the militia was disbanded and the Royal Guernsey Light Infantry was formed, consisting of two battalions. The men of the 1st (Service) Battalion were allowed to serve overseas, whilst the 2nd (Reserve) Battalion remained in Guernsey. This also coincided with the island's authorities bringing in military conscription in line with the same conditions as were imposed on the rest of the British mainland.

The Military Services Act 1916, which allowed for men to be lawfully conscripted into the British Army, came into effect on 2 March 1916. It determined that all men between the ages of 18 and 41 were eligible to be called up to serve in the British Army. The exceptions to this, were married men, widowers with dependent children, those already serving in the Royal Navy, a minister of any religious denomination, or a man who was working in what had been officially recognised as a reserved occupation. In May 1916, the Act was amended by the authorities, so that all men between the ages of 18 and 41, regardless of their marital status, were liable to be conscripted, and those men who had previously been declared medically unfit for military service were liable to be re-examined. There would be three more amendments to the Act before the end of the war. The third was in April 1917, the fourth in January 1918, and the fifth and final change came in April 1918.

An interesting point surrounding the subject of conscription was that in the eighteen months between August 1914 and the introduction of the first Military Service Act in January 1916, some 3 million men had volunteered for military service. In the thirty-three months between January 1916 and the end of the war, an estimated 2.3 million men had been conscripted.

The Royal Guernsey Light Infantry did not fare well during the First World War. According to Wikipedia, of those from the island who left their homes and families to go to war, 327 were killed, another 667 were wounded and a further 250 were captured and became prisoners of war.

The men of the 1st Battalion, Royal Guernsey Light Infantry saw their fair share of action during their time spent on the Western Front – at Ypres, Passchendaele, Cambrai in 1917 and Lys, Estaires, and Hazebrouck in 1918.

A brief history of the Royal Guernsey Light Infantry

17 December 1916 – Founding of the Royal Guernsey Light Infantry. This consisted of one unit, the 1st (Service) Battalion. Many of the men who had previously served with the Royal Guernsey Militia volunteered to join the island's newly formed regiment; others were conscripted from their civilian lives.

Fort George 1917 – This is where the men of the Royal Guernsey Light Infantry, began their military training. It is situated in St Peter Port, Guernsey and was built as the island's main military headquarters, housing the Barracks. The construction of the Fort began in 1780, but it would be another thirty-two years before it was completed and ready for use. Over the course of time the number of troops stationed on the island was greatly increased to act as a deterrent against the possibility of a French invasion. They also used the area at L'Ancresse, which included beaches and a large common, and at Beaucamps.

1 June 1917 – Training in England – The regiment left Guernsey and travelled to England for infantry training at Bourne Park Camp, Bishopsbourne, near Canterbury in Kent. They became part of 202 Brigade, 67th (2nd Home Counties) Division, which carried out Home Defence duties, as well as recruitment, training and the re-supplying of overseas units with replacement soldiers. During the Second World War, besides other purposes, it was used as a D-Day Marshalling area.

July 1917 – 2nd (Reserve) Battalion – It was decided that the regiment needed to be increased in size. This saw the formation of the 2nd (Reserve) Battalion, which allowed for more recruits to enlist and be trained up as future replacements for those men who were wounded and killed whilst serving in the 1st (Service) Battalion. With the number of casualties that the Royal Guernsey Light Infantry sustained on the Western Front, having a second battalion proved to be extremely useful.

September 1917 – Final Leave – With deployment to France just over the horizon, the men of the 1st Battalion, Royal Guernsey Light Infantry were sent home on leave to spend some time with their friends and loved ones. For some, although they didn't know it at the time, this would be farewell.

26 September 1917 – The journey to France – A total of 44 officers and 964 men from the other ranks, travelled by train to Southampton, from where they were transported across the English Channel to France. They landed in Le Havre the next day, before then travelling by train again, to their base at 'Stoke Camp' in the Belgian village of Proven, close to the border with France, where they became part of 86 Brigade of the 29th Division.

Instead of leaving for France with their comrades, two officers and fifty-three other ranks, returned home to Guernsey where on arrival they were posted to the regiment's 2nd (Reserve) Battalion, either because they had been unfit, too old or too young to be sent to the front.

The Battle of Poelcappelle 9–14 October 1917 was the first action that the men of the Royal Guernsey Light Infantry fought during the First World War. Part of the Third Battle of Ypres (Passchendaele) it was fought in the Flanders region of Belgium. The regiment lost four men during this campaign, the first men from the regiment to lose their lives during the First World War. All were killed on 14 October were buried at the Cement House Cemetery in the West-Vlanderen region of Belgium.

Major Archibald Henry Pingston **Davey** (36) was the son of William John and Emily Davey, of London and husband of Hester P. Davey, of 5, Springfield Terrace, King's Rd., Guernsey.

Private (22) John **Bourgaize** (27) was the husband of Mabel Le Pelley Bourgaize, of Lukis House, Grange, St Peter Port, Guernsey.

Private (470) Philip **Guille** (25) was the son of Philip and Lizzie Guille, of 'La Tour', Sark.

Cement House Cemetery.

Private (213) Wallace Henry Le Poidevin (20) was the Son of Isaac and Mary Le Poidevin, of 8, Mont Morin, St Sampson's, Guernsey.

October and November 1917 – Saw the officers and men of the 1ˢᵗ Battalion, Royal Guernsey Light Infantry undergoing training for the forthcoming Battle of Cambrai.

20 November – 3 December 1917 – Battle of Cambrai – This was a defining moment of the First World War, in that it was the first time in modern warfare, that large numbers of tanks were used in battle by the British Army. The commander of the newly formed Tank Corps, Brigadier General Hugh Elles, had come up with the idea for such a collaboration so that he could demonstrate the worth of his tanks.

It was also the first time that tanks, some 500 to begin with, eight infantry divisions, elements of the Royal Flying Corps, artillery units which included some 1,000 guns, and five cavalry divisions, had all worked together in the war. The logistics of moving so much equipment and so many men to Cambrai, without alerting the Germans to what was taking place, was no mean feat, but it was achieved, with 6.20am on 20 November 1917, designated as zero hour. The enemy were taken totally by surprise and their front-line positions, were quickly overrun, with British forces pushing some five miles into enemy held territory.

The battle was also a watershed moment in the regiment's existence. It certainly started well. The Royal Guernsey Light Infantry had been tasked with pushing through the Hindenburg Line after the first wave of British troops to take an area that was known as 'Nine Wood' or the Bois des Neufs, to the north of Marcoing. Their fight started in the early hours of the afternoon and the Guernsey men achieved their objective.

By 30 November 1917 the Germans had recovered from the shock of the initial British attack on their positions and counter-attacked. The Royal Guernsey Light Infantry were ordered to move south to the village of Les Rues Vertes on the south side of the St Quentin Canal, but to do so they had to cross the canal from the north to provide support for the other British units that had already engaged the enemy, entering the village unopposed from the south.

The village's narrow streets meant close quarter combat between the British and German forces, was the order of the day. Sometimes bloody and brutal, sometimes hand-to-hand fighting, over a two-day period they lost and regained control of the village twice. After it was all over the men from Guernsey, who had fought spiritedly, had sustained heavy casualties, with some 40 per cent of their number either missing, killed or wounded. But they were a determined bunch of men who eventually withdrew from their position only because they had been ordered to do so.

Many of the wounded were sent back to Guernsey, rather than mainland Britain, for further medical treatment. The more serious cases ended up at the Victoria Military Hospital at Amherst and the less seriously injured, and those who needed rest, recuperation and convalescence, were sent to the hospital at Les Touillets in Castel, Guernsey.

What was left of the regiment were still in France. Initially, they were given a well-deserved rest; lost and damaged equipment was replaced and physical fitness was maintained for the men's wellbeing and discipline. The main problem which the regiment then had to face was finding suitable replacements for the men who had been lost. Because of the high level of casualties sustained, there simply were not enough suitably qualified and abled-bodied Guernsey men available as replacements. This meant that as 1917 drew to a close and a new year fast approached, the regiment was split 50/50 between Guernsey and non-Guernsey men.

By the time the fighting was over at Cambrai both sides had lost an estimated combined total of 80,000 officers and men, who had either been wounded, killed or missing. The Commonwealth War Graves Commission website records that between 20 November and 3 December 1917, the Royal Guernsey Light Infantry, had a total of 118 men who were either killed in action or who died of their wounds, illness or disease.

January to early April 1918 – For the first three months of the year, the men of the Royal Guernsey Light Infantry, were not involved in anything too traumatic. They undertook a few duties in the front-line trenches at Sint-Jan, north-east of Ypres and were also involved in training, as well as being detailed as work parties. They were also in the front-line trenches at Poelcappelle, in the Belgium province of West-Flanders, at the end of March.

The first week of April saw them once again tasked with front-line trench duties, this time in the Passchendaele sector, but the most exciting thing that happened to them was when they were suddenly moved out of the line and transported by lorry to the nearby French town of Vieux-Berquin in the Lys area. The reason for this unexpected re-deployment was because a surprise German offensive had broken through the Allied lines in that area.

The Battle of the Lys 10 – 14 April 1918 – During the Battle of the Lys just east of Hazebrouck, the Allied lines were breached by elements of the German Sixth Army. What was left of the Royal Guernsey Light Infantry had arrived in the area earlier to bolster the already fragmented defensive positions, in an effort to stem the German advance. On their arrival they had a strength of 503 officers and men but, hopelessly outnumbered, the best they could do was to slow down the German advance, by performing a fighting retreat from Le Doulieu to near Merris.

Before the men of the 1st (Service) Battalion, Royal Guernsey Light Infantry were relieved by units from the Australian 1st Division, it is fair to say that they took a hell of a battering.

The *London Gazette* of 21 October 1918 included the despatches of Field Marshal Douglas Haig, part of which included the following comments:

> After very heavy fighting, in the course of which the 1st Battalion, Royal Guernsey Light Infantry, 29th Division, Major-General D E Cayley, CMG. commanding the division, did gallant service...

The Commonwealth War Graves Commission website records that between 10 and 14 April 1918, a total of 113 officers and men of the regiment were killed or died of their wounds, meaning that out of the 503 members of the Royal Guernsey Light Infantry who arrived in the Lys area on 10 April, there were only 110 of fighting strength left – 393 of them were wounded during that same four-day period which equates to 78 per cent casualties.

Royal Guernsey Light Infantry, withdrawn from the 29th Division and 86 Brigade – 27 April 1918 – The effort and sacrifice that the Royal Guernsey Light Infantry had made, had not gone un-noticed by the Army's top brass. They were removed from front-line commitments and sent to guard Field Marshal Haig and his staff of the British Expeditionary Force, who were located in the French town of Montreuil in the Pas de Calais. Haig travelled the two miles each morning and evening between his headquarters and where he slept at the Chateau Beaurepaire under the protection of his 'Guernsey bodyguards'.

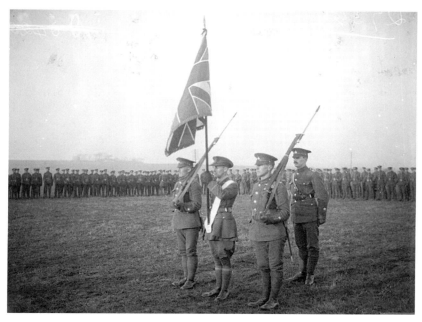

Colour Party, Royal Guernsey Light Infantry at Montreuil 1919.

Haig and the rest of his staff remained at Montreuil until 5 April, because although the Armistice had been signed, the war still wasn't officially over. It didn't finally come to an end until 28 June 1919 when Germany signed the Treaty of Versailles.

With the war over and their work finally done, the remainder of the Royal Guernsey Light Infantry, who were from the island, made their way back to Guernsey, on board the SS *Lydia*, arriving there on 22 May 1919. The *Lydia* had been built in 1890 as a passenger vessel for the London and South Western Railway, sailing between Southampton and Guernsey. In 1915 she had been attacked by a German submarine whilst at sea, but fortunately for the crew and passengers on board at the time, the torpedo missed.

The following men of the regiment were awarded various orders and medals:

Order of St Michael and St George (Companion) (3rd Class)

Lieutenant Colonel Thomas Lyttleton de Havilland.
Royal Victorian Order (5th Class)

Lieutenant N.R. Ingouille
Military Cross

SS Lydia.

Captain T. Hutchesson
Lieutenant F. de M. Laine
Lieutenant H.A. Le Bas
Second Lieutenant E.J. Stone
Second Lieutenant H.E.K. Stranger
Distinguished Conduct Medal

Corporal 569 W.H. Budden
Serjeant 586 H.L. James
Serjeant 590 W.J. Le Poidevin
Military Medal

Private 841 T.R. Robins
Private 610 C.H. Yeaghers
Corporal 843 J. Seally
Corporal 335 W. Gannicott
Private 458 G. Ruaux
Medaille Militaire **(French version of Military Medal)**

Corporal 843 J. Seally
Mentioned in Despatches

Lieutenant Colonel Thomas Lyttleton de Havilland
Lieutenant E.A. Dorey
Lance Corporal 438 C.W. Hockey
Lieutenant H. Jones
Lance Corporal 226 Lance Corporal
Lance Corporal 1131 W.T. Robinson

One of the photographs in the Alderney Museum shows sixty-one officers and men from Alderney in a group photograph taken somewhere in France in 1917, but only twenty-nine of the men are actually identified. The names of these men are as follows:

I first checked the Medal Rolls Index Cards, that cover the period of the First World War, for William **Angel**, there were twenty men recorded with that name. Of these, one, a William H. Angel, was a Gunner (102851) in the Royal Garrison Artillery. I make mention of this, as two other men in the same photograph, served with artillery units. I then checked a list of British soldiers who died in the First World War. This showed Gunner (192308) William Angel, who enlisted at St Peter Port, Guernsey and joined the 41st Siege Battery, Royal Garrison Artillery. He died of his wounds on 21 March 1918, the first day of the German Spring Offensive, and is buried at the Roye New British Cemetery, in the Somme region of France.

B. **Antequil**. I could find no mention of anybody with this name.

John **Baker**. I found a John Nicholas Baker, who at the outbreak of the war was 14 years of age. He was shown as being a stone worker who lived at Braye Street, St Annes, Alderney. I could find no trace of any military connection with a John Baker, living anywhere in the Channel Islands.

George **Baron**. I could find no direct match for this man, this included a search of the Medal Rolls Index, for men who served in the British Army during the period of the First World War. It showed a total of 13 men with the name George Baron. Two of them, Bombardier (92919) George F. Baron, and Gunner (192259) George J. Baron, served in the Royal Garrison Artillery.

Frank **Bideau** was a Gunner (192266) and a member of the 109th Field Company, Royal Garrison Artillery. It would appear that Bideau and Blondin enlisted at the same time as they have consecutive Army service numbers. The chances are that these two men knew one another and it is quite possible that they were good friends. He survived the war.

John Lucas **Blondin** was Gunner (192265) who served with the 109th Field Company, Royal Garrison Artillery. His name is not one of those included on the Alderney War Memorial, so I can say with some degree of certainty that he survived the war.

Jack **Buckle**. The Medal Rolls Index Cards for the First World War, showed three men with the name of Jack Buckle. One served with the Bedfordshire Regiment, another with the Yorkshire Regiment and the other with the Royal Army Medical Corps. The Jack Buckle in the photograph could be one of these three men, but I have no way of being able to distinguish which one it is for certain. The 1911 Channel Islands Census showed nothing for a Jack Buckle.

Ben **Chivers**. Once again, I could find no direct match to this man.

Ned **Cherry**. I found nothing from the 1911 Census for this man and also checked military records, once again, with a negative result.

Reg **Cleal**. Nothing for him in the 1911 Channel Islands census, but I found a Gunner (192267) Reginald A. Cleal, with the Royal Garrison Artillery. The photograph that had his name added to it, was of artillery men, so there is a strong possibility that is one and the same person. The Medal Rolls Index Cards for the First World War also showed a Lance Corporal (27631) Reginald Cleal, who was a with the 1st Battalion, Somerset Light Infantry. He was killed in action in France on 4 October 1917.

Art **Goring** and F. **Goring**. The 1911 Channel Islands census shows the Goring family living at Breche Philipe, Alderney, which includes a 15-year-old Arthur Goring and a younger brother, Frederick, who was 12. There was an elder brother, Thomas, who was 18 and three sisters, Louisa (21), Annie (18) and Ethel (10). The Medal Rolls Index Cards, for the First World War, records seven men with the name Arthur Goring. One of these men, Gunner (192278) Arthur H. Goring, was in the Royal Garrison Artillery, whilst another, Driver (219966) Arthur Goring, was in the Royal Field Artillery. He had previously served with the Army Service Corps.

Also recorded are seven men with the name Frederick Goring. Of these two served in the Royal Garrison Artillery. Gunner (192277) Frederick R. Goring served in the Royal Garrison Artillery and Driver (111624) (202940) Frederick T. Goring served in both the Royal Field as well as the Royal Garrison Artillery.

As Frederick R. Goring (192277) and Arthur H. Goring (192278) have consecutive service numbers, and both served as Gunners in the Royal Garrison Artillery, it could be assumed with some degree of certainty, that they are the two men who are named in the photograph in the Alderney Museum.

Charles Harold **Hammond** was 26 years of age, and a Gunner 1922799, serving with the 226th Siege Battery, Royal Garrison Artillery, when he was killed in action on 13 August 1918. He was buried at the Gonnehem British Cemetery in the Pas de Calais. His parents' home was in the High Street, Alderney. Charles was the middle of five sons born to William and Elizabeth Hammond, with the youngest of the family being their daughter, Violet Maud Hammond.

One of Charles's younger brothers, Gunner (91352) Arthur Louis Hammond, who was with D Battery, 155th Army Brigade, Royal Field Artillery, was killed in action some ten months before Charles, on 26 October

1917. He is buried at the Buffs Road Cemetery in the West-Vlaanderen region of Belgium.

Helya. Although I believe this was somebody's surname, rather than their first name, a search of the 1911 Channel Island census, revealed nobody with that name. It was exactly the same result when checking the same name against the Medal Rolls Index Cards.

Sid **Lucas**. The Medal Rolls Index Cards for the British Army show twenty-eight men with that name, who served during the First World War, four of whom served with Artillery units.

Gunner (96750) Sidney R. Lucas, Royal Garrison Artillery

Driver (L/17852) Sidney Lucas, Royal Field Artillery

Driver (106161) Sidney C. Lucas, Royal Field Artillery

Gunner (192158) Sidney C. Lucas, Royal Garrison Artillery

There was no trace of a Sidney Lucas on the 1911 Channel Islands census.

Morton. A check of the 1911 Channel Island census shows only five men with the surname Morton, and only three of them would have been old enough to have served in the military. One of them was Private (8051) Frank Howard Morton, of the King's Own Royal Lancaster Regiment, who first arrived in France on 15 January 1915. He had originally enlisted on 16 December 1903, and was medically discharged from the Army, as a result of an unspecified sickness, on 18 May 1916. He was accordingly awarded a Silver War Badge (3564), indicating that he had been medically discharged from the Army. Wearing the badge stopped medically discharged soldiers from having to convince members of the public that they had done their bit for king and country. The badges were only issued once and could not be replaced.

Although detailed in its description, this does not mean this man is the same one referred to in the photograph. The obvious doubt that immediately comes to mind is the fact that he wasn't serving with an artillery unit.

Emile **Ogier**. The Medal Rolls Index Cards shows an Emile Ogier, who served as a Gunner (192201) in the Royal Garrison Artillery. He died of his wounds on 4 April 1918 whilst serving on the Western Front with the 253rd Siege Battery and is buried at the Picquigny British Cemetery on the Somme. One of his brothers, John Ogier, enlisted in the American Army at Akron, Ohio on 5 June 1917.

Henry **Oliver**. The 1911 Channel Island Census shows a Henry G. Oliver living at 1 Little Street, Alderney, Channel Islands. By the end of hostilities he would have been 20 years of age, more than old enough to have served during the First World War. A check of the Medal Rolls Index Cards shows a Bombardier (192293) Henry G. Oliver of the Royal Garrison Artillery. It also shows another Henry G. Oliver who served with the Royal Field Artillery as a Corporal (L/46065), and who was later transferred to the 9th Lancers. Of the two possibilities, I would opt for the first one as being the Henry Oliver named on the photograph.

I was, however, unable to find any information about Jim **Oliver,** Patrick **Reals,** Frank **Palzard** or Archie **Rowe** in either the 1911 Channel Islands census or the Medal Rolls Index Cards.

The 1911 Channel Islands census records an Albert **Simonet**, aged 13 and living at Longy Road, Alderney with his parents and his five brothers and sisters. A check of the Medal Rolls Index Cards shows an Albert J. Simonet as a Gunner (192299) in the Royal Garrison Artillery.

Harold John **Squires** enlisted on 26 January 1917 at Alderney, when he became a Gunner (192300) in the 109th Company, Field Artillery. He was posted to the 1st/1st (SAR) Battalion on 22 July 1918, to the 4th/1st (SAR) Battalion, on 5 August 1918, before ending up 2nd/1st (SAR) Battalion, Royal Garrison Artillery, where he was posted on 8 March 1919. He died at the 2nd Eastern General Hospital, Brighton on 24 March 1919, when he was just 20 years of age, of broncho-pneumonia and a cerebral abscess. He was buried at the Brighton City Cemetery, Bear Road, Brighton.

His parents, Richard and Elizabeth Squires, lived at Lower High Street, Alderney. There is a form, W.5080, which is part of his Army Service Record, and dated 17 June 1919, which shows that he had two brothers, Ernest, who was 22 years of age and Alfred, who was 19, who were both stationed at Fort George, Guernsey, but it does not record what regiment or corps they were serving with.

There was no trace of a Jack **Talbot** in the 1911 Channel Islands Census, or on other military records. Nor could I find information on Alfred **White**, other than during the First World War, 377 men with that name died whilst serving with different units of the British and Dominion forces. There was no direct match for anyone with the surname **Trustam**, although the name has Channel Island connections.

In relation to the surname **Rolls**, I found a Frederick John Rolls, and although he didn't serve with an Artillery unit, he was a 29-year-old Private (1196) in the 1st (Service) Battalion, Royal Guernsey Light Infantry, who was killed in action on 27 April 1918, which was after the date of the group photograph in question. He is buried at the Tournai Communal Cemetery, Allied Extension in the Hainaut region of Belgium.

It would have been extremely interesting to have the names of all of the men in the photograph, to see who survived the war and those that unfortunately didn't.

Here are some other relevant moments of the year 1917 which involved the Channel Islands and its people.

On Sunday, 14 January 1917 a newspaper article reported that a Mr James John Walkey appeared before the Royal Court in Jersey charged under the Defence of the Realm Regulations, with having circulated a rumour that the

Great Western cross-channel steamer *Ibex* had been torpedoed whilst on a voyage to the Channel Islands. He was found guilty as charged and fined the princely sum of £1. Unfortunately, the report did not include how the matter came to be reported and what if any reason Mr Walkey had for spreading such a rumour.

The 1911 Census shows a John James Walkey, aged 49 years, who lived with his wife Henrietta and their three children, Jack, May and Doris at 61 St Saviour Road, Jersey. He was employed as a chauffeur. John and Henrietta had married in 1890, a union which had seen the birth of six children over the years, but by 1911, the census of that year recorded that three of them had already died.

On Saturday, 10 March 1917, the following letter was received by the editor of the *Belfast News Letter*. It had been sent by Mr James P. De Veulle, who was the Hon. Secretary of the London Channel Islanders' Society Comforts Fund, of 153 St Asaph Road, Brockley, London.

> *Sir,*
>
> *As my committee would be glad to have the help of a few local residents to act as voluntary visitors to the wounded men in the hospitals in your district, I venture to ask whether you would kindly insert this letter in your paper.*
>
> *The wounded men in whom we are particularly interested, all originate from the Channel Islands; therefore, this request for voluntary helpers is a special appeal to those of your readers who formerly resided in the Channel Islands. The necessary funds for providing a weekly parcel of comforts for the wounded Channel Islanders in the various hospitals have been generously contributed to our comforts fund by residents in the islands and by members and friends of the London Channel Islanders' Society.*
>
> *Therefore, may I ask those who are willing to help by occasionally visiting the wounded men in your district to write to me at the above address, and I shall be happy to send fuller particulars. I should also be obliged if matrons of hospitals, nursing sisters and others would send me a postcard if they have any wounded or sick men from the Channel Islands under their charge.*

This seemed to be a common theme for wounded soldiers from the Channel Islands who were in hospitals up and down the country, where letters requesting similar assistance for them appeared in many local newspapers.

A general theme for many of the newspaper articles about the Channel Islands during the First World War consisted mainly of stories about cattle, beef, flowers, tomatoes or potatoes, all of which, with the possible exception of the flowers, usually appertained to how these items helped to sustain the population of Britain throughout the war years. The winter of 1916/17 was particularly severe. One of the knock-on effects was a late potato harvest throughout the islands due to snow and frost which continued until 15 February 1917, meaning that the planting which usually began at the end of January, was delayed by a month, with the crop then not being available until May 1917. With potatoes being part of the nation's staple diet, the shortage was a real issue.

An announcement was made in the Press in April 1917 about, a marriage having been arranged between Lieutenant Colonel J.A.C. Forsyth DSO, of the Royal Field Artillery, who was from Dorset, and Ethel Winifred Robin, of Steephill, Jersey. Ethel was one of four children born to Charles Janvrin and Henrietta Robin. Her father who had been a banker and a barrister, was very well off, enabling the family to employ seven servants. Charles died in 1912, and in his Will, he left £72,930 9s 4d. With the value of the £ of 1912 being worth £112.04 in today's (2018) money, he left the equivalent sum of £8,171,650.54.

Charles had two sons, Charles junior, who was born in 1887, and Guy, in 1889. According to the 1911 Census, Guy was a university undergraduate and Student at Law, whilst Charles, had studied at University College, Oxford. Charles joined the Jersey Militia in 1907 and was gazetted to the Royal Fusiliers the following year, but because of ill health, he resigned his commission in 1910. At the outbreak of the war in August 1914, he was mobilized with the rest of the Jersey Militia and in 1915 he was attached to the York and Lancaster Regiment and sent to Egypt. In 1916 he went to France and was killed in action on 11 May 1917 at Gavrelle and buried at the Military Cemetery, Bailleul-Sir- Berthoult in the Pas de Calais. A fellow officer wrote of him:

> *He was always ready to go anywhere and do anything, he was utterly unselfish and continually helping others in any way he could.*

Another officer wrote of him:

> *I had the greatest admiration for the way he carried out his work without any idea of sparing himself.*

Charles was a married man, his wedding to Yvonne Lempriere, of Rosel Manor, Jersey, the daughter of Reginald Raoul Lempriere, the Seigneur of Rosel and Viscount of Jersey, having taken place on 17 September 1913. The couple's first child, Raoul Charles Robin, was born on 6 September 1914.

The evening of Sunday, 29 July 1917 saw the death of Mrs Elvina Braine, of the Wellington Hotel, Gloucester, the wife of Alderman Henry Richard James Braine of Gloucester. The cause of her death was arteriosclerosis, which is the hardening and loss of elasticity of the arteries.

Mrs Braine was the daughter of the late Captain George Allix, who was a prominent ship owner from the Channel Islands. It was whilst on a visit to Jersey that Mr Braine first met his future wife. They married in Jersey in 1885 but decided to settle in Gloucester rather than the Channel Islands where they had four children, two sons and two daughters. During her husband's year as the Mayor of Gloucester, she managed to juggle the roles of being a mother and a supportive wife, having to oversee many receptions and other social functions attached to his official appointment. Her well-attended funeral took place in her adopted home at Barnwood in Gloucestershire on the 1 August 1917.

On 11 August 1917 an amended Army Order was issued in relation to the award of the Silver War Badge, for men who had been discharged after service, having served overseas. It incorporated anybody who had served in the British military, including those from the Channel Islands, after 4 August 1914. This meant that thousands of men from Guernsey, Jersey, Alderney and Sark, who had been wounded fighting for their country, would get to wear the Silver War Badge. Each badge had an individual number which could be directly connected to the man it was issued to. No replacements were issued in the event of its loss.

Saturday, 15 September 1917 saw the tragic death of 19-year-old Lieutenant Reginald Walter Le Gallais of the Royal Flying Corps, who was killed when part of his aircraft broke away whilst he was flying at a great height. The inquest into his death was held at Faversham Guildhall on Monday, 17 September 1917 by the Deputy Coroner, Mr E.C. Harris.

Major Gerald Allen, the officer commanding the squadron that Lieutenant Le Gallais was part of, told the inquest that the deceased was an experienced pilot who had flown on active service in France. On the day of his death he was flying a single-seater 100hp tractor scout aircraft. It was a brand new aircraft, which had flown for sixty-four hours since leaving the factory, and it was thirty-eight hours since it had last been checked over.

At around 3pm Major Allen saw Lieutenant Gallais' aircraft falling from about 1,000ft up, and obviously out of control. As the aircraft turned, he could clearly see that the left wing had fallen off. His theory was that the under-plane strut had broken, which caused the top left part of the wing to collapse. The bottom left-hand wing then collapsed, causing the stricken aircraft to plummet to the ground. The actual machine had been flown earlier that day for a period of 54 minutes.

Walter Edgar Lilley, 2nd Class Air Mechanic and rigger, told the court that he had examined the aircraft before Lieutenant Gallais had taken it up and everything appeared to be fine with it. He said that the aircraft had been in the air for about 20 minutes, carrying out routine manoeuvres, when he saw it suddenly nosedive towards the ground and crash. He could offer no reasonable explanation as to why the aircraft should have performed the way that it did.

The deputy coroner in summing up, said that this was one of those cases where they would never be able to get to the bottom of what caused the accident. All that was available was supposition, theory and guess work, although an official enquiry into the matter was planned. He did not feel it was possible to delve any further into the matter at that time and that the correct course of action was to leave it with the relevant authorities to discover the truth.

During the evening of the day of the inquest, Lieutenant Gallais' coffin was conveyed on a gun carriage from the mortuary at Faversham Cottage Hospital and taken to the railway station for the onward journey for burial at St Saviour Churchyard, Jersey.

Lieutenant Gallais' brother, Captain Edmund Mark Gallais, who was also a pilot in the Royal Flying Corps, survived the war.

An incident in Jersey in October 1917 caused some humour in other parts of the country, when it was revealed that an un-named local man had gone before Military Tribunal in Jersey. It wasn't so much the detail of his application for requesting an exemption from having to undergo military training, but more the outcome. Evidently the good people of Jersey did not take an optimistic view as to the possibilities of there being an early end to the war, as the panel provided the man with a temporary exemption, but not for three months, nor six, not even nine, but eleven and specifically 30 September 1918. Maybe the committee members knew something that nobody else did. But that wasn't the end of the matter. Just to reinforce their apparent lack of optimism as to how soon they felt the war would end, they added the condition, 'not renewable'. It showed that those who sat on the tribunals in the Channel Islands, were more than capable of hardening their hearts, when the occasion so required. With the war finally coming to an end in November 1918, the Military Tribunals in Jersey appeared to have got it just about right.

November 1917 saw mention of how Berwick had become something of a haven for men from the Channel Islands. On Thursday, 22 November 1917 a Berwick and Spittal ferryman, who was also a noted sailor of many years experience, and whose travels had taken him all over the world, was buried at Berwick Cemetery. Mr Henry 'Harry' Demee, was 75 years of age when he passed away at his home in Church Street, Berwick, after a short illness. He was born in Jersey in 1841 and, coming from a seafaring island, he naturally took to a career on the ocean wave, like a fish to water.

Two other men in recent times who found themselves in Berwick, and who were born in the Channel Islands, were General Godfray and Edward Molley, who were both stationed at Berwick Army Barracks where they were serving with the King's Own Scottish Borderers.

An interesting article appeared in the *Yorkshire Post* on Saturday, 8 December 1917 which reflected extremely well on the fighting men of the Channel Islands. The important events of the last week of November and first week of December 1917 in what history has recorded as the Battle of Cambrai, had prevented Field Marshal Sir Douglas Haig from making any previous comment on the first appearance in the fighting line of a unit of Channel Islands troops.

The casualty lists, amongst which the Press had been allowed to make reference to the 'Guernsey Battalion', was in fact the Royal Guernsey Light Infantry. Early in the fighting the regiment lost its adjutant when Captain Alfred Frank Cyril Borrett was killed in action on Saturday, 24 November 1917. Although having never been in action before, the men from the Channel Islands were noted to have fought just as bravely as any others and with the steadiness of veterans. They consisted of a Service Battalion of the Guernsey Militia which provided most of the officers for the overseas unit.

It was noted that the men of Guernsey, had for many years been obliged to serve in the militia, which consisted of artillery, engineers and infantry soldiers, but that they were not under any compulsion to serve overseas. But once the war began there had been no lack of volunteers for the Service Battalion. The Channel Islanders had ties not just to Britain, but to France as well, and having undergone their baptism of fire they had done their bit for both Allied nations.

As the war approached its final year the steely determination and bravery, that the men of the Royal Guernsey Light Infantry had shown throughout the fighting at the Battle of Cambrai, had been noted. The fight was now on to finish the job once and for all, a fight in which the men of the Channel Islands would play their part.

CHAPTER FIVE

1918 – The Final Push

Acting Captain Allastair Malcolm Cluny McReady Diarmid VC, of the 17th (Service) Battalion, Middlesex Regiment, and who was 29 years of age, was awarded the Victoria Cross for his actions on 30 November and1 December 1917 for leading successful attacks against German positions, during the Battle of Cambrai.

The citation for the award of his Victoria Cross, read as follows;

In the Moeuvres Sector, France, when the enemy penetrated into our position, and the situation was extremely critical, Captain McReady-Diarmid led his company through a heavy barrage and immediately engaged the enemy and drove them back at least 300 yards, causing numerous casualties and taking 27 prisoners. The following day the enemy again attacked and drove back another company which had lost all its officers. The captain called for volunteers, and leading the attack, again drove them back. It was entirely due to his throwing of bombs that the ground was regained, but he was eventually killed by a bomb.

He has no known grave, but his name is commemorated on the Cambrai Memorial.

One man who had been stationed on Guernsey before the First World War, was awarded the Victoria Cross. Add to this his connection with the Belgian town of Marcoing, where the Royal Guernsey Light Infantry saw action during the Battle of Cambrai, and a 'story' linking the man with Adolf Hitler, makes this a tale worth telling.

Henry 'Napper' Tandey was born in Leamington in Warwickshire on 30 August 1891. His father, James Tandey, who had also been a soldier, died when Henry was still a very young boy. After leaving school he initially became a boiler attendant at a hotel in his home town and then took the decision to follow in his father's footsteps and enlisted in the British Army when he was 19 years of age in August 1910, initially becoming a Private (9545) in the 3rd Battalion, Alexandra, Princess of Wales's Own (Yorkshire Regiment) also known as the Green Howards. In his early years he served in South Africa and on his return to the United Kingdom he was stationed at Guernsey, more than likely at Fort George. This is where his connection with the island came from.

He first arrived in France on 5 October 1914 with the regiment's 2nd Battalion and almost immediately found himself in the thick of things, seeing action during the 1st Battle of Ypres, which took place between 19 October and 22 November 1914. Two years later he was wounded during the fighting of the Battle of the Somme, when he sustained a gunshot wound to one of his legs which resulted in his being sent back to the UK for treatment. Having recovered from his wounds, he was sent back to the Western Front, but now part of the 9th Battalion, with which he fought with during the Battle of Passchendaele in November 1917 and where he was once again wounded. When he was released from hospital he was posted to the regiment's 12th Battalion in France. On 26 July 1918 the 12th were disbanded, which resulted in Tandey and his colleagues being attached to the 5th Battalion, Duke of Wellington's Regiment.

On 28 August 1918, during fighting at Vaulx-Vraucourt in northern France, his actions resulted in him being awarded the Distinguished Conduct Medal. The citation for his award read as follows:

Private Henry Tandey, VC, DCM, MM.

> *Private 34506 H. Tandey, 5th Battalion, West Riding Regiment (TF) (Leamington).*
>
> *He was in charge of a reserve bombing party in action, and finding the advance temporarily held up, he called on two other men of his party, and working across the open in rear of the enemy, he rushed a post, returning with twenty prisoners, having killed several of the enemy. He was an example of daring courage throughout the whole of the operations.*

Two weeks later, on 12 September, he once again displayed his heroism, where during fighting at Havrincourt he was responsible for the capture of more German prisoners. For his actions that day he was awarded the Military Medal.

The award of the Victoria Cross came about as the result of his actions on 28 September 1918, for conspicuous bravery at Marcoing, this was the same location where the 1st Battalion, Royal Guernsey Light Infantry fought so bravely during the Battle of Cambrai on 30 November 1917.

The citation for the award of his Victoria Cross, which appeared in the *London Gazette* on 14 December 1918, read as follows:

> *For most conspicuous bravery and initiative during the capture of the village, and the crossings at Marcoing, and the subsequent counter attack on September 28th, 1918. When during the advance on Marcoing,*

his platoon was held up by machine-gun, he at once crawled forward, located the machine gun, and with a Lewis gun team, knocked it out. On arrival at the crossings he restored the plank bridge under a hail of bullets, thus enabling the first crossing to be made at this vital spot.

Later in the evening, during an attack, he, with eight comrades, was surrounded by an overwhelming number of Germans, and though the position was apparently hopeless, he led a bayonet charge through them, fighting so fiercely that 37 of the enemy were driven in to the hands of the remainder of his company.

Although twice wounded, he refused to leave till the fight was won

One of Private Tandey's comrades, Private H. Lister, gave the following account of what he witnessed that day.

On 28th September during the taking of the crossing over the Canal de St Quentin at Marconing, I was No.1 of the Lewis gun team of my platoon. I witnessed the whole of the gallantry of Private Tandey throughout the day. Under intensely heavy fire, he crawled forward in the village when we were held up by the enemy machine gun, and found where it was. He then led myself and other comrades with the gun in to a house from where we were able to bring Lewis gun fire on the machine gun and knock it out of action.

Later when we got to the canal crossings and the bridge was down, Private Tandey, under the fiercest of aimed machine gun fire, went forward and replaced planks over the bad part of the bridge to enable us all to cross over without delay, which would otherwise have ensued. On the same evening when we made another attack we were completely surrounded by Germans, and we thought the position might be lost. Private Tandey, without hesitation, though he was twice wounded very nastily, took the leading part in our bayonet charge on the enemy, to get clear. Though absolutely faint, he refused to leave us until we had completely finished our job, collected our prisoners and restored the line.

Tandey was also Mentioned in Despatches, five times relating to further acts of courage and bravery.

Now for the final part of this interesting story which brings in Private Tandey's supposed connection with Adolf Hitler. In 1938, the then British Prime Minister, Neville Chamberlain, visited Adolf Hitler at his alpine retreat in the Obersalzberg in the Bavarian Alps, near Berchtesgaden, known as the Berghof. The purpose of the meeting was for discussions which ultimately led to the Munich Agreement, which was an attempt to prevent war, some would say an appeasement. In essence it allowed Nazi Germany to annexe parts of Czechoslovakia, which ran parallel to its own borders, that in the main were inhabited by German-speaking people.

Whilst at the Berghof, Chamberlain, as the story goes, was taken by a painting hanging on one of the walls, as it quite clearly was a portrayal of British soldiers during the First World War. He asked about its relevance. Hitler is said to have replied:

> *That man came so close to killing me that I thought I should never see Germany again; Providence saved me from such devilish accurate fire as those English boys were aiming at us.*

So the story goes that Hitler asked Chamberlain to pass on his best wishes and gratitude to Tandey, which he agreed to do, promising to phone him personally on his return to England, something which he 'supposedly' did.

Before taking this further, let's look at a few facts. Firstly, the painting in question does actually exist. It was commissioned by the Green Howards Regiment in 1923 and depicts a British soldier carrying a wounded comrade at the Kruiseke Crossroads in 1918, somewhere north-west of Menin. The painter was Italian artist, Fortunino Matania, and the main soldier in the painting who is carrying his wounded comrade is supposedly Private Henry Tandey.

Besides being an extremely brave and courageous individual, Tandey had proved on many an occasion, that in the heat of battle he was more than capable of killing the enemy to prevent his friends and himself from being killed. But he also had a reputation for not killing if he didn't have to. An example of this was at Marcoing on 28 September 1914 after he had led the bayonet charge. As the day's fighting finally came to an end and the remaining German troops were either captured or made good their escape, a wounded German soldier, who was a short distance away, limped into Tandey's line of fire. Although armed the German soldier did not raise his rifle and, although Tandey took aim at the man, he did not open fire, unable to shoot an enemy who was clearly wounded and who posed no immediate threat. The man, possibly realising his good fortune, nodded at Tandey and the two men went their separate ways.

Tandey's award of the Victoria Cross was announced in the *London Gazette* on 14 December 1918, and a year later on 17 December 1919, he was personally decorated by King George V at Buckingham Palace. In covering the presentation of his Victoria Cross, the press published a photograph of a sketch of Tandey carrying his wounded colleague after the Battle of Ypres, an image which would eventually be immortalized by the renowned artist, Fortunino Matania.

The question is, did either incident actually take place? It would appear that Hitler did in fact have a large photograph of the painting by Matania. An article about Henry Tandey on Wikipedia includes a piece about Dr Otto Schwend, who was a member of Hitler's personal staff, and who during the

First World War had been a medical officer during the First Battle of Ypres in 1914. He treated a senior British Army officer, Lieutenant Colonel Maxwell Earle of the 1st Battalion, Grenadier Guards, who had been shot in the head and leg at Gheluvelt, Belgium, on 29 October 1914. The wound to his leg came about when an orderly who was treating him was shot in the back at close range by a German soldier, the bullet passed through the orderly, striking Earle in the leg. After the war, Schwend and Earle stayed in touch and in 1936 Earle sent his friend a copy of the painting which, it would appear, he passed on to Hitler.

Claims that Chamberlain telephoned Tandey to pass on Hitler's gratitude, cannot be correct, as in 1938 British Telecommunications Archive Records show the address where Tandey was living, 22 Cope Street, Coventry, did not have a telephone.

As to the wounded German soldier whom Tandey did not shoot. This could not have been Hitler for three reasons. Firstly, Hitler was on a period of leave on 28 September 1918, and wasn't at Marcoing. Secondly, Hitler's unit, the 16th Bavarian Infantry Regiment, were nowhere near Marcoing on the date in question, and thirdly, Hitler was wounded on three separate occasions during the First World War, none of which included 28 September 1918.

It would appear that either Hitler or his propaganda machine, decided to make the outlandish claim of a connection with Henry Tandey, possibly because of the latter's heroic past. Whoever was behind the claim, obviously hadn't done their homework.

As for Henry Tandey, if he did in fact allow a wounded German soldier to live, rather than shoot him, on 28 September 1918, then it most definitely wasn't Adolf Hitler.

On Monday, 23 December 1918 an inquest took place at Guernsey on the body of a sailor found near the fishing ketch, *Iris*, that was wrecked off the island's north coast on 20 December. The body was identified as being that of the vessel's mate, Reginald Lewis Collings, by Captain Winterflood, of Aimvell, who had spent some time with him the previous week at Fowey.

After all of the evidence had been heard a verdict of 'found drowned' was returned. None of the other crew members had been found dead or alive.

The British Army Pension Records that cover the period of the First World War, show the following individuals from Guernsey who were in receipt of Army pensions.

Private (2163) Louis Francis **Bachelet,** was discharged from the 2nd Reserve Battalion, Royal Guernsey Light Infantry on 17 September 1918, as no longer physically fit for wartime military service. He had appeared before an Army Medical Board on 27 August 1918, where because of his medical history, it was determined that he should be discharged from the Army. He was 28 years of age and had served for just 254 days, having enlisted on 7 January 1918, and was stationed at Fort George, Guernsey. Prior to military service he had earned his living as a general labourer. When he sat his Army medical all that was noted was that he had a depressed scar on the front of his neck and that he was undergoing medical treatment, neither of which were deemed not sufficiently bad enough for him to be rejected.

On 12 February 1918, just after a month after having enlisted, he was admitted to hospital in Guernsey suffering with bronchitis. It was so bad that he was not released until 1 June 1918, 110 days later. He had only been out of hospital for one day before he was re-admitted suffering with asthma. He wasn't released until 23 July 1918 after a stay of 52 days. His medical sheet was endorsed with, 'suffers from chronic asthma and is not likely to improve'. By the time of his discharge, he had spent more than half of his military service in hospital.

Neither of his ailments were deemed to have been aggravated due to his brief Army service. He had been suffering from bronchitis and asthma-related problems for more than ten years. His mother had also suffered with the same conditions. Louis was not strong physically and was only 4ft 11in inches in height. He was a married man who lived with his wife at St Mare Cottage, L'Islet, St Sampson, Guernsey.

Private (2149) Albert Edward **Bond** had enlisted in the 2nd Reserve Battalion, Royal Guernsey Light Infantry on 28 December 1917, at which time he was shown to be 5ft 10 inches tall and was still only 18 years of age. His home was at 10 New Street, St Peter Port, Guernsey.

He arrived in France on 27 May 1918 and two days later he was posted to the 1st (Service) Battalion, Royal Guernsey Light Infantry. He had served in France for ten months during which time he was admitted to the 7th Canadian General Hospital at Etaples on 17 January 1919. He left France on board the SS *Golden Eagle* on 1 March 1919 and on his arrival back in the UK he was re-united with his old comrades in the 2nd Reserve Battalion, Royal Guernsey Light Infantry. He was also admitted to the War Hospital at Chester where he stayed between 2 and 5 March 1919. On the day of his discharge he was sent to Winsford Lodge VAD hospital to recuperate where he remained until 15 April 1919.

The writing on his medical record is not totally legible, but he appears to have been suffering from heart and lung problems which resulted in dizziness, headaches and fainting. His ailments have been recorded as having been aggravated by his military service, which resulted in him being medically examined by a major with the Royal Army Medical Corps, at Guernsey Hospital on 7 October 1919. He was discharged from the Army on 5 November 1919, but his pension, of 12s a week, which began on 6 November 1919, lasted for just six months and finished on 11 May 1920.

Private (206) Arthur **Bougourd** enlisted on 5 December 1916 when he was 39 years old, in the 2nd Reserve Battalion, Royal Guernsey Light Infantry. Prior to joining the Army he had been employed as a gardener.

Whilst serving at Cambrai in France on 30 November 1917, he contracted malaria, although he remained on duty, possibly because he was not fully aware of his condition and assumed that he had nothing more sinister than a cold. The next day he was treated by the 89th Field Ambulance unit, before being admitted to the 21st Casualty Clearing Station hospital at Etaples. A week after this, on 7 December 1917, his medical history sheet records that he had been transferred back to England where he was admitted to the 22nd General Huddersfield War Hospital, the result of being buried alive, due to a German shell exploding near his position, when he also sustained a small shrapnel wound to his left thumb. He remained there until 22 April 1918.

It also shows that he was sent to the Command Depot Hospital, 3rd Royal Naval Division, No.4 Camp, Perham Down, on 26 April 1918 'for effects of burial by shell explosion', and on 23 September 1918 he was sent to hospital in Guernsey suffering from the effects of malaria, remaining there until 7 October 1918. The entry on his medical history sheet is confusing as it leaves it unclear as to whether he was buried by a shell explosion once or twice.

His case went before an Army Medical Board in Guernsey on 26 November 1918, and it was decided that Arthur Bougourd should be medically discharged from the Army as no longer physically fit for wartime military service. It added that although he was strong and healthy, he was unable to bend his back, or stoop due to the pain and the effects of having been buried alive by a German shell. He was a married man who lived at Les Cornus, St Martin, Guernsey, with his wife Amy, and their nine children.

Acting Lance Corporal (421) Clifford Henry **Bougourd** enlisted in the Army on 9 February 1915 and joined the 1st (Reserve) Battalion, Royal Guernsey Light Infantry. He sustained gunshot wounds to his left arm, side, hand and leg. All of these wounds subsequently healed causing him no further trouble, but he also suffered with lumbago which prevented him from bending, stooping or lifting. Before he had recovered sufficiently to leave hospital, he had been treated at four separate medical facilities: North Evington Military Hospital, Leicester, the VAD Hospital at Long Eaton, the 5th North General Hospital, Leicester, and the New Zealand General Hospital, at Brockenhurst in Hampshire.

Private (615) John **Carre** was 37 years of age when he enlisted in the Royal Guernsey Light Infantry on 2 January 1917 in the regiment's 2nd Reserve Battalion. On 9 January he was transferred to the 1st Reserve Battalion, before being posted back to the 2nd on 15 April 1917. Prior to enlistment he had been a gas worker and lived at Grand Bouet, St Peter Port, Guernsey.

After completing his initial training, he arrived at Le Havre in France on 27 September 1917. He was wounded when he sustained gunshot wounds to his left leg on 26 November 1917, with his initial medical treatment being carried out by the staff of No. 37 Field Ambulance. His wounds were such

Perham Down Camp, Wiltshire.

that it was necessary for him to be sent back to the UK for further treatment at the 22nd General War Hospital, Newcastle. One of the bullets had struck him in the upper part of his left thigh, whilst another struck him in the lower part of the same leg, which restricted movement in his ankle. The scarring which resulted was painful and caused him to walk with a slight limp.

He was admitted to the Command Depot Hospital, which was part of the 63rd Royal Naval Division at Perham Down, near Tidworth in Wiltshire, on 21 February 1918 for further treatment. He remained until 30 May 1918, a period of 99 days.

On his release from hospital on 28 May 1918, he was returned to his unit, before being demobilized on 9 March 1919 and transferred to Class Z of the Army Reserve.

Private (2046) Arthur **Couch** served in the 2nd Reserve Battalion, Royal Guernsey Light Infantry, having enlisted on 22 October 1917 when he was 18 years of age. He was sent to France on 5 July 1918, before returning to the UK three months later on 17 October. He underwent a medical examination at North Evington War Hospital in Leicester the following day.

As a result of stomach pains, he underwent an operation on 6 January 1919 for appendicitis, before he was transferred to the Royal Victoria Military Hospital, Netley, near Southampton on 24 January 1919. He was demobilized on 25 February 1919 and placed in Class Z of the Army Reserve, at which time he was provided with a pension of 3s 6d per week for twenty-six weeks.

Private (7665) Fred **Dodd** enlisted in the 2nd Reserve Battalion, Royal Guernsey Light Infantry on 11 September 1918 when he was 19 years of age. On 2 June 1919 whilst stationed in Guernsey and undergoing his initial

Army training, he went absent at 2315 hours, not returning until 2130 hours on 11 June 1919. For this breach of Army discipline, he was punished with a week's military detention.

His British Army Medical Sheet records that he was suffering with, 'congenital mental deficiency'. Under the heading of 'What is his present condition?' the hand-written answer states: *He is very dull & stupid, obstinate & liable to be mostly if not an idiot, but is not quite up to normal intelligence, & is quite unfit for retention in the Army.* The report also noted that he was of 'poor physique'. The report, dated 12 August 1919 and signed by a captain from the Royal Army Medical Corps, finished with the comment 'discharge as permanently unfit'.

What is most remarkable about Fred Dodd's case is that he underwent an initial medical at the time of his enlistment, which determined he was physically fit enough to undertake military training, yet just eight months later he is deemed to be 'stupid and dull, and no longer physically fit enough for wartime military service'. It is hard to take in that a young man could undergo such a rapid mental decline in a relative short period of time and poses the question whether this was not a case of a recruitment serjeant – who was paid a sum of money for each man he signed up – simply turning a blind eye.

Private (429) Charles **Ducellier** joined the 1st Battalion, Royal Guernsey Light Infantry on 29 January 1916 when he was 21 years of age. At the time of his enlistment he was 100 per cent physically fit, according to the medical that he underwent at that time at Guernsey Military Hospital, but sometime during the initial period of his basic Army training, he was diagnosed as having a hernia which resulted in his being admitted to hospital for treatment on 7 October 1916. He remained there for five weeks, finally being discharged on 14 November 1916. He had a subsequent relapse and was re-admitted to hospital on 5 June 1918, which resulted in the removal of his right testicle, causing him pain and discomfort in his groin, but despite this he remained in the Army.

In February 1919, he was once again admitted to hospital, in France, this time suffering with the effects of flu and chronic bronchitis, the latter of which led to slight heart problems. His condition worsened, causing him to be sent back to the UK where he was treated at the Nell Lane Military Hospital, West Didsbury, where he arrived on 11 March 1919, before being discharged from the Army on 7 April 1919, as no longer physically fit enough for wartime military service.

Private (1014) Edwin William **Dunne** enlisted in the 2nd Reserve Battalion, Royal Guernsey Light Infantry on 30 January 1917. Prior to joining the Army he lived at 4 Sir William Place, La Plaiderie, St Peter Port, Guernsey.

His First World War military service saw him firstly in France for two months, then in Belgium for a further two months, where he was initially reported as missing in action on 1 December 1917. He had in fact been captured and taken as a prisoner of war, and then spent the remaining thirteen months of the war incarcerated in a camp at Minden in Germany where he arrived on 14 December 1917. Prior to his capture he had been admitted to hospital in Tournai, Belgium, because of a hernia problem. During his enforced stay in Germany, he had a ruptured hernia. This was a long-term medical condition which he had prior to enlisting in the Army. He told the doctor who examined him at his initial medical and was given a truss to wear.

At the end of hostilities he was released from the camp in Germany and repatriated to the UK. On 23 February 1919, he was discharged and transferred to Class Z of the Army Reserve. This consisted of men who had previously served in the British Army but who were held in reserve just in case there were any problems with the Armistice that was in place with Germany. The Z Class of the Army Reserve was abolished on 31 March 1920.

His subsequent request for an Army pension was rejected, although the Army authorities did supply him with a truss. His military service with the Royal Guernsey Light Infantry had also seen him stationed in India and South Africa.

Private (821) Sidney John **Duquemin** enlisted on 12 January 1917 in Guernsey, joining the 2nd Reserve Battalion, Royal Guernsey Light Infantry. He served in France from 26 November 1917 to 2 April 1918, by which time he had reached the rank of lance corporal. On his arrival at Le Havre he had problems with his right knee, which resulted in his having to attend both the 72nd and 37th Field Ambulance on the same day. On 29 November he had to attend the 41st Stationary Hospital. Two days after that he was sent to the 1st Australian General Hospital and on 28 December 1917 he was sent to the 2nd Command Depot Hospital.

On 27 March 1918 he was wounded when he suffered from the effects of a German gas attack. Initially he was treated at the 64th Casualty Clearing Station, before being moved to the 35th General Hospital four days later. On 2 April 1918 he was sent home to the UK for further treatment on board the Hospital Ship, *Princess Elizabeth*. On arrival in England he was initially sent to the 4th Northern General Hospital in Lincoln, where he stayed between 3 April and 21 May 1918. This was followed by a stay at the Command Depot Hospital at Perham Down in Wiltshire between 22 May and 19 June 1918.

On 24 November 1919 he underwent a medical examination in Guernsey. His subsequent medical sheet stated that his 'heart action was normal, his pulse was 72 and there was nothing in his lungs'. On finally leaving hospital he was sent on a rifle course at Hayling Island in Hampshire, which he passed, qualifying as a 1st Class instructor. He was demobilized and transferred to the Army Reserve on Christmas Eve 1919, by which time he was a married man with five children, and had reached the rank of acting corporal.

Private (993) John **Gallienne** enlisted in the 2nd Reserve Battalion, Royal Guernsey Light Infantry. After having completed his initial military training he was sent to France, arriving there on 26 September 1917, but after being wounded in action, he was sent back to the UK for medical treatment, on

16 October 1917. At the age of 31, having served for a year and 136 days, he was discharged from the Army on 13 June 1918 in Guernsey, as no longer physically fit for wartime military service, as a result of being wounded in action when he was shot in the right hand and thigh. Prior to the war, John had earned his living as a gardener and lived at La Salive, St Peter Port, Guernsey.

Private (905) Thomas John **Gaudion** enlisted in the 1st Reserve Battalion, Royal Guernsey Light Infantry on 19 January 1917 when he was 22 years of age. After his initial training he was sent to France, arriving at Le Havre on 27 September 1917.

After having served in Belgium and France for six months, he was wounded in a gas attack in France on 28 March 1918 and treated at the 64th Casualty Clearing Station, before being transferred to the 31st General Hospital in Calais and at another one in Boulogne. He was discharged from hospital on 23 May 1918 and re-joined his battalion in the field. On 30 October 1918 he returned to the UK on two weeks leave and whilst back home in Guernsey, the fighting came to an end and the Armistice was signed. He still had to return to France, which he did on 14 November 1918 and re-joined his battalion, where he remained for the next three months in the immediate aftermath of the end of the war. On 3 February 1919 he was admitted to the 56th General Hospital, which was run by the staff from the Royal Army Medical Corps, to be treated for boils and carbuncles. He returned to the UK less than two weeks later on 16 February.

His combined injuries ultimately resulted in his discharge from the Army on 15 April 1919 and transfer to Class Z of the Army Reserve. The Army provided him with a pension of 5s 6d, but only for a period of six months. He remained living at Columbia Villa, St Sampson, Guernsey and returned to his pre-war job as a fisherman.

Private (2033) Louis **Guegan** had been a farmer before he enlisted in the British Army on 12 October 1917 in the 2nd Reserve Battalion, Royal Guernsey Light Infantry. He was just 19 years of age, born in Guernsey on 17 August 1899.

Whilst serving in France he contracted pneumonia on 28 October 1918. This resulted in him experiencing pain in his limbs and heart which was followed by broncho-pneumonia, but by the time he had undergone a medical examination which took place on 9 January 1919 at the North Staffordshire Infirmary, his condition, 'was rapidly clearing up'. His medical sheet also shows an entry for when he attended the Newcastle-under-Lyme War Hospital, in Stoke-on-Trent, which was an Army Dispersal Hospital, which he attended on 11 January 1919. This part of the form is signed by a Captain R.N. Berman of the Royal Army Medical Corps.

He was demobilized and transferred to Class Z of the Army Reserve on 8 February 1919, but his application for an Army pension was rejected by the military authorities on 31 January 1919.

Private (36079) Arthur Frank **Hearnden** enlisted in the British Army on 7 November 1916 at Rotherhithe, when he was just 18 years of age, although he wasn't mobilised until 16 February 1917. Initially he joined the 2nd (Home Service) Battalion, North Staffordshire Regiment. On 9 August 1917 he was transferred to the 17th Battalion, Royal Defence Corps and just eleven days later he was once again transferred, this time to the 2nd Reserve Battalion, Royal Guernsey Light Infantry as Private (1932). On 24 January 1918 he was posted to the 1st (Service) Battalion, Royal Guernsey Light Infantry and was sent out to France the same day.

He was wounded in action on 11 April 1918 whilst serving in France, suffering a gunshot wound to his lower right leg. Over the course of the following two days Arthur was treated at the 87th (1st West Lancashire) Field Ambulance, the 17th Casualty Clearing Station at Remy Siding, Lijssenhoek, near Ypres – where ambulance trains brought in casualties from the battlefields and evacuated them to base hospitals – and then the 20th General Hospital, which had been located at Camiers in the Pas de Calais from 15 May 1915.

He arrived back in England on board the Hospital Ship *Princess Elizabeth* on 16 April 1918 and was admitted to the 1st Southern General Hospital at Kidderminster where he remained until 12 August 1918. On 5 October 1918 Arthur was admitted to the VAD Infirmary at Les Touillets, Guernsey where he remained until 14 January 1919. He had spent a total of 220 days in hospital in the previous nine months. Arthur's war was over and he was demobilized on 13 February 1919 and placed in Class Z of the Army Reserve.

Private 21844 Albert Edward **Howlett** enlisted on 28 June 1915, aged 24, but was not mobilized until 5 September 1915. On 4 October 1915 he was transferred to the Royal Irish Fusiliers and was sent to France as part of the British Expeditionary Force, but on 24 October 1916 he was transferred to the 1st (Service) Battalion, Royal Guernsey Light Infantry as Private (34). He was posted to the 2nd (Reserve) Royal Guernsey Light Infantry on 9 October 1917, before being posted back to the 1st (Service) Battalion on 13 March 1918 and sent back to France where he stayed until 4 March 1919. He returned to the UK the following day and was immediately demobilized and placed on the Army Reserve.

Before enlisting, he lived at Brompton Place, Piette Road, St Peter Port, Guernsey. He went on to serve in Belgium for three months followed by a further twenty-one months in France, before his war came to an end when he was caught in the blast of a German shell on 5 September 1916, which left him with a shrapnel wound to the spine. Thankfully it did not leave him with a permanent disability. He ended up in the Crag Head VAD Hospital in Manor Road, Bournemouth.

Private 3/11306 Herbert **Jowett** was born in Bradford on 10 January 1888 and had been a grocer in North Shields before the war. He had enlisted in the British Army on 26 August 1914, initially in the 3rd Battalion, West

Riding (Duke of Wellington's Regiment), then the West Yorkshire Regiment as Private (20855), (29 April 1916) before moving on to 2nd Battalion, North Staffordshire Regiment as Private (24590) (1 November 1916), then the 17th Battalion, Royal Defence Corps as Private (62744) (9 August 1917). Finally, he ended up as Private (7628) of the 2nd (Reserve) Battalion, Royal Guernsey Light Infantry (31 January 1918).

He survived the war and was demobilized on 15 March 1919. It was whilst he was serving with the North Staffordshire Regiment that he was admitted to hospital in Guernsey on 7 March 1917, for what was described as 'a severe sprain of the left ankle'.

He spent all of his wartime service in the United Kingdom. His injuries were a fractured ankle and rheumatism, which saw him spend a period of time as a patient at Fort George Military Hospital in Guernsey. He claimed that the injury to his ankle occurred as a result of working with the Royal Engineers and trying to remove the branch of a tree from telegraph wires, when the ladder he was standing on slipped from underneath him, throwing him to the ground. He underwent a medical examination on 14 February 1919 in Guernsey, when it was noted by the examining medical officer that he had had a 'fractured ankle and rheumatism'.

He further noted that Herbert had never received hospital treatment for rheumatism. His claim to having sprained his left ankle was dismissed by the medical officer, on what basis, is not clear, especially as the same medical record showed that he had been treated in hospital in Guernsey for the ankle, which was bad enough to require a total of 67 days treatment between 17 March and 12 May 1917 before the ankle was cured. His subsequent application for an Army pension was rejected by the military authorities.

During his military service his disciplinary record was far from exemplary. On three occasions he was disciplined for being absent from his barracks, which resulted in his being confined to barracks for a total of fourteen days, as well as a further two week period of detention and forfeiture of three days' pay.

Private (1428) Douglas Peter **Laine,** aged 20, lived at 'Richmond', St Saviour, Guernsey. After he enlisted on 11 April 1917 in Guernsey he joined the 2nd (Reserve) Battalion, Royal Guernsey Light Infantry. He was posted to the Regiment's 1st (Service) Battalion on 7 November 1917, as part of the BEF in France, first arriving at Le Havre on 10 November 1917. But after only two weeks his war was over when he was captured and taken prisoner by the Germans. He spent the next year incarcerated in a camp in Germany and was not released until 17 December 1918.

Whilst held as a PoW, Douglas was admitted to Minden Hospital where he was treated for a combination of ailments. He had a weak heart and suffered with his nerves, both of these issues came about as a result of his treatment whilst held captive in Germany, along with the sound of nearby

Minden PoW Camp.

continuous shell fire. Whilst stationed in Guernsey, before leaving for France with the BEF, he was twice admitted to hospital suffering with scabies. The first occasion was for five days between 12 and 16 April 1917 and the second was for two days, 22 and 23 May 1917. On both occasions he returned to his unit on his release.

Douglas was demobilized and transferred to the Army Reserve on 21 February 1919. He was awarded an Army pension of 5s 6d for six months beginning on 22 February 1919, due to his nerves and weak heart, which it was accepted were the result of being a prisoner of war.

Frederick Adolphus **Lepage** was another member of the 2nd (Reserve) Battalion, Royal Guernsey Light Infantry. He was 39 years of age when he enlisted on 15 June 1917 in Guernsey. When he joined the Army, he must have already been suffering with Myalgia, as on 16 July 1917, just one month after his enlistment, he was admitted to the Military Hospital in Guernsey. There he remained until 28 February 1918. He was then only out of hospital for one week before he was re-admitted on 7 March 1918, where he was still a patient as of 9 October 1918 when he was medically examined. A question on the medical report, asks, 'What is his present condition?' and was answered by the medical officer who completed the report:

> *He is a strongly built man, but suffers from chronic Myalgia, of which he makes the most. He is stiff in all joints, feels the cold very much, and is of no use as a soldier.*

He refuses to undergo treatment at Bath and makes no attempt to help himself. He refuses to make any effort.

A large period of the sixteen months he spent serving in the Army was spent as a patient in hospital. Despite this and the fact that he was discharged from the Army for being physically unfit, he was given an Army pension of 5s 6d per week for 27 weeks for an ailment which he more than likely had before he had even enlisted.

Private (445) William **Lockyer** enlisted in the Army on 9 December 1915 at Guernsey, joining the 2nd (Reserve) Battalion, Royal Guernsey Light Infantry. His solitary act of misconduct occurred on 15 October 1916; whilst on guard duty at his barracks in Guernsey, he left his position unattended and was charged with neglect of duty. He was found guilty and punished by losing his lance corporal's stripe. He was transferred to the 1st (Service) Battalion on 17 December 1916, and nine months later on 27 September 1917 he arrived in Le Havre, France, where he remained until 26 March 1919. Whilst serving abroad he was treated by medical staff at a field ambulance for influenza. His condition was so severe that he was admitted to the medical unit for four days.

He was demobilized and placed on Class Z of the Army Reserve on 23 May 1919, by which time he was 36 years of age and a married man with three children. He applied for an Army pension, but his application was rejected by the military authorities.

He reported sick on 28 February 1919 whilst serving in France suffering with headaches, pains and bronchitis, all of which combined saw him diagnosed with influenza. He was returned to the UK and admitted to the Bradford War Hospital on 27 March 1919, where he underwent a medical examination on 11 April 1919, before being released on 24 April 1919. The same day that he was released from the Bradford War Hospital, he was admitted to the Keighley War Hospital, where he remained for just one day. He had previously suffered with a bad case of bronchitis in June 1917 which meant he had to rest for fifteen days before he was fit enough to re-join his battalion.

His mother, Mrs E. Lockyer lived at 5 St Clements Road, St Peter Port, Guernsey.

Private (7418) William **Locock** ended up in the 2nd (Reserve) Battalion, Royal Guernsey Light Infantry, which he joined on 3 April 1918, but he had begun his military career serving as a private with the Royal Sussex Regiment, before being transferred to the Royal Irish Fusiliers. He initially enlisted on 21 May 1915, when his medical examination noted that at the time he was suffering with haemorrhoids, but that they were not sufficiently bad to result in his being rejected from army service.

After completing his basic training, he first arrived in France on 18 February 1916, where he remained until 18 March 1918. On his return to the UK he was treated at New End Military Hospital at Hampstead, London, between 9 and 23 March 1918. On the same day he was discharged, he was admitted to a VAD Convalescent Hospital in Eastbourne. On 22 April 1918 he was admitted to hospital in Guernsey suffering with Tonsillitis where he remained a patient until 14 May 1918. He was re-admitted to hospital in Guernsey on 27 July 1918 suffering from Trench Fever and spent the next 171 days there as a patient, not being released until 13 January 1919. He had been diagnosed with the contagious condition caused by lice whilst serving in France on 14 February 1918.

William was married to Elsie and they had two daughters, Elsie and Rita. He was transferred to Class Z of the Army Reserve on 12 February 1919, and despite having Trench Fever, which he could only have contracted whilst he was in the trenches, his application for an Army pension was rejected by the military authorities. This was possibly to do with the fact that by the time he underwent a medical examination with a view to possibly being medically discharged from the Army, the doctor who examined him, Captain P.C.H. Ryan of the Royal Army Medical Corps, could not find that Locock had any disability. This was more a case of his health having improved rather than his not being unwell in the first place.

Private (2527) Charles Thomas **Lowe** enlisted in the Army on 9 February 1915 and served in the 2nd Reserve Battalion, Royal Guernsey, Light Infantry. He first arrived in France 17 December 1915 and served there with his battalion for a period of two years and 145 days, although he did return to the UK on leave on two occasions, between 21 January and 6 February 1917, and 7 November to 22 November 1917.

Prior to that he served with them in South Africa for 347 days. He was previously a Private (3278) with the 6th Service Battalion, Royal Irish Regiment in India for three years and 21 days. Before the war, Charles had been an Insurance Agent, working for the Royal Liver Friendly Society. On 31 December 1918, Mr Charles Daws, the Society's Secretary, wrote a letter to the Ministry of Labour, informing them that they were prepared to offer him immediate employment on his return to civilian life.

He was demobilized and transferred to the Army reserve, Class Z, on 11 February 1919. Despite suffering with bronchitis through prolonged exposure in the trenches and receiving gun-shot wounds to one of his arms and both thighs, on 11 April 1918, his subsequent application for an Army pension was rejected by the military authorities. The injuries he sustained from his gunshot wounds, were initially treated at the 17th Casualty Clearing Station, before he was transferred to the 8th Stationary Hospital later the same day. On his return to the UK on 11 May 1918 he was admitted to the Kitchener Hospital at Brighton to be treated for Bronchitis. After being discharged from there, he was admitted to the Military Convalescent Hospital at Woldingham, where he remained from 13 June to 9 September 1918, and from there he was admitted to the Command Depot Hospital of the 63rd Royal Naval Division at Perham Down, Wiltshire, before leaving there on 25 September 1918.

Private (1640) Thomas Frederick **Martel** enlisted in the Royal Guernsey Light Infantry. He was discharged from the Army on 12 February 1919 as no longer physically fit for wartime military service. The pension he was awarded was a one-off award of £5.

Private (1533) Frederick John **Miller** enlisted in the 2nd Reserve, Battalion, Royal Guernsey Light Infantry on 15 May 1917, but on 12 January 1918, he was posted to the regiment's 1st (Service) Battalion, and arrived in France the following day. He was wounded in action on 11 April 1918.

His medical sheet shows that he was admitted to hospital in Guernsey between 26 November and 19 December 1917 for dental problems. He underwent three further terms in hospital. The next was between 17 April and 29 May 1918 at the Norfolk and Norwich Hospital in Norwich, where he was treated for a head wound. The same day that he was discharged from hospital in Norwich, he was admitted to a convalescent hospital in Derby where he remained until 10 July 1918, and from there he was transferred to the Command Depot Hospital, which was part of the 63rd Naval Division, at Perham Down in Wiltshire, where he remained until 24 July 1918.

After investigating Frederick's case in more detail, it turns out that on 11 April 1918, whilst in France, he received a gunshot wound to the head, apparently from a German machine gun. This possibly explains the treatment he received whilst he was admitted to hospital in Norwich. Although no doubt a serious injury, it apparently wasn't life threatening and appears to have struck him in the region of his left ear. His initial treatment in France was carried out by the medical staff at the 87th Field Ambulance, before he was transferred to the 3rd Canadian General Hospital on 13 April 1918 and then returned to the UK four days later. Frederick's war over, he was demobilized and placed on the Army Reserve on 8 March 1919. He was left with a 2½ inch scar on the side of his temple, as a memento of his lucky escape, although on his medical sheet it is also described as being only a 'flesh wound'.

He was a married man who lived with his wife, Alice, at 11 Ville au Rue, St Peter Port, Guernsey.

Private (1952) Reginald George **Moore** enlisted in the Royal Guernsey Light Infantry on 18 October 1916. He sustained a gunshot wound to his left upper arm during fighting in France on 12 April 1918, which resulted in his being returned to the UK and admitted to a military hospital in Norwich.

On 10 January 1919 he sustained a fracture to the fibula of his right leg whilst playing in a football match which had nothing to do with his military duties. His medical record states that this incident resulted in disciplinary action being taken, but it does not clarify if it was taken against Reginald Moore, or the person who fractured his leg. He was transferred to Class Z of the Army Reserve on 20 February 1919 and was provided with an Army pension for a year. The first six months his pension was worth 8s 3d per week and for the following six months he was paid 5s 6d per week. His pension was then reviewed and it was decided to continue his pension for a further six months at a rate of 5s 6d per week.

Private (R/258691) John **Musgrave** was originally in the Remount Squadron of the Army Service Corps, the unit he enlisted in on 16 November 1915 in Leeds. By birth, he was a Yorkshire man, born in Leeds in 1878. Despite enlisting, he was placed on the Army Reserve and not mobilized until 6 February 1917, during which time he had been free to continue his work as an assistant tailor. Two months later on 20 April 1917 he was transferred to the 2nd Reserve Battalion, Royal Guernsey Light Infantry, as a Private (7435). All his wartime service was on the home front, where he was demobilized on 1 March 1919, when he was living with his wife, Annie, at 104 Town Street, Armley in Leeds.

He was admitted to hospital in Guernsey on 12 June 1918 for a period of seventeen days, suffering with what was initially thought to be Myalgia, pain in the muscles. It was an ailment which had first been recorded back in 1855 and was also known by the name, Myoneuralgia. This was later re-diagnosed as pulmonary tuberculosis, which left him confined to his bed.

A pension of 11s 8d was provided for John Musgrove's two children, Marie and Kenneth, for a six-month period from 2 March to 2 September 1919, and then 23s 6d for his wife and the two children, from 2 September to 9 November 1919, when John Musgrove died as a result of his tuberculosis. Thankfully for his wife and children, the payment of an Army pension was continued and increased after this date, until 31 March 1920.

Private (351) Henry James **Osborne** who lived with his wife, Amy, at 6 Park Street, St Peter Port, Guernsey, enlisted on 2 January 1917 in the 2nd Reserve Battalion, Royal Guernsey Light Infantry. On 13 January 1917 he was transferred to the regiment's 1st (Service) Battalion, but less than three months later on 7 April 1917 he was posted back to the 2nd Reserve Battalion, before once again being posted back to the 1st (Service) Battalion on 1 December 1917, which he joined in Rouen, France on 4 December.

On 19 January 1918, he was treated by the 88th Field Ambulance Unit, before being transferred to the 44th Casualty Clearing Station, which was staffed by nurses of the Queen Alexandra's Imperial Military Nursing Service, and surgical and dressing teams of the Royal Army Medical Corps, on 23 January. He was again transferred to the 26th General Hospital at the large medical facility at Etaples, for which no admission or discharge registers have survived.

Henry Osborne was sent back to the UK on 6 February 1918 on board the Hospital Ship, *Princess Elizabeth*. On arrival, he was sent to the County of Middlesex War Hospital, at Napsbury, St Albans, where he remained for 93 days until 9 May 1918. From there he was transferred to the Military Heart Hospital at Colchester, where he remained until 31 May. At both locations he was treated for disordered action of the heart, or DAH. This was a condition that was believed to have come about as a result of a combination of over exertion, mental stress and fatigue, all of which were applicable to a soldier who had experienced combat and was attributed to cardiac related problems where there was some kind of abnormality of rhythm and heart rate, rather than heart disease.

Despite still being treated in hospital at the time, he was discharged from the Army on 9 May 1919, as no longer being physically fit for wartime military service.

Point number 15 of his medical sheet, dated 3 April 1919 and signed by a captain of the Royal Army Medical Corps, asks the question; 'What is his present condition?', part of the hand-written reply, states that he was suffering from the effects of 'Trench Fever', a serious condition which is transmitted by body lice.

Private (136) Sidney **Osborne**'s was an interesting case, as he enlisted in the Guernsey Depot Service Company on 23 November 1916, having informed the recruiting serjeant that he was 18 years of age, although it was later determined that he was in fact only 16 years and 11 months. On 17 December 1916 he was posted to the 1st (Service) Battalion, Royal Guernsey Light Infantry, before ending up with the 2nd Reserve Battalion of the same regiment on 4 January 1917.

On 1 April 1918, whilst still in Guernsey, Sidney was tried and convicted by a District Court Martial for 'sleeping at his post'. He was sentenced to eleven days' detention. If he had committed and been found guilty of the same offence whilst serving in France, he could have faced a firing squad. On 18 June 1918, he arrived in France, but after just two months he was sent home on leave for two weeks, not returning to France until 28 August 1918.

On 6 October 1918, suffering with a bad case of influenza, he was admitted to the 7th Canadian General Hospital at Etaples, which by this time consisted of some thirty-five wooden huts, with more than 2,200 beds, a number it managed to maintain until the end of the war. After being treated in hospital for a week, Sidney's condition had not improved and he was sent home to the UK on board the Hospital Ship *Brighton* on 14 October 1918, and just eleven days later he was medically discharged from the Army, as no longer physically fit for wartime service owing to tuberculosis of the skin.

Like his brother Henry, he had survived the war and had finished his military service by being medically discharged.

On the British Army's First World War Pension Records there are two records, one is for Sidney Osborne and the other is for Sydney William Osbourne. Both men are shown as being Private (136) of the 1st (Service)

Battalion, Royal Guernsey Light Infantry. Both men were 18 years of age when they enlisted. Both had worked as sweet makers before they had enlisted, and both were medically discharged for tuberculosis of the skin. It is fair to assume that they are one and the same person.

Private (1610) Harry **Ozanne** enlisted on 28 February 1917 but was not mobilized until 8 June 1917 when he was 33 years of age. He joined the 2nd Reserve Battalion, Royal Guernsey Light Infantry. On 7 August 1917, whilst still undergoing his initial military training, he was admitted to Guernsey Military Hospital, because of an inflammation of the stomach. Whatever the problem was, it must have been reasonably bad as he remained in hospital until 28 February 1918. It turned out to be a long-standing ailment which, coupled with indigestion, had been aggravated by the fear of having to go to war. The inflammation had become so bad that he was unable to eat his Army rations, although it was felt that if he was at home living on soup, he would be quite well. He was diagnosed as suffering with dyspepsia and after serving for a year and 180 days, he was medically discharged from the British Army on 4 December 1918, for no longer being physically fit enough for wartime military service. He was awarded a pension of 5s 6d per week for thirty weeks, which began on 11 December 1918 and finished on 8 July 1919.

Private (47) Douglas **Ozanne** enlisted in the British Army on 8 February 1919 and served in the 2nd Reserve Battalion, Royal Guernsey Light Infantry. Prior to this he had served as a Private (3308) with the 6th Service Battalion, The Royal Irish Regiment. He arrived in France on 17 December 1915 and was wounded in action when he sustained a gunshot wound to his right ankle during fighting at Loos on 10 June 1916. Four days later he was shipped back to the UK for further treatment at West Riding Military Hospital, but despite this, he was still left with a 20 per cent disability, and accordingly he was provided with an Army pension of 5s 6d per week for twenty-six weeks, which commenced on 19 February 1919.

He was discharged from the British Army on 18 February 1919, as no longer physically fit enough for wartime military service. This was the result of a medical examination at Guernsey Military Hospital on 20 January 1919. At this time the wound is recorded as having healed nicely, although it was in the form of a large scar which ran from the point of the tibia to below the point of the ankle. The subsequent movement of the ankle and the heel were very painful, especially during cold weather.

Private (2521) Frederick **Pallot** enlisted on 25 September 1915 in the 2nd Reserve Battalion, Royal Guernsey Light Infantry, but eventually rose to the rank of a company serjeant major, before being transferred to the Army Reserve on 7 November 1919. Whilst fighting in Armentières in France he received a gunshot wound to his right elbow on 11 April 1918. He was initially treated by medical staff of the 87th Field Ambulance before being transferred, later the same day, to the 2nd Australian General Hospital at Wimereux. The date of Frederick's injuries coincided with the period when the Germans were shelling the town with mustard gas, which eventually forced British forces to retreat from the area. The Germans had dropped so many mustard gas bombs on the town that their troops had to wait for two weeks before they were able to enjoy the spoils of their hard-won victory because the gas still hung so thickly in the air.

Frederick Pallot was admitted to the East Leeds War Hospital on 15 April 1918, the same day he arrived in England, and where he remained until 15 June 1918. He was then admitted to the Military Hospital in Guernsey on 27 June 1918 for electrical and massage treatment, where he remained until 12 February 1919. Although the bullet had caused no movement issues with his elbow, it had resulted in some weakening of the grip to his right hand.

On 7 November 1919, he was transferred to Class Z of the Army Reserve. For the bullet wound to his elbow, he was awarded a provisional payment of 7s 6d, and from 1 February 1919, he was granted a 'bonus payment' of 17s 6d per week.

Private (21924) William **Pollitt**, a single man and a butcher by trade, enlisted in the Army on 7 August 1915 in Preston, Lancashire, and initially served in the Loyal North Lancashire Regiment. On 30 August 1917 he was transferred to the Army Service Corps Remount as Private (R/11394) and on 22 May 1918, he was further transferred to the 2nd Reserve Battalion, Royal Guernsey Light Infantry, as Private (7583) although he wasn't a Guernsey man by birth and came from Bolton in Lancashire.

Although William served in the Army for just under four years, he only spent seventy-six days of that time in France, between 18 November 1918, a week after the signing of the Armistice, and 1 February 1919. On 19 January 1919 whilst in France he was diagnosed with having lumbago. On his arrival back in the UK he spent fifty-one days being treated in hospital for the effects of his lumbago, before on 25 March 1919 being transferred to the Military Convalescent Hospital at Eastbourne, where he remained until 4 April 1919. He was demobilized on 8 May 1919 and placed on the Army Reserve list.

Private (1630) Walter James **Renault** was 23 years of age when he enlisted in the Army on 15 June 1917 and joined the 2nd Reserve Battalion, Royal Guernsey Light Infantry. He was transferred to the regiment's 1st (Service) Battalion on 1 December 1917 and three days later he had arrived in Rouen, France. On 20 March 1918 he was wounded in action when he received a gunshot wound to his right thigh and was treated at the 87th Field Ambulance. He wasn't sent back to the UK for further treatment and, once recovered, he re-joined his unit. With the Armistice signed and the fighting at an end, Walter was granted two weeks annual leave which entitled him to return to the UK, but he still had to return to France after he had finished his leave. On 10 March 1919, whilst he was still serving in France he was admitted to the 7th Canadian General Hospital with sickness.

Walter underwent a further medical examination on 12 August 1919 at the Military Hospital in Guernsey when he was seen by a captain from the Royal Army Medical Corps. He explained that he was still experiencing pain down the region of his right side where he had been shot. His medical sheet had been endorsed with the comment that the gunshot wound to his right thigh was 'quite superficial'. It also stated that he was in 'good health before enlistment. Never had any fever, troubles or venereal diseases. Had never had any serious illness only pain in right side whilst in the Military Hospital in Colchester. Doesn't complain of anything.'

He was demobilized on 10 September 1919 and placed on the Army Reserve list and was awarded a pension of 5s 6d per week for a period of six months, beginning from 11 September 1919.

Private (1158) Frederick John **Renouf** was born at St Peter Port, Guernsey on 19 September 1884, and lived at 12 Norman Terrace, Amherst, Guernsey. He was 33 years of age when he enlisted in the Army on 16 February 1917 at Guernsey, joining the 2nd (Reserve) Battalion, Royal Guernsey Light Infantry. He was a married man with four children.

He first arrived in France on 26 September 1917 and after just two months he accidentally fractured his 9th rib on his right side, on 19 November 1917. He was at Bullecourt whilst advancing on the enemy, when he was blown into a trench hole by a German shell, fell awkwardly and fractured his rib.

He was treated by medical staff at the 37th Field Ambulance, before being transferred to the 55th Casualty Clearing Station the following day, where he had his side strapped up. From there he was sent to the 24th General Hospital at Etaples the same afternoon. It was determined that his injury was bad enough to warrant sending him back to England on board the Hospital Ship *Ville de Liège* for further treatment, where he arrived on 2 December 1917. He was admitted to the Queen Mary's Military Hospital at Whalley, Lancashire, where he remained until 29 January 1918.

He was demobilized and transferred to the Army Reserve on 21 March 1919, but his application for an Army pension was rejected, as, according to his medical record there was 'no disablement'.

Private (2061) Stanley Theodore **Renouf** was a draper's assistant living at 12 Coronation Road, Guernsey before his enlistment on 31 October 1917. He had just turned 18 years of age when he joined the 2nd (Reserve) Royal Guernsey Light Infantry, but on 27 May 1918 he was posted to the regiment's 1st (Service) Battalion and sent to France. He had only been there for five days when he reported sick. His medical sheet doesn't record the reason why, but after he had been treated in hospital, he re-joined his battalion on 10 June 1918. There is a non-detailed comment near the end of the report which refers to his having some kind of heart-related problem as well as suffering with bronchitis.

On 8 July he reported sick and was once again admitted to hospital at Etaples and didn't return to his battalion until 1 August 1918. On 27 August

1918 he was admitted to the 56th General Hospital at Etaples, and on 30 August he was sent back to the UK on board the Hospital Ship *Newhaven* and was re-posted to the regiment's 2nd (Reserve) Battalion. On arrival he was admitted to the 2nd Southern General Hospital at Bristol, where he was treated for bronchitis. On 16 October 1918 he was transferred to a nearby hospital in Plymouth and treated for the same ailment, where he remained for the following fifteen days.

On 4 November 1919, he was transferred to the Army Reserve, at which time his home address was shown as 14 Coronation Road, St Peter Port, Guernsey, which was next door to his father, who lived at number 12. He was awarded an Army pension of 5s 6d, for a period of six months, payable from 5 November 1919.

Private (7619) Thomas James **Roberts** was a farmer before he enlisted on 20 July 1918. He was 33 years of age when he joined the 2nd (Reserve) Battalion, Royal Guernsey Light Infantry, but just four and a half months later, his military career was over. He had been in the British Army for just 143 days when he was medically discharged as no longer physically fit enough for wartime military service, on 9 December 1918. He had appeared before a medical board on 8 December who had decided that he would be permanently unfit. Just ten days after enlisting he was admitted to hospital for a period of eleven days at Guernsey suffering with 'debility'. He was released on 9 August 1918. On 24 August he was re-admitted to the same hospital and treated for appendicitis, finally being released on 10 October 1918. On 21 October, he was once again returned to hospital, this time suffering with Colitis, which he had been suffering with on and off, over the previous fourteen years. It was during this period in hospital, that the medical authorities first considered medically discharging him.

Private (1178) Hedley **Roberts** enlisted on 19 February 1917, a month before his thirty-third birthday, in the 2nd (Reserve) Battalion, Royal Guernsey Light Infantry. On 24 October 1917 he was posted to the regiment's 1st (Service) Battalion and sent to France, arriving in Le Havre the next day. He had only been in France for five weeks when he was reported as missing in action, and on 17 December 1917 the German authorities confirmed that they had captured Private Roberts and that he was being held as a prisoner of war in their camp at Minden, in the state of North-Rhine Westphalia.

At the end of the war he was repatriated to the UK where he arrived on 26 November 1918. On 24 November 1919, he underwent a medical examination at the Military Hospital Guernsey, where his hand was examined. The following was noted: *There is a small scar at end of 2nd finger on left hand, which appears to be the result of a Whitlow. The movement of the finger is poor, and no disability.*

A Whitlow is a rare, yet painful infection of the finger, caused by the herpes virus. The symptoms are a red, painful and swollen finger. A person can contract the virus if they touch a cold sore, or the blister of another infected person. It is an infection that can return and remains in the body for life. He was demobilized and transferred to the Army Reserve until 24 December 1919, but his application for an Army pension was declined as the authorities did not consider that he had a disabled hand. His medical sheet records, however, that he had a 'disabled hand' and received treatment for it whilst he was being held at Minden prisoner of war camp, but there was no explanation as to what his disability actually entailed.

Private (1801)Cyril **Robin** enlisted in the Army on 22 April 1915, having successfully undergone a medical examination, at the Military Hospital at Guernsey. He served in the 2nd (Reserve) Battalion, Royal Guernsey Light Infantry. Having completed his basic training, he sailed from Folkestone on 17 September 1915 and arrived in Boulogne the same day.

He was admitted to the 30th General Hospital in Calais on 26 March 1918 with the symptoms of Gastritis. His condition worsened and he was invalided back to the UK for further treatment. On arrival in England he was admitted to North Evington Military Hospital in Leicester on 6 April 1917 where he was treated for twenty-six days, before he was finally discharged on 2 May 1917. On 4 January the following year, he was admitted to the military hospital in Guernsey, where he remained for five days being treated for an abrasion of the skin, the details of which were not included on his medical sheet.

On 16 March 1918 he returned to France and, after three days acclimation, he re-joined his battalion. He had only been back in the field for twenty-three days, when he received a gunshot wound to his left hand. Over the next three days he was treated by medical teams at the 87th Field Ambulance, the 2nd Casualty Clearing Station and the 2nd Australian General Hospital, at Wimereux, France. On 16 April 1918, he was admitted to the Bradstones Auxiliary Hospital West Derby, Liverpool, to be treated for the wound to the second and middle fingers of his left hand. His treatment and recuperation lasted until 8 May 1918, when he was transferred for further treatment to yet another hospital, the name of which was illegible on his medical sheet, where he remained until 5 July 1918. He was then transferred yet again, this time to hospital for a fifth time, as a patient at the 1st Western General Hospital at Fazakerley in Liverpool. The reason for his admission on this occasion was to have the middle finger of his left hand amputated. He was discharged from there on 9 August 1918.

Although he was not awarded an Army pension, he was given a gratuity of £65 on 15 December 1918, which by 2018 would have been worth somewhere in the region of £2,100, a large sum of money. By way of example, for £3,000 in 1977, it was possible to purchase a three-bedroomed, terraced house.

Private (125) John Frederick **Savident** was an 18-year-old fisherman when he enlisted in the Army on 20 November 1916 at Guernsey. Initially he was allocated to the Depot Company but on 17 December 1916, he was transferred to the 1st (Service) Battalion, Royal Guernsey Light Infantry.

7th Canadian Hospital, Etaples.

After completing his basic training he was sent to France as part of a Lewis Gun team on 27 September 1917. During fighting on 1 December 1917, he sustained a gunshot wound to his left thigh. As a result of that day's actin he was captured and taken prisoner by the Germans. Whilst in their care his left leg was amputated, high up on the thigh, on 4 December 1917. He wasn't repatriated to the UK until 8 October 1918, and on his return he was posted to his regiment's 2nd (Reserve) Battalion.

He was admitted to the 1st London City of London, General Hospital on 12 October 1918 and was treated there until 9 November 1918. On 5 December 1918 he became a patient at the Queen Mary's Convalescent Hospital at Roehampton where he was fitted with an artificial leg, and he remained there until 22 January 1919. The amputation was so far up the leg, that John Savident was left with only a 5-inch stump.

He was medically discharged from the Army on 23 January 1919. His home was at Richmont, St Saviour, Guernsey. His medical record did not show how much Army pension or the amount of pay out he received for the loss of his leg taking into account the fact that Private Cyril Robin, who had to have a finger amputated, received a payment of £65.

Private (13/16458) John Percival **Saville** enlisted on 9 September 1914, initially in the 13th Battalion, Durham Light Infantry, before transferring as a Private (66143) to the 17th Battalion, Royal Defence Corps, and finally becoming Private (2467) Royal Guernsey Light Infantry. He sustained a gunshot wound to his right arm on 10 July 1916 which resulted in his return

Beaufort War Hospital, Bristol.

to the UK for treatment at the County of London War Hospital where he remained until 20 October 1916.

A medical board which heard Private Saville's case on 18 June 1918, determined that he should be medically discharged from the Army, which he duly was on 10 July 1918. A medical report considered by the board described him as a healthy man and included the information that he had a deep scar on his right arm near the insertion of his deltoid, which would have been a result of the gunshot wound. It was interesting to note that he was still undergoing medicals once a year up to 1921. This may have been to see what improvement there was in his condition, so the medical authorities could determine by how much they could reduce his pension.

Private (3935) George **Tandy** attested on 1 December 1915 and was then placed on the Army Reserve. He was mobilized at the age of 33, on 31 May 1918 and joined the 2nd (Reserve) Battalion, Royal Guernsey Light Infantry, stationed at Worcester. He was discharged from the Army on 16 November 1918 as no longer physically fit for wartime military service, having served for just 169 days. Of this, 155 days were spent in hospital from 6 June to 26 October 1918 suffering from a combination of Myalgia and influenza. His pension, which began on 17 November 1918, was for 8s 3d a week for three months, after which he was provided with a further three months pension of 15s 8d. This was marked as 'Final Weekly Allowance'.

Private (1240) Clifford Francis **Tostevin** was 29 years of age and lived at 'La Villette' before he enlisted in the Army on 26 February 1917 at Guernsey, joining the 2ⁿᵈ (Reserve) Battalion, Royal Guernsey Light Infantry. Less than a month later, his son Clifford was born on 16 March 1917. With his son just six months old he was sent to France, arriving in Le Havre on 27 September 1917.

Whilst serving in France on 23 November 1917, he sustained a gunshot wound to his right knee which left him with an 8-inch scar on the outer side of his right knee. He was initially treated by staff at the 89th (1st Highland) Field Ambulance, the 48th Casualty Clearing Station, as well as the 24th General Hospital. On 5 December 1918, he was transferred back to England on board the Hospital Ship, *Ville de Liège*. Back in England he spent time in three different hospitals: Queen Mary's Hospital, Stratford, Command Depot Hospital at Perham Down and the VAD Hospital in Guernsey. As he healed, his movement was affected to such an extent that he had to partly rotate his right hip. On 21 March 1919 he was demobilised and transferred to Class Z of the Army Reserve, meaning that his injury may not have been as bad as it sounded, because if it had been, he would have been medically discharged rather than placed on the Army Reserve.

Private (1642) Thomas **Tostevin** enlisted in the Army on 15 June 1917 at Guernsey and joined the 2ⁿᵈ (Reserve) Battalion, Royal Guernsey Light Infantry. It became apparent during his basic training that he was having difficulties when it came to marching due, as it was claimed, by pain in the right ankle. This led to his being admitted to the military hospital in Guernsey, on three occasions, twice in relation to his ankle (12 November–27 December 1917 and 20 November–16 December 1918) a third occasion (19 March–22 June 1918) when he was suffering with Gastritis, an inflammation of the stomach. He was discharged from the Army on 16 December 1918 as no longer physically fit for wartime military service, at which time he was given an Army Pension of 7s 10d for a total of thirty weeks, which included allowances for his children.

Private (3926) Walter John **Tostevin** was only 19 years of age when he enlisted in the Army on 29 May 1918 in Guernsey and served in the 2ⁿᵈ (Reserve) Battalion, Royal Guernsey Light Infantry. Prior to enlisting he had worked as a painter and decorator. He was sent to France on 15 October 1918 and on arrival he was posted to the regiment's 1st (Service) Battalion. He spent six days of acclimatisation and administrative work, before joining up with his new battalion on 21 October 1918. Just eight days later he was admitted to the 7th Canadian General Hospital at Etaples.

Private Tostevin's condition did not improve and so he was sent back to the UK on board the hospital ship *St Denis* on 6 November 1918, arriving in England the following day. He was admitted to the Beaufort War Hospital in Bristol for further treatment, where he remained until 25 January 1919.

He was transferred to Class Z of the Army Reserve on 27 February 1919, at which time he was provided with a pension of 5s 6d per week for six months, payable from 28 February 1919, as he was suffering with general debility and anaemia. His ailments had officially been recognised as having their origins as of 29 October 1918 whilst he was serving in France.

He was re-admitted to the Beaufort War Hospital in Bristol for follow up treatment nine months after he had been placed on the Army Reserve, staying there for thirty-two days between 23 November and 25 December 1919. Why he had to travel back to Bristol for treatment and couldn't have been seen at the Military Hospital in Guernsey is not clear.

Private (693) Richard **Verron of** 3 Union Street, St Peter Port, Guernsey served in the 2nd Reserve Battalion, Royal Guernsey Light Infantry. He had enlisted on 21 December 1916 when he was 24 years of age. After his basic training he was sent to France, arriving at Le Havre from Southampton on 27 September 1917. During fighting on 1 December 1917 he was reported as missing in action, but was later confirmed as having been taken prisoner by the Germans. He was repatriated on 7 December 1918. On 14 May 1919, he was transferred to Z class Army Reserve, before being finally demobilized on 11 June 1919. There is a note on his pension record which states: *He is debilitated and suffering from DAH due to strain and hardship while a prisoner of war in Minden, Germany.* DAH stands for Disordered Action of the Heart. A further note dated 29 March 1919, said: *Discharged, being no longer physically fit for war service,* but it was crossed through and the words *cancelled, entered in error* were added.

Private (1541) Walter Charles **Wherry** joined the 2nd Reserve Battalion, Royal Guernsey Light Infantry, having enlisted on 16 May 1917 when he was 34 years of age. When he underwent his pre-recruitment Army medical examination, it was noted that he was receiving unspecified dental treatment and that he wore glasses due to defective sight. Walter, a baker by trade, was a married man who lived with his wife, Amy, at St Thomas Village, Victoria Road, St Peter Port, Guernsey.

He was transferred to the Army Reserve on 23 December 1919. He had suffered with pleurisy during the war which had resulted in his spending time in hospital in Guernsey between 21 and 31 December 1917. In addition to this he had two further spells in hospital because he was suffering from influenza. The first time was between 20 January and 9 February 1918 and the second, between 17 and 19 July 1918. On all three occasions he was returned to his unit on being discharged. Having been in military service for two and a half years, he made a request for an Army pension. This was rejected by the military authorities who wrote on his Army papers that there were 'no grounds for award'.

The war is full of sad stories. One such story was about four men from the 245th (Guernsey) Army Troop Company, Royal Engineers. The men were billeted in a building in Berchem, a district of Antwerp in the Flemish Region of Belgium. With the Armistice signed and a week having passed, the men could afford to relax somewhat and not have to worry that the harbinger of death might consider paying them a visit.

Four of them, Sapper (324456) John William Rihoy (41), of Victoria Road, Guernsey; Sapper (324585) George Hilary Robert (40), of 7 Rockwell Terrace, St Martin, Guernsey; Sapper (324516) John Oliver Duquemin (38), of Grandes Rocques, Castel, Guernsey, and Pioneer (324529) Thomas Henry Kimber (31), of 6 Church Hill, St Peter Port, Guernsey, were the company's cooks.

The four men all slept in the same room, so as not to cause too much commotion to the other men when they awoke at 5am to start preparing breakfast. Each was married and had children.

On the evening of 18 November 1918, everything was quite normal amongst the men. Some were playing cards, some were reading, whilst others were having a smoke or a hot drink. During the evening about 9.45pm, Sapper Robert went out for a smoke with one of the men from the adjoining room, but they were back indoors by 10pm having a cup of cocoa with other comrades including Sapper Rihoy.

The following morning, 19 November at 5am sharp, the four cooks were called by Sapper Carre, one of the men from the adjoining room, so they could start preparing breakfast. But he was unable to rouse any of them from their night's sleep and quickly went to inform Corporal Oliver, saying, 'I believe they are all dead,' despite later giving evidence before an official board of enquiry held in relation to the incident, on 23 November, that 'two of the men, Duquemin and Kimber were snoring but I could get no answer from them'.

Medical staff were called from the nearby 105th Field Ambulance Unit, but sadly Sappers Rihoy, Robert and Duquemin, were all pronounced dead at the scene. Kimber was alive, but died the following day.

There was a coal-burning stove located in the middle of the room, which had an outlet feed pipe to let out the smoke and fumes from the stove, via the open bedroom window. The situation in the men's room was discovered to be somewhat different. Instead of hanging out of the window, the end of the pipe was leaning against the wall and the window was closed, meaning that not only was the room not properly ventilated, but the fuel from the burning charcoal was trapped and breathed in by all of the men, which sadly led to their untimely deaths.

Major J.R.N Kirkwood gave evidence to the board of enquiry that he had inspected the men's room as recently as 16 November and found the stove and pipe to be in good working order, and that the ventilation was good. It was his opinion that the stove's pipe could not possibly have accidentally fallen into the position it was found in on the morning of 19 November, and that it must have been removed by one of the men in the room, who was mistakenly under the impression that the coals in the stove were extinguished. He added that all the men were fully aware of the potential dangers from inhaling the coke and charcoal fumes from the stoves.

The deaths were recorded as, misadventure by carbon monoxide poisoning, each of the men having inhaled the charcoal fumes from the stove whilst they slept.

CHAPTER SIX

Red Cross Nurses From The Channel Islands

At the beginning of the First World War there were already thousands of volunteer VAD members serving with the organisation. Founded in 1909, it was a joint venture between the British Red Cross and the St John Ambulance Society. Once the war began, thousands more quickly enlisted, eager to do their bit for king and country.

The one thing that nobody in authority appeared to have fully considered, were the extremely large numbers of casualties that the war was going to bring with it. The wounded could almost be counted on an industrial scale and there were literally hundreds of military and auxiliary hospitals situated up and down the country to deal with them. This was where the VAD nurses proved invaluable. They were never intended to replace trained and qualified nurses, and there was sometimes friction between the VADs and professionals. A large number of the VAD nurses were from well-to-do families. Many of these well-intended young women had never undertaken even basic domestic chores, as their families employed servants to carry out such work. Many of the VAD volunteers struggled with the concept of being told what to do by nurses whom they saw as below them in the social structure of society.

VAD nurses were not there to replace qualified nurses, but to supplement them. For every VAD nurse who could bandage, change and clean a wound dressing, make a bed, serve a meal, wash and clean their patients, change and clean linen or a ward, a qualified nurse was free to concentrate on actual nursing matters in helping doctors and surgeons to save lives. Although not exclusively so, the vast majority of VAD nurses were utilised in auxiliary hospitals, where wounded and sick men were sent after they had been operated on and had their wounds treated. Auxiliary hospitals were where these soldiers were sent for recovery and to get them back fighting again.

Every county had VAD sections. Most were staffed by women, but there were also male VADs, who were used mainly in such roles as orderlies or ambulance drivers.

Each of the women's detachments consisted of a male or female commandant. If the commandant was not a qualified doctor, then that section would have a medical officer. There was also a female superintendent, who needed to be a qualified nurse; a male or female quartermaster to look after equipment, medicines, food and the like; a pharmacist, along with twenty women, of whom four had to be qualified cooks.

Each VAD detachment was registered with its governing body and allocated an individual number by the War Office. Mentioning a VAD section just by the name of the town it was stationed in wasn't sufficient as some towns had more than just one.

To become a VAD nurse working in a military hospital, applicants had to be between 21 and 48 years of age for home service, but to work abroad they had to be between 23 and 42 years of age. They also had to complete a one-month probationary period which, if completed successfully, they then signed a six-month contract, which was paid at a rate of twenty pounds per annum. For each further six-month contract they received an additional £2 10s per annum, which increased up to a maximum of £30.

On the wards it was lights out at 9pm each evening, a rule that was strictly adhered to, and rigorously enforced by the night sister and her staff.

The following is a list of women from Guernsey, Alderney and Sark, who during the First World War, served, in one capacity or another, as members of the British Red Cross. In most cases this meant leaving their homes and families and travelling to mainland Great Britain, not knowing when they would return.

Miss Grace Emily Jane **Bye** lived at 7 Grange, Guernsey. She was initially employed as a probationary nurse on 24 April 1918, working on a full-time basis, at the 2nd/1st Southern General Hospital in Birmingham, on a wage of £20 a year. By the time her services were no longer required by the British Red Cross, on 3 July 1919, her pay had risen to £22.10s.

Mrs Havillema **Byrch** lived at 14 Sausmarez Street, Guernsey. On 4 April 1917 she began working for the Guernsey VAD 1114 section in the VAD free canteen in Guernsey as a volunteer. She continued to work there until its eventual closure, on 16 November 1919.

Miss Gertrude **Campbell**'s home was at Sutherland House, London Road, Deal, Kent, but like lots of women who wanted to do their bit during the war, she went where she was needed the most. As a full-time qualified nurse, between January and August 1918, that was at the Military Hospital, Guernsey. She was then transferred to the Netley Military Hospital, near Southampton, which catered for a wide range of wartime injuries, including 'shell shock' or what today would be referred to as Post Traumatic Stress Disorder. Gertrude was still working there until at least 18 June 1919.

Miss Doris Emmeline **Carey**, lived at a house named 'Rozel' in Guernsey, with her parents, Lionel and Blanche and her elder brother Cedric, who was a lawyer. The family were affluent enough to be able to afford three live-in servants. Doris began working for the Guernsey VAD 1114 unit, as a volunteer, part-time housemaid at the Les Touillets Military Hospital,

Netley Military Hospital.

Guernsey, in February 1918. She worked there for just six months and left in August 1918.

Miss Eileen Fanshawe **Carey** lived at 52 Hauteville, Guernsey, with her parents, Lecie and Helen, and her elder sister, Daphne. Because of her father's work, as a successful lawyer, the family could afford to employ four live-in servants to look after them. In February 1918, when she was 18 years of age, Eileen enlisted with the Guernsey VAD 1114 unit, as a volunteer, part-time housemaid, and began working at the Les Touillets Military Hospital. It was a role she undertook for a period of just six months, leaving there in August 1918.

Miss Mabel Colebrook **Carey** lived at 'Beechwood', Guernsey, with her parents, William and Frances, her elder sister, Bessie, and three live-in servants. Her father was the island's chief magistrate. Mabel, despite coming from such an affluent family, still wanted to do her bit for the war effort, and so began working for the VAD as a volunteer cook at the Red Cross Hospital at Waverley Abbey, in Farnham, where she worked for only a six-week period. On 4 September 1917, she began working for the Guernsey VAD 1114 section, as a volunteer, part-time clerk, at the Fort George Military Hospital at Guernsey, until 31 March 1918. After that date, she continued to be employed as a clerk, but in a full-time, paid capacity, until 31 March 1919.

Miss Vera Elizabeth **Carey** lived at Sausmarez House in Guernsey. When she started working for the VAD on 21 July 1915 she was 24 years of age, but unlike most of her peers who chose to work on the island close to home, she went to work at the Hursley Park Officers' Military Hospital, at Winchester, although it isn't clear from her VAD Service Card, in what capacity she did so. She remained there until 21 February 1916.

Miss Violet **Carey** lived at 2 Grange Terrace, Guernsey, with her mother Alice, her younger sister, Lily, and two servants. Her father, Peter Francis Carey, had died on 15 October 1904, aged 57. He was a nautical man by profession, but to what degree is unclear, although he was awarded his Certificate of Competency as a Second Mate on 17 February 1872 when he was 25 years of age, by the Committee of Privy Council for Trade. When he died he left his wife, Alice, the princely sum of £11,516 17s 10d. Today, that would be worth £1,333,411.92. Whatever it was that he did for a living, he was certainly very successful at it.

Violet, had a younger brother, Peter Dudley Carey, who was a vet by profession. In 1912 he joined the Army Veterinary Corps, and served with them during the First World War, rising to the rank of captain. He was still serving with them in 1922.

On 25 September 1917 Violet enlisted with the Guernsey VAD 1114 Unit and became a part-time, volunteer assistant quartermaster. Her main duty throughout her service, was being in charge of the VAD Free Canteen, which opened every morning at the unearthly hour of 3am to provide breakfast to the soldiers arriving by the early boat, up until 8am. She did this each and every morning, apparently with a smile on her face and a welcoming word, all the way through until 19 February 1919.

Miss Marjorie **Carre** who lived at Le Bouillon, Guernsey, began working for the VAD in October 1917 as a part-time volunteer, on Sundays for three hours, as a cleaner on the wards at St Dunstan's in Brighton, which was a specialist hospital for soldiers who had lost their sight during the war. She was still in post as of 5 July 1919.

Miss Evelyn Grace **Cohen** lived at 31 High Street, Guernsey. She began working for the Guernsey VAD 1114 Section in October 1917, as an unpaid volunteer worker at the VAD Free Canteen for Soldiers in Guernsey, a position she continued in until February 1919.

Miss Olive **Cohen** lived at Rouge Huis Lodge, Brock Road, Guernsey. She was a Pharmacist by profession and began working for the Guernsey VAD 1114 section in a full-time capacity on 1 January 1916, for which she was paid £2 4s per week. But instead of remaining in Guernsey, she was sent to the Cambridge War Hospital in Aldershot, where she remained until the end of the war.

Miss Edith M. **Collings** lived at The Grange, Guernsey, and enlisted with the Guernsey VAD 1114 Section on 1 April 1917, on an initial six-month contract, which saw her paid at the rate of £20 per annum. She continued to work for the VAD at the same location when her contract expired, but from then until she left on 31 March 1919, she undertook part-time unpaid work.

She began her time working as a full-time nurse for the VAD at the British Red Cross Hospital at Netley, for six months between 1 April and 1 October 1917, for which she was paid at a rate of £20 per annum. From

16 December 1917 until 23 August 1918, she undertook unpaid voluntary work, as a nurse at the Les Touillets Military Hospital, Guernsey, amassing a total of 1,368 hours. She then took a couple of weeks off before commencing part-time voluntary work at the Victoria Hospital, Guernsey on 10 September 1918, where she remained working until 31 March 1919 having amassed a further 920 hours – a truly remarkable effort.

Miss Louise Bonamy **Collings** was a local Guernsey girl, who began working for the Guernsey VAD 1114 Section as a paid, full-time nurse, on 26 September 1916, but the first six months of her service saw her working at the 4th London General Military Hospital, in Denmark Hill. She finished her six-month stint there on 16 March 1917. She then took a nine-month break from nursing, before continuing as a nurse, by now having returned to Guernsey, at the Les Touillets Military Hospital on Guernsey, between 7 December 1917 and 10 June 1918.

Miss Mary Bonamy **Collings**, according to the 1911 Channel Islands Census, lived at 24 Saumarez Street, St Peter Port, Guernsey, whilst her VAD Service Card, shows her living at 'La Verdure' Guernsey. When she started working for the Guernsey VAD 1114 Section, at their Free Canteen, on 6 October 1915, she was already 69 years of age.

She must have had a vast knowledge of the nursing profession as she was made an Honorary Serving Sister when she commenced working at the Free Canteen, and had been awarded a Medallion in 1886, what for exactly was not explained on her service card. She had also supervised at all lectures and practices for the St John Ambulance Association that were connected to the VAD.

She passed away on 4 August 1935, when she was 85 years of age. In her will she left £6,308. With the British pound of 1935 having an equivalent value today of an estimated £58, Mary Collings left the equivalent of £365,864.

Miss Elizabeth **Cox** lived at 'Grendahr Rohais', Guernsey, with her parents, John and Elizabeth Cox, but between 14 April 1916 and 1 June 1917, when she was 29 years of age, she was employed as a full-time nursing sister at the Red Cross (Weir) Hospital, in Grove Road, Balham, London. She was an only child and her father was a master mariner.

Miss Elsie **De Garis** lived at Villa Warnbrook in Brock Road, Guernsey, and became a member of the Guernsey VAD 1114 Section on 10 December 1917 as a part-time, volunteer nurse, working at Fort George Military Hospital. She continued working there for a period of six months, having finished her contract on 15 June 1918, which she did not renew.

Mrs Victoria L.E. **De Garis** lived with her husband, Adolphe De Garis, who was a master grocer, at 'Belle Vue', St Peter in the Wood, Guernsey. She was 36 years of age when she enlisted in the Guernsey VAD 1114 Section on 4 October 1918, where she was a part-time, volunteer nurse at the island's Victoria General Hospital. Her time spent there was a short one, as she left on New Year's Eve 1918.

Central Prisoners of War Committee.

Miss Dorothy Grant **de Jersey** had a very interesting and varied time during the war. Her home was at Cote de Vauxlauriers, Cambridge Park, Guernsey – not that she saw much of it during those hectic times. Between

October 1915 and December 1916 Dorothy was serving as a VAD nurse at the 24th General Hospital at Etaples, on the north coast of France. Her main duties were acting as the secretary to the matron as well as working in the mess. Due to unspecified ill health, she had to leave her position in France and soon afterwards it was determined that because of her illness she was no longer fit enough to continue working as a nurse. Despite this, she still wanted to do something towards the war effort. On her return to England she utilised her secretarial skills and entered general service. In February 1917 she was sent to work at the Royal Herbert Hospital in Woolwich, where she remained until October of that year, at which time she was forced to take a break owing to a serious illness that had befallen her mother. She was once again able to use her nursing skills in looking after her mother. After eight months of caring for her mother, she returned to work in May 1918 when she took up a position with the Central Prisoners of War Committee, which was located at Nos.3 and 4, Thurloe Place, London.

This lasted for just six months at which time she left owing to her own ill health. Because of her earlier service in France, she was entitled to the 1914–1915 Medal.

Dorothy Grant de Jersey's sister Miss Margery Grant de Jersey began working for the VAD in March 1916 as a full-time head cook, a role for which she was paid one guinea a week. She initially began work at the Kings Langley Hospital in Hertfordshire but was only employed there for three months before moving on to the Michie Hospital at 184 Queens Gate, Streatham, which was an affiliated auxiliary hospital to the Queen Alexandra Military Hospital, Millbank, London. She continued working there until at least January 1919.

Miss Marie **de La Rue**, who lived at Kings Mills, Castel, Guernsey, began working for the Guernsey VAD 1114 Section on 1 December 1917, as a part-time, voluntary housemaid at the Les Fouillets Military Hospital, Guernsey. She remained working there until 23 August 1918.

Mrs Bertha Ellen **de Putron** was living in Oberland Road, Guernsey, when she enlisted as a part-time, volunteer member for the Guernsey VAD 1114 Section, on 2 November 1917. She was sent to work at the Fort George Military Hospital, where she undertook general household duties, on alternative day and night duties.

Miss Rose Marie **de Ste Croix** lived at St Saviour's Rectory, Guernsey, when she enlisted on 16 April 1916 as a part-time, volunteer in the Guernsey VAD 1114 Section. She worked as a housemaid at the island's Military Hospital, at Les Touillets, remaining for more than two years, until 23 August 1918.

Miss Helen May **Duke** was living at Ivy Gates, Guernsey, when she enlisted in the Surrey VAD 56 Section in March 1915 in a nursing capacity. Prior to this she had worked at Mrs Ellecombe's Red Cross Hospital at Ash

Nurses at Waverley Abbey Military Hospital.

Vale in Surrey. Her wartime VAD work saw her working in the kitchen of the Waverley Abbey Hospital as a Pantry Maid, and out on the wards, undertaking a multitude of tasks. She worked there on two occasions: from March to September 1915, and March 1916 until March 1917.

Before the war, Waverley Abbey Hospital, was a private residence, the home of Rupert and Amy Anderson and their five children, but at the outbreak of the war, they offered the premises to the Government for use as a military hospital. It was a gesture that was gratefully accepted, and with Mrs Anderson also being the Commandant of the No.56 VAD, it was also extremely helpful. Opening as Waverley Abbey Auxiliary Military Hospital in September 1914, it became one of the first country houses to be converted into a military hospital.

Helen's younger sister, Miss Sybil Dorothy **Duke**, also enlisted in the Surrey VAD 56 Section, carrying out the same work as her sister, a pantry and ward maid at Waverley Abbey Auxiliary Military Hospital. She began working there on 11 January 1916, and spent fifteen months at the hospital. Her VAD service card states that she also worked at other un-named hospitals during the war. Her termination of employment with the VAD was on 12 December 1918.

Helen and Dorothy's father, Joshua Duke, retired from the Army in November 1902 as a lieutenant colonel and medical officer with the Indian Medical Service. At the outbreak of the First World War, he re-joined the Army at his previous rank and went to work at the York Place Indian Hospital at Brighton, which before the war had been a school, remaining there until 1915 when he moved on to the Bermondsey Military Hospital in Ladywell Road,

London, where he served until 1917. He died on 13 February 1920, at Rohais in Guernsey where he is buried. His son, Herbert, also became a doctor, going on to work for the Colonial Service in Uganda.

Miss Winifred Leila **Duquemen** lived at 65 Victoria Road, Guernsey, but when the First World War arrived she sailed to England in 1916 and joined the London VAD 40 Section, working as a full-time, paid nurse at three hospitals. Between 1 and 31 October 1916, she worked at the 2nd Western Hospital in Manchester. Between 1 November 1918 and 10 May 1919, she worked at the Kings College Hospital, 4th London General Royal Army Medical Corps, (Territorials) at Denmark Hill. Her third and final posting was at the Queen Alexandra Hospital Home for Discharged Soldiers, Gifford House, Putney Park Lane, Roehampton, Auxiliary Hospital, where she worked between 19 May 1919 and 26 June 1919. This may well have been even longer. The last date was when her VAD Service Card was completed, and when she was definitely known to have still been working at Roehampton.

Mrs Phyllis Maud **Elliot** lived at Manor Farm, St Martin, Guernsey, when she enlisted in the County of London Reserve VAD Detachment. She was employed as a full-time clerk and paid 31s 6d per week at Charterhouse Military Hospital, in Godalming, Surrey. She had to resign her position on 3 December 1918 as she was about to be married to Mr E.K. Sutherland-Richards.

Miss E. Florence **Elliott** lived at Le Douit Farm, St Saviour, Guernsey during the war years. On 1 June 1918 she enlisted in the Guernsey VAD 1114 Section and went to work at the VAD Free Canteen at Guernsey, where she helped to serve breakfasts to returning troops on the 3am ship. She continued working there until 19 February 1919.

Mrs Evelyn Pattie **Elliott** lived at Grange Place, Guernsey, when she enlisted with Guernsey VAD 1114 Section as a part-time, volunteer nurse. She was sent to work at the Victoria Military Hospital, between November 1916 and May 1917, and the Hospital at Fort George, between January and May 1918.

Mr John **Enright** lived at Les Conus, St Martin, Guernsey, with his wife Eveline and his mother Bridget. He was 33 years of age when he started to work for the VAD on Guernsey as a full-time ambulance driver, on 11 April 1918. For this he was paid 35s a week, to begin with, and by the time he had finished his work, on 4 December 1918, this amount had risen to 36s 6d.

Prior to his work for the local VAD, he had undertaken similar work for the St John Ambulance No.18 Section in the Montdidier region in Argonne, France. His occupation before the war was a gardener. On his eighteenth birthday, 24 March 1903, he enlisted in the Royal Navy, as a seaman and went on to serve on board seven different ships, before finishing his service on 7 June 1906, when he was medically discharged due to being diagnosed as suffering from epilepsy.

The home address for Miss Lilian Vernon **Forsdick**, was shown on her VAD Service record card as being the Victoria Military Hospital, Guernsey. Despite this she worked for the Surrey VAD as a full-time nursing sister at Redhill War Hospital, Earlswood Common, for which she was paid £50 per annum.

Mrs Amy Gertrude **Friend** lived with her husband, Edward, and their two children, Stanley and Joan, at La Marettes, St Martin, Guernsey. She enlisted with the Guernsey 1114 VAD Section on 21 May 1918 as a paid, part-time kitchen worker, but, despite being married and the mother of two young children, she was sent to the Royal Victoria Hospital at Netley near Southampton for six months, finally returning home on 29 November 1918.

Miss Eva Jane **Fuzzey** lived at 22 Mill Street, Guernsey and was a 41-year-old spinster, by the time she enlisted in the Guernsey VAD 1114 Section on 17 October 1917. She was put to work as a housemaid and waitress at the 14th Canadian Military Hospital in Eastbourne. She continued working there until 9 June 1919. According to the 1911 Channel Islands Census, Eva, was, at that time living at 60 Hauteville, Guernsey, which was the home of her elderly mother.

Miss Lilian Frederica **Galliatt** lived at 'Carmel', St Martin, Guernsey. Her VAD Service Card only recorded that she was a trained nurse and that she only served for just over two months, between 20 August and 1 October 1817.

Miss Beatrice May **Gallienne** lived with her parents, Thomas and Alice, her sister Maud and her two brothers, Harold and Herbert, at The Ponchez, Castel, Guernsey. Her father, Thomas was a farmer, Beatrice and her and sister worked as milk maids on his farm. On 7 December 1917 Beatrice enlisted in the Guernsey VAD 1114 Section as a part-time volunteer, at the rank of general service member. She was then allocated as a housemaid at Les Touillets Military Hospital, Guernsey, where she worked for only four months, until April 1918.

Miss Mary **Gavet** was the second youngest of seven children born to John and Marie Cavet, with the family living at Beanham, St Andrews, Guernsey. She enlisted at 24 years of age in the Guernsey 1114 VAD Section on 25 September 1917, and during the following two years, she was sent to work at the following locations: 25 September 1917 to 6 December 1917 – VAD Free Canteen; 8 December 1917 to 20 January 1918 – housemaid at Le Touillets Military Hospital; 21 January 1918 to 18 July 1918 – VAD nursing probationer at the same hospital where she was paid at the rate of £20 per annum; 30 September 1918 to 14 February 1919 – Voluntary, part-time VAD nurse, Victoria Hospital Guernsey. It is believed that she was still working until at least 5 July 1919 at the Le Touillets Military Hospital.

Her youngest brother, Edward, enlisted in the Guernsey Light Infantry, becoming Private (1359) in the 2nd (Reserve) Battalion. He was discharged on 9 June 1917 as no longer physically fit for wartime military service, having served in the Army for just seventy-four days. This was due to having been diagnosed as having tuberculosis of the lung. It was deemed by the members of the Medical Board who heard Edward's case, that he did not qualify for an Army pension, but he was eligible for a one-off gratuity payment of £25. Edward died on 6 July 1917 aged just 24.

Miss Annie **Gould** lived at 12 Upper Canichers, Guernsey and became a full-time general service member of the Guernsey VAD 1114 Section on 6 October 1917, for which she was paid £26 a year. She was allocated as a VAD housemaid at Fort Lodge Hospital, Guernsey. Her contract was for the duration of the war, but she was still in post, during the early months of 1919.

Mrs Edith Gertrude **Gould** lived at Uplands, Guernsey. She enlisted in the Guernsey VAD 1114 Section in September 1917 as a part-time, volunteer nurse, and was sent to work at the Fort George Military Hospital. She continued in her role until July 1918.

Miss Gertrude Annie **Grut** was 24 years of age when she began working for the VAD. She lived at The Evergreens, Upland Road, Guernsey, with her father Herbert, who was a fancy draper. Prior to enlisting in the Jersey VAD 4 on 5 December 1917, Gertrude worked as an assistant in her father's business. She became a full-time, paid nurse at the 4th Southern General Hospital, in Plymouth, where she remained until 27 March 1918.

Miss Mabel **Grut** lived at Elmleigh, Elm Grove, Guernsey. She was 26 years of age when she enlisted in the Lincoln 32 VAD Section on 7 April 1916 as a nurse and, according to her VAD Service Card, she was sent to the Kitchener Hospital at Brighton, which was the largest of the three hospitals in the town that catered entirely for wounded Indian soldiers. This somewhat contradicted what I had read elsewhere, which stated that nursing at the Kitchener Indian Hospital, was carried out by men, and that women were never employed there, even as nurses. Regardless of which of those facts was correct, the hospital could accommodate more than 1,700 wounded and sick men at any time, and if necessary 1,000 more patients could be accommodated in the grounds of the adjacent racecourse.

On 26 October 1916 Mabel was transferred to go and work in Salonica, where at the time there were more than twenty military hospitals, including both general and stationary ones. Which one Mabel was sent to is not stated on her service card. After more than a year she left Salonica and moved on to work in Italy, where she remained between 21 January 1918 to 7 May 1918. So good was she at her work that she was awarded two efficiency stripes on 1 May 1918.

Mrs Alice H. **Hickey** was the commandant and in charge of recruiting for the Guernsey VAD 1114 Section, between 6 October 1915 and 27 March 1919, and possibly later, but her VAD service card was no more specific. It clarified that she was not paid for either position, but not whether she worked part-time or in a full-time capacity.

During her time as commandant, she helped organise some seventy-five parades, as well as providing instruction on stretcher drill, and giving twenty-five lectures on hygiene and massage. He role also saw her conduct all interviews of general service staff, and she was heavily involved in the island's VAD Free Canteen that was provided all year round.

She lived at 'Arosfa', Les Gravees, Guernsey with her husband, Vincent Hickey, who worked for the Post Office as a sorting clerk and telegraphist. Vincent's claim to fame was that he had fourteen brothers and six sisters.

Miss Louisa Emily Victoria **Hicks** lived at 3 Vannert Terrace, Guernsey, and was a qualified nurse. Her VAD service card isn't clear in its detail, but she worked for what appeared to be the 'Training Nurses Department' but where that was, isn't stated. What the card does reveal is that she served with the VAD between 6 March 1916 and 31 July 1919, and that her starting pay was £1 1s per week and rose to £1 4s per week by the time she had finished.

Miss Annie Frances **Hubert** was 31 years of age and lived with her parents, Francis and Ann Hubert, her younger sister, Elsie De Garis Hubert, and her brother Wilfred George Hubert, at 'Mount Vernon', Doyle Road, Guernsey, when she enlisted in the Channel Islands VAD 8 Section on 7 July 1916. Between then and 9 April 1917 she was working as a nurse at the 1st Eastern General Military Hospital in Cambridge. On 10 April 1917, she was sent out to work in an unspecified military hospital in France, where it is known that she was still working on 29 July 1919.

Miss Emma Giffard **Isemonger** who lived at St Jacques House, Guernsey, was one of four children of Thomas and Mary Isemonger, and along with her older sister, Eva, she enlisted in the VAD during the First World War. Emma's VAD Service Card shows that rather than remain on Guernsey, she travelled to England and joined the Devon 16 VAD Section and in April 1915, became a full-time, paid dispenser at Exeter War Hospital until 12 October 1918. Her wage was £114 per annum, less the cost of her board and lodgings

Miss Eva Maude **Isemonger**'s story was very similar to her sister Emma's in that she too travelled to England, enlisted with the Devon 16 VAD Section, and worked at the Exeter War Hospital as a dispenser, between 12 April 1915 and 22 July 1918.

Miss May **de Jersey** lived at The Villocq, Castel, Guernsey, with her mother, Marguerite, her brother, John, and her sister, Adele. When May was 22 years of age, she travelled to England and enlisted in the Devon 86 VAD Section. She worked at the 4th Southern General Hospital, at Plymouth as a full-time telephonist on the hospital's telephone exchange. She began working there on 15 January 1916, when her wage was 20s per week. By the time she left on 12 September 1918, her wages had risen to 37s 6d a week.

At the beginning of the First World War, Miss Olive Clare **Le Mottee**, who was born in the North-West Providence of India, lived at May Trees, Hauteville, Guernsey, with her father, George Herbert Le Mottee, a retired lieutenant colonel with the Royal Army Medical Corps, her mother, Josephine, Clara Le Mottee, her older sister, Caroline, and three servants.

In June 1916 Olive left for England and enlisted in the Southampton, Hampshire 2 VAD Section, where she ended up working full-time as the assistant quartermaster at the Red Cross Hospital, Highfield Hall, Southampton. She was still working there on 25 June 1919.

Miss Miriam **Leale** lived at The Hanchorus, St Sampson, Guernsey, with her parents, John and Amelia Leale, her younger brothers, John and Roy, and a servant named Frances. By trade her father was an ironmonger. Miriam travelled to England and enlisted in the East Lancashire VAD 222 Section, but was then sent to the University War Hospital, Southampton, as a full-time nurse. She worked there from 21 September 1917 to 17 April 1919.

Miriam's brother, Roy, went on to become a lieutenant, firstly, in the Royal Guernsey Light Infantry, and later attached to the 7th Battalion, Royal Fusiliers. The UK Army Register of Soldiers effects, records that Roy died on 21 April 1919, but it does not include the details of how and where he died. The Commonwealth War Graves website does not show any record of Roy's death.

Miss Marie Ogier **Le Patourel** lived at La Ramee, St Peter Port, Guernsey, and was the middle of seven children of Alfred and Emily Le Patourel. Her three older siblings were, Marcus, Alfred and Harry, the younger three being Emily, Freda and Hilda. Marie's father, Alfred, was a farmer and cattle breeder. Marie enlisted in the Channel Isles 8 VAD Section on 3 January 1916 when she was 23 years of age, as a nurse, and was sent to work in the 3rd Northern General Hospital in Sheffield, but she was only there for exactly a month, leaving there on 3 February.

The British Army Medal Rolls Index Cards that cover the period of the First World War, record a Marcus James Le Patourel, who was a Private (1528) in the Royal Guernsey Light Infantry. Fortunately, his Army Service Record, also survived. Its shows that he was in the 2nd (Reserve) Battalion. He enlisted on 14 May 1917 at Guernsey, when he was 31 years of age, prior to which he had been a ploughman and driver on the family farm. His attestation form shows that on 16 December 1916, he was discharged from the Army from what appears to be the Royal Garrison Artillery, but the writing is not totally legible.

After five months of basic training, he left Guernsey on 24 October 1917, arriving in Le Havre the following day, having been posted to the regiment's 1st (Service) Battalion, and became part of the 46th Infantry Base Depot, on 27 October 1917. On 3 November 1917, he joined his battalion in the field, and just over a month later on 1 December 1917, he suffered a gunshot wound to his left thigh. He was initially treated by the 89th Field Ambulance, which was provided by the Royal Army Medical Corps, who were responsible for providing the initial medical treatment and assessment. Later the same day he was transferred on to 48 Casualty Clearing Station. Despite his gunshot wound he remained in France.

Between 25 and 30 January 1918, he was once again treated by the 89th Field Ambulance unit for Myalgia, a form of muscular rheumatism, and again on 22 March 1918 for sores to his legs. His condition worsened and he was transferred to the 3rd Australian Casualty Clearing Station on 30 March 1918, when they were located near Poperinghe, Belgium. Marcus was returned to England for further treatment, arriving there on 4 April 1918. Between 24 August 1918 and 13 January 1919, Marcus was admitted to hospital in Guernsey, again suffering with Myalgia. It is clear to see by the length of time that he subsequently spent in hospital being treated and recovering from it, just how debilitating the ailment could be.

His conduct sheet records that he was in trouble with his senior officers for an infringement of Army discipline on 21 June 1919 when he faced two charges. The first was for being absent from a parade, and the second was for quitting camp without permission. He was found guilty and his punishment was 'confined to barracks for three days'.

It is quite common to find a template letter attached to a soldier's service record from the employer they worked for immediately before enlistment. It reads as follows:

I/we (Name of employer or Company name) hereby declare that (Name, service number and regiment/corps the man served with) was in my/our employ previous to August 4th, 1914, and that I am/we are prepared to take him back in to our employment as (Job title) on his return to civil life.

There was such a letter attached to Marcus's service record submitted by Marcus's father, the farmer whom he worked for. Marcus was demobbed from the Army on 20 March 1919.

Miss Gertrude D. **Lukis** lived at Le Douit Farm, St Saviour, Guernsey, and enlisted in the Guernsey VAD 1114 Section on 10 January 1918, remaining with them until 19 February 1919. During that time she worked as a part-time volunteer, house maid at the Les Touillets Military Hospital, and afterwards she worked in the VAD's Free Canteen, serving cups of tea and breakfasts to returning soldiers on the early boat which arrived in Guernsey at 3am each morning.

Miss Lukis is shown in the 1911 Channel Islands Census as having been born in Nantes, France in 1870, and living at Moulin De Haut, Guernsey, with her occupation recorded as by 'private means'. Living at her address as a boarder was a Miss E. Florence Elliot who was recorded as being a companion.

Miss Annie Rosalee Mary **Mackay** lived at Seaton Villa, Bosq Lane, Guernsey. She enlisted in the Guernsey VAD, which particular section is not mentioned on her service card, on 15 May 1918 when she was 38 years old. She was sent out to work in an unspecified military hospital in France, but she was only there for just a week, her work as a VAD coming to an end on 22 May 1918, with no explanation as to why.

According to the 1911 Channel Islands Census she was working as a servant and housemaid for the Gruchy family who were living at Ronceville, Jersey.

The entry on the Red Cross website for Miss Aline R. **Mahy** is somewhat confusing as there are two VAD Service Cards in her name, but with slight variations.

Card number one is for Miss Aline Rachel Mahy which contains the following information. Her home address is recorded as being at 24 Scotts Avenue, Shortlands, Kent. She was 39 years of age when she began working as a full-time cook for the Guernsey VAD 1114 Section on 27 June 1918 at the Royal Naval Infirmary at Deal, Kent. She remained working there in the same capacity until 17 April 1919. On 12 May 1919 she started work at one of the hospitals in Huddersfield. On 12 August 1919 she then transferred to the 'Brecon', presumably the Brecon Military Hospital, where she was still working on 11 September 1919.

Card number two is for Miss Aline R. Mahy who this time is shown as living at Les Tilleuls, Vale, Guernsey. She began working for the Guernsey VAD 1114 Section on 28 May, but it doesn't clarify which year. It shows that she was a full-time worker who was paid £26 per annum and worked as a cook at the Royal Marine Infirmary, in Deal, Kent but that is all the information the service card contains.

Miss Marie Helene **Mahy** was the younger sister of Aline Mahy and lived at Les Tilleuls, Vale, Guernsey, with her parents Thomas, who was a farmer, and her mother Rachel. On the 1911 Channel Islands Census there was no sign of an Aline Mahy, but there was another sister, Constance Mahy, who was a year younger than Marie. The census did show an Aline Mahy, along with two other sisters and two brothers.

Marie began working for the VAD 1114 Section on 10 July 1918 as a paid full-time nurse. Her first posting saw her being sent to the 1st Southern General Military Hospital in Birmingham, where she remained until 9 February 1919. By 3 August 1919 she had moved to the Brook War Hospital, at Shooters Hill, Woolwich, which had the capacity for 1,000 beds, and where she was still working in September 1919.

Miss Clarissa **Major** lived at St Peter Port, Guernsey, joined the Worcester VAD on 20 March 1918 and, according to her service card, ended up working in 'Highbury' as a full-time house maid, which could be Highbury in North London or Highbury St John's Hospital, Moseley, Worcestershire. She finished her wartime volunteer work, sometime in early 1919.

For the next person, there are three VAD service cards in existence, all with a slight variation in the name. Mrs Lauretta Anscell **Martel** lived at

2 Amphill Place, Victoria Road, Guernsey. She enlisted in the island's VAD on 9 November 1918 as a clerk when she was 44 years of age. Her service card does not clarify if she was a volunteer or was paid for her work, or whether she was full-time or part-time. What is known is that she continued with her VAD duties until 23 September 1919.

Her work began at the Walton-on-Thames Auxiliary Hospital on 9 November 1917, where she worked for only one month, before moving on to the Prees Heath Military Hospital at Whitchurch, Shropshire on 7 December 1917 where she worked for just three weeks until 29 December 1917. The hospital was a hutted camp with capacity for 609 patients.

Her work then took her to an unknown Canadian Military Hospital where she worked between 28 March and an unknown date in April 1918. Next on her list of places was the Red Cross, Kimbolton Auxiliary Hospital, between 11 May 1918 and 16 December 1918. Her last posting, which lasted for a period of just three months, was at the Barry Road Auxiliary Hospital in Northampton, between 20 January and 8 April 1919. Her VAD wartime career ended at their headquarters where she worked between 26 May and 23 September 1919, before returning to her pre-war life.

The second VAD service card for this woman, has the name spelt slightly differently: Lawretta A. Martel, who lived at the same address. It covers the period 28 November to 28 December 1917. On this occasion, she is shown as having been a housekeeper at the local VAD headquarters, paid 31s 6d per week in wages. The third VAD service card for this individual is in the name of Lauretta Airsdell Martel. It contains a lot of the information which is included on the other cards, and covers the period, 11 May to 16 December 1918.

Miss Merea Courteney **Martel** was the younger sister of Lauretta. She enlisted in the Guernsey 2 VAD Section on 29 April 1918, when she was 18 years of age, as a housemaid at the following locations:

26 April 1918 to 2 June 1919 – Cooden Beach Canadian Military Convalescent Hospital, Bexhill, Surrey.

2 June 1919 to 18 August 1919 – Oakham. This might refer to the hospital at Hambleton Hall.

18 August 1919 to 13 September 1919 – Llangammarch Wells (Breconshire) Officers' Hospital.

Miss Margaret Isabel **Massey** lived at Castle Carey, Guernsey, and enlisted in the Guernsey 2 VAD Section. During her time with the unit she worked as an unpaid volunteer, canteen worker, a housemaid as well as in a nursing capacity at the following locations:

November 1915 to April 1916 – assistant at 'The Dug-Out' a canteen for New Zealand troops, at 1 Victoria Street, London.

November 1916 to January 1917 – housemaid at the British Red Cross VAD Auxiliary Michie Hospital, 184 Queens Gate, London.

October 1918 to March 1919 – Victoria Cottage Hospital, Guernsey.

Mrs Kate **McLean** lived at 'Hermes', La Plaque, Castel, Guernsey, with her husband, Robert, a telephone manager for the States of Guernsey, and 19-year-old William Gill, a boarder and nighttime telephone operator.

By the outbreak of the First World War, Robert and Kate had been married for thirteen years but had no children. She enlisted in the Guernsey 2 VAD 1114 Section on 20 December 1917, as a part-time, general service volunteer, and worked there until 23 August 1918, as a housemaid at the Les Touillets Military Hospital.

Miss Violet Kathleen Sybella **Mockler** enlisted as a full-time general service member with the Guernsey 2 VAD 1114 Section in September 1914, working in both a volunteer and paid capacity. Between September and November 1914, she worked in a nursing capacity at the Victoria Cottage Hospital, Guernsey, as a part-time volunteer. Between December 1914 and January 1915, she went to work in France at the Hôpital du Chateau St Malo as a volunteer nurse. She remained in France and between April and July 1915 worked as a volunteer at the Hôpital de Mondeville, possibly named after the French surgeon, Henri de Mondeville. Next on the list of hospitals in France, was the Church Army Hospital. She was there between July 1915 and April 1916. After what appears to have been a short break from her stressful and demanding work, she took up where she had left off, this time at the Hôpital d'Arc-en-Barrois, where she worked between July 1916 and January 1917.

This was an emergency evacuation hospital for the French 3rd Army Corps, but the staff were nearly all British volunteers, who were provided by

Hôpital d'Arc-en-Barrois 1915.

the British Red Cross VAD. It was situated in the Chateau d'Arc-en-Barrois, in the Haute-Marne region of France. Violet remained in France, but was getting nearer and nearer to the coast, when in July 1917 she began working at the British Expeditionary Force's No.30 General Hospital in Calais, where she remained until February 1918, where she was paid at a rate equivalent to £20 per annum.

By March 1918 she had finally made her way back to Guernsey, when she began working at the Fort George Hospital, as a part-time, voluntary nurse, but she only stayed there for three months and she was off again. With the war fast drawing to a close she took up a paid position at the King George's Hospital at Waterloo in London, where she was between July and December 1918.

Violet had spent the entire war in the service of others. She had dealt with badly wounded men in France, England and Guernsey, and had no doubt seen death on more occasions than she cared to. She did what she could to comfort those she was tasked with caring for, with her professionalism, a smiling face and a friendly word.

Miss Bertha Julia **Moullin** who lived at Chislehurst, Baissieres, Guernsey, was 23 years of age when she enlisted with Guernsey VAD 1114 Section on 24 September 1916. She was sent out to work at one of the numerous military hospitals in Malta – 'the nurse of Mediterranean' as she was also affectionately referred to. There were twenty-seven in total which had an overall capacity to treat 25,000 wounded men, and by the end of the war had treated some 135,000 men, mainly from the fighting at Gallipoli in Turkey and Salonica in Greece. Many of those who were treated in Malta were sick,

Staff on steps of Hôpital d'Arc-en-Barrois.

suffering with such ailments as malaria and dysentery, due to both the heat and lack of proper sanitation.

Bertha remained working in Malta until 22 May 1917 then returned to England, where after a few months rest, she returned to nursing, but this time, according to her VAD service card, at the military hospital at Chatham, probably Fort Pitt. She worked there as a nurse between 8 August 1917 and 8 August 1918.

Miss Annette Le Patourel **Ogier** lived at Vrangue Manor, St Peter Port, Guernsey. She was the eldest of five children born to John and Emma Ogier, her father being a farmer. She was 23 years of age when she enlisted in the Channel Isle 8 VAD Section on 3 January 1916 as a nurse and was sent to work at the 3rd Northern General Hospital in Sheffield. She worked there some nineteen months, finally leaving on 11 August 1917.

Annette's younger sister, Miss Miriam Flere **Ogier**, also enlisted in the VAD, but for her it was the Guernsey 2, 1114 Section that she joined on 10 October 1917, as a VAD nursing probationer, for which she was paid £20 per annum. She was still serving as of 25 May 1919, and during her service she had worked at Fort George Military Hospital as well as Castlemount Military Hospital at Dover. She died on 9 October 1992, just seven months short of her 100th birthday.

Miss Dora Christine **Ogier** lived at Lower Rohais, St Andrews, Guernsey. She worked for the VAD between 2 May 1917 and 5 December 1918 as a nurse and was sent to work at the Fovant Military Hospital in Salisbury, Wiltshire.

Miss Elsie Sylvia **Ozanne** lived at North View, Cobo, Castel, Guernsey. She worked as a nurse for the London 40 VAD Section between 31 March 1917 and 27 September 1919. She began working at the Connaught Hospital, Aldershot on 31 March 1917, staying there until 1 June 1918. From there, having volunteered for overseas attachments, her VAD service card, shows that she went to work at an unspecified French military hospital, between 1 June 1918 and 2 July 1919. She then took a two month break before being sent to the Royal Naval Hospital Chatham, between 1 and 27 September 1919.

Mrs Frances Hind **Ozanne** who lived at Le Palton, Guernsey, began working for the Guernsey 2 VAD 1114 Section, in September 1914 and continued until October 1917. She started at the Victoria Cottage Hospital in Guernsey, on a part-time voluntary basis, between September and October 1914. The following month she left Guernsey for France, and started working full-time on a voluntary basis, at the Hôpital du Chateau St Malo, where she stayed until the end of December. From there she moved on to the Hôpital de Mondeville, where she was a full-time voluntary worker between April and September 1915. According to her VAD service card, she had a break for about eighteen months before she returned to nursing at the Red Cross Hospital near Netley, working on a full-time voluntary basis, for a month between March and April 1917. Her time working for the VAD came to an end after she had worked for two months between September and October 1918, as an assistant at the Guernsey VAD Free Canteen for returning soldiers to the island who arrived on the early boat.

Frances's husband, Edward Chepmell Ozanne, who was the Bailiff of Guernsey between 1915 and 1922, would later be knighted. Sir Edward and Lady Frances Ozanne lost a son in the war. Captain Edward Graeme Ozanne, 3rd Battalion, Royal Fusiliers was killed in action, aged 32, on 14 February 1915.

Miss Helen C. **Ozanne** lived at 1 Choisi Terrace, Guernsey, and her time working in the VAD, was certainly a varied one. She enlisted in the Guernsey 2 VAD 1114 Section on 25 September 1917 carrying out a multitude of tasks. She started out as a part-time volunteer assistant at the VAD Free Canteen in Guernsey, finishing there on 19 February 1919. She also carried out other VAD work. Between 6 January and 10 May 1918, she worked as a volunteer housemaid at Les Touillets Military Hospital, Guernsey. She remained at the hospital and became a full-time clerk, a job for which she was paid a weekly wage of 28s 4d. She remained working there until 27 March 1919.

Miss Ruth **Ozanne** was the daughter of the Bailiff Edward Ozanne and his wife Frances, living at Le Platon, Guernsey. She became a general service member of the VAD, working in Guernsey, France and England. Between September and November 1914, she worked as a part-time volunteer at the Victoria Cottage Hospital, Guernsey, in a nursing capacity. Between 1 December 1914 and an unspecified date in January 1915, she worked as a full-time volunteer at the Hôpital du Chateau in St Malo. She remained in France and moved on to Caen, where she worked at the Church Army Hospital as a full-time volunteer between July 1915 and April 1916. In July 1916, she started working at the Hôpital d'Arc-en-Barrois as a full-time volunteer. Leaving there in January 1917. Her next move took her to Calais where she worked full-time at No.30 General Hospital, between July 1917 and February 1918, for which she was paid at a rate of £22 per annum. From there it was back to Guernsey to work at the Les Touillets Military Hospital, where she spent the months March through till May 1918, and was once again a part-time volunteer. Her time with the VAD came to an end in England, where she worked full-time at the King George Military Hospital in Stamford Street, London.

Author William Parker published Ruth's diaries in a book entitled, *Life in Occupied Guernsey – The Diaries of Ruth Ozanne – 1940-1945* which was her personal account of living in German occupied Guernsey during the course of the Second World War.

Miss Marie **Quesne** lived at 12 Upper Canichers, Guernsey, and enlisted in the Guernsey 2 VAD 1114 Section, as a full-time cook, a role for which she was paid £26 per annum. She began working as a cook at Fort Lodge, Guernsey, on 12 November 1917, and she was still working there on 27 March

1919. The 1911 Channel Islands Census records a Marie Quesne, who was a domestic servant working for Adelina De Montey, at 8 Grange Road, Guernsey, and was the only person with that name recorded on the census.

Miss Marie Louise Mansell **Randall** lived at Magnolia, Guernsey. She enlisted as a nurse in the Jersey 2 VAD Section on 12 August 1915. Between that date and 20 September 1916, Marie's VAD service card, records that she went to work at an unnamed military hospital in France. She then went to work at what has been recorded as a Camberwell Military Hospital, this might have been the Maudsley Military Hospital, at Denmark Hill, Camberwell. She worked there between 20 January and 20 July 1917.

There is a second VAD service card in the name of Miss Marie Randall, who is more than likely the same person. This one records her as living in St Saviour, Jersey and being a nursing member of the VAD Jersey 2 Section. It also shows her as having enlisted in the VAD in June 1915, and between then and 11 August of the same year, she was working at a hospital in Guernsey. On 12 August 1915, she went out to France and began working at the No.10 General Hospital, which by 1915, was in Rouen. There was also a No.10 British Red Cross Hospital that was set up in Le Tréport, but that wasn't until June 1916.

She remained working in Rouen until 20 September 1916. The service card then then records her as working at the 1st London General Hospital in Camberwell, but the dates are slightly different. On the second card she is shown as working there between 20 January and 31 July 1917. In 1918 she went to Holland to work in a YMCA hut for British prisoners of war, but there is no record of where exactly that was.

Miss Clara Lilian **Randell** lived at Grove End, Doyle Road, Guernsey, and enlisted in the Guernsey 2, VAD 1114 Section, in September 1917, as a volunteer worker in the VAD Free Canteen. She stopped working there in September 1918. According to the 1911 Channel Islands Census, Clara was 41 years of age and a head teacher at a primary school on the island, living with her elderly widowed mother and two of her sisters, Maud E. **Randell** and Mabel Agnes **Randell**, who also enlisted in the VAD.

Maud joined the Guernsey 2, VAD 1114 Section on 6 October 1915 as a section leader, in which capacity she had been involved in the detachment's training since its formation in October 1915. She was also an unpaid volunteer on the unit's ambulance, and between 25 September 1915 and February 1919, she worked as an assistant in the VADs Free Canteen.

Mabel, who like her sister Clara, was also the head teacher of a local primary school, had followed suit and joined the same VAD Section as her sisters, working for them between September 1917 and December 1918 as a part-time, volunteer at the VAD's Free Canteen in Guernsey.

Mrs Hilda N.C. **Renouf** who lived at Victoria, Ville au Roi, Guernsey, enlisted in the Guernsey 2, VAD 1114 Section on 20 August 1917, as a cook.

Between 20 August 1917 and 15 October 1917, she worked at the Les Islets Military Isolation Hospital, Guernsey as a volunteer, but from 16 October 1917 until 16 October 1918 she was taken on as a paid, full-time cook at the same establishment, for which she was paid £26 per annum. She continued in the same role until 14 December 1918, but for the last two months, she worked as a volunteer. The 1911 Channel Islands Census, records that she was living at Holborn Villa, Collings Road, Guernsey with her husband, William, who worked as a managing clerk at an auctioneers.

Mrs Elsie Georgina **Richings** lived at Lower Havelet, Guernsey. She enlisted in the Guernsey 2, VAD 1114 Section in a nursing capacity, which saw her working at the Horton War Hospital at Epsom in Surrey for one year, and the Magdalen Camp Hospital, Winchester, but her VAD service card, does not provide specific dates for both postings. The Horton War Hospital, which opened on 12 March 1915, came under military rule on 9 April that same year. Prior to this it had been the Horton Asylum which provided accommodation and care, for more than 2,000 patients, who were moved out to various other asylums. It ended up with a capacity of 2,532 beds for wounded soldiers. By the end of the war it had treated an estimated 45,686 patients, of whom only 351 died, which is less than 1 per cent. The Magdalen Camp Hospital was established at an Army base situated near Winchester and had a maximum capacity of 252 beds. Elsie continued serving in the VAD until at least 14 May 1919.

Miss Edith Emma **Robilliard** lived at La Pictu, Guernsey and enlisted in the Guernsey 2 VAD on 1 January 1917 as an assistant cook, her first posting, albeit for only three days, was at the Auxiliary Hospital at Clandon Park, which before the war had been the stately home of Lord and Lady Onslow, but they offered it to the War Office for use as a military hospital. There was sufficient room for 100 patients, and their first batch of patients, 101 Belgian soldiers arrived rather abruptly on 12 October 1914. The hospital remained open until 1 May 1919, when the last patient was discharged. A total of 5,059 soldiers had been treated there throughout the war, and 747 operations were carried out.

The other location where Edith worked was the Royal Victoria Hospital at Netley, near Southampton. She was there for three months between 25 September and 15 December 1918, at which time she was paid £1 12s 18d a week.

Mrs Florence Francis **Robilliard** lived at Dereham Brock Road, Guernsey, with her husband, William who was a carpenter, and their son William. She enlisted in the Guernsey 2, VAD 1114 Section, and began working as a part-time volunteer on 22 September 1917, at the VAD's Free Canteen. She continued at the canteen until the early part of March 1919.

Miss Kathleen **Robilliard** lived at La Piette, Guernsey, with her four older sisters and her parents, Peter and Isabella Robilliard. Her father was a timber merchant who was doing sufficiently well to employ a servant.

On 14 January 1918, when Kathleen was 20 years of age, she enlisted with the Guernsey VAD 2 Section as a nurse, for which she was paid £20 per annum, and was sent to work at Les Touillets Military Convalescent Hospital on the island, which ironically in the Second World War became the Nazi headquarters during Germany's occupation of the Channel Islands. Kathleen was still working at the hospital on 9 October 1919.

Mr William Nicholas **Robin** was 44 years of age when he began working for the VAD as an orderly on 6 December 1917, a role for which he was initially paid 28s per week. By the time his services were no longer required, 27 November 1918, this sum had risen to 32s per week. His VAD service card was very sparse on information. There was nothing on it to indicate what hospitals he had worked at, other than 'France'. William lived at Carlton, Baissieres, Guernsey.

Dr Ernest Laurie **Robinson** lived at Melrose, St Peter Port, Guernsey, and between June 1916 and 1919 he was the County Director of the VAD on the island.

Miss Kathleen Bainbridge **Robinson** lived at Melrose, St Peter Port, Guernsey and worked for the Guernsey 2 VAD 1114 Section between 16 October 1916 and 27 March 1919. She was employed as a full-time volunteer, section leader and spent all of her wartime service at the Michie Hospital, Queen's Gate, London.

Miss Sybil Edith **Roper** lived at Menheniot Vineries, Guernsey, and on 25 May 1917 she enlisted in the Guernsey 2, VAD 1114 Section as a general service clerk earning £1 a week, but by the time she had finished working for the VAD on 14 February 1919, she had been promoted to the position of head clerk on a wage of £1 14s 6d per week. Her VAD service card only says that she worked at a Military Hospital on Guernsey, without specifying which one.

Mrs E.M. **Scott** lived at Les Reveaux, St Peter Port, Guernsey. She became a volunteer home worker and served between 15 May 1916 and 18 November 1918.

Miss Edna Mary **Scott** was single and just 19 years of age when she enlisted in the Kent 130 VAD Section on 4 June 1917. She was sent to work at the Auxiliary Hospital, Gifford House, Roehampton, as a nurse, where she remained until 1 March 1918.

Mrs Amy Frances **Scrimshaw** lived at The Bungalow, Icart, St Martin, Guernsey, and was 48 years of age when she enlisted in the Sussex 176 VAD. She started out as a nurse, but by the time she had finished serving with the VAD on 12 June 1919, she had reached the rank of commandant and was also a matron. She worked at numerous different locations during her nearly four years of service, but none of them were in Guernsey.

Miss Elizabeth May **Scudamore** lived at Castle Carey, Guernsey and enlisted in the Suffolk 20 VAD Section on 11 June 1915 as a full-time volunteer nurse until 14 January 1919. During this time, she worked at four different locations, none of which were in the Channel Islands.

Miss Alice **Smith** who lived at Yalta Villa, La Couture, Guernsey, served with the Guernsey 2, VAD 1114 Section as a volunteer worker at the VAD Free Canteen in Guernsey, between 1 October 1917 and 19 February 1919.

Miss Elsie **Smith** who lived at Dracaena Lodge, Collings Road, Guernsey, worked as an assistant at the VAD Free Canteen between 19 April 1918 and 19 February 1919, having enlisted in the Guernsey 2, VAD 1114 Section.

Miss Hilda **Tanner** was 22 years of age when she enlisted in the Guernsey 2 VAD, on 20 November 1916 as a full-time nurse, a role for which she was paid £20 per annum. She began by working at the University War Hospital, Southampton between 20 November 1916 and 22 June 1917, where she was paid £20 per annum. She then moved on to the New Zealand Hospital at Walton-on-Thames, where she was stationed between 12 September 1917 and 31 July 1918. She received 10s a week in wages. There were two New Zealand Hospitals in Walton, one at Mount Felix which was the No.2 New Zealand General Hospital and the other was at nearby Oaklands Park, which was used as an extension to the main site. Between October and December 1918, she also worked at the Victoria Cottage Hospital in Guernsey. Miss Tanner was born in Guernsey and lived at Vanvert House.

Mrs Edith Maugena **Tracey** lived at Bon Accord, Mount Row, Guernsey, and on 7 October 1917 she enlisted in the Guernsey 2, VAD 1114 Section, and worked as a part-time volunteer nurse at the Fort George Military Hospital. She continued working there until 23 August 1918.

Miss Ethel Rose **Tracey** lived at 9 Belmont Road, Guernsey, and became a part-time volunteer VAD member, enlisting in the Guernsey 2, VAD 1114 Section. She was sent to work at the Fort George Military Hospital, where she spent the rest of her service which ended on 23 August 1918.

Miss Mabel **Tracey** was Ethel's sister and her VAD service card, shows the same details as her sister's.

Miss Louisa **Warry** who lived at St Jacques, Guernsey enlisted in the Guernsey 2, VAD 1114 Section on 1 June 1918 as a section leader. Her service was spent as a canteen assistant at the VAD's Free Canteen at Guernsey which finished on 19 February 1919.

Miss Rita Cochrane **Webber** was 33 years of age and lived at 3 Newlands Terrace, Near Durand, Guernsey. She enlisted in the Guernsey 2 VAD on 3 November 1916 and went to work at the Alexandria Military Hospital, Cosham as a full-time medical and surgical nurse, where she remained until 20 March 1918. The following day she went to work at the 56th General Hospital at Etaples, France, staying there for a year until 26 March 1919. On 30 April 1919 Rita Webber was informed that she had been awarded two efficiency stripes for her consistently good work.

Miss Vera Maud **Webber** was Rita Webber's younger sister who enlisted in the VAD on 29 July 1916, but unlike her sister she chose the Jersey 2 Section. Her first appointment was at the 2nd Southern General Hospital at Bristol where she served for only a month between 29 July and 25 August 1916. After taking a seven-month break, she then moved on to Southwark Military Hospital where once again, she only remained for a month between 1 March and 3 April 1917. Her next posting took her to Parkhurst Military Hospital on the Isle of Wight, where she stayed for more than two years, between 2 May 1917 and 8 August 1919. She ended her wartime VAD service working at the No.1 Australian General Hospital at Sutton Veny from 11 September, to at least 14 November 1919.

Miss Dorothea **Webster** aged 22 years, was living at The Grange, Guernsey when she enlisted in the Guernsey 2 VAD on 17 October 1917 and was sent to work at the Canadian Military Hospital at Eastbourne. Her VAD service card doesn't mention whether she was part-time or full-time. She finished on 2 June 1919.

Miss Margaret **Wild** lived at Choix, Guernsey and enlisted in the Guernsey 2, VAD 1114 Section on 30 July 1917, and worked for them until 14 February 1919, as a full-time clerk earning 33s 6d per week. Her VAD service card only says that she worked at a military hospital in Guernsey.

Miss Florence **Workman** lived at Les Blanches, St Martin, Guernsey. She enlisted with the Guernsey VAD 1114 Section on 24 August 1918 and was employed as a full-time housemaid at the Les Touillets Military Hospital. She was paid £22 per annum, a role she was still undertaking as of 27 March 1919.

Miss Florence Margaret **Wright** lived at Baidar House, La Couture, Guernsey. She enlisted in the Guernsey VAD 1114 Section on 5 September 1917 and remained working with them until 31 March 1919. During her time with the VAD she split her duties, allowing herself to undertake numerous different roles. Between 25 September 1917 and 19 February 1919 she worked as a volunteer at the VAD Free Canteen in Guernsey, accumulating a total of 564 hours during that period. Between 2 January 1918 and 15 July 1918, whilst still working at the canteen, she also worked as a housemaid at the military hospital at Les Touillets, where she amassed a total of 320 hours. She also had two stints of working at the Victoria Nursing Hospital, between 30 July 1914 and 15 March 1915, and then again between 30 September 1918 and 31 March 1919, amassing a total of 1,058 hours of voluntary work.

Alderney

Miss Dorothy Grant **de Jersey** who was 31 years of age and lived at Butes House, Alderney, enlisted in the London 110 VAD Section on 2 November 1915 and was sent to work at an un-named military hospital in France, where she remained until December 1916.

Sark

Mrs Mary Cameron **Kay** was 28 years of age when she enlisted in the VAD organisation on 8 July 1918 and was then sent to work as a full-time, paid nurse in the 2nd London General Military Hospital in Chelsea, a role she continued in until 30 March 1919.

The VAD service card for Mrs Amy **Pickthall** shows that she was living at Dixcart on the Island of Sark, but before this she was living at Shillingford Bridge House, Shillingford in Devon. She served in the Oxford 8, VAD, which adds to the confusion. What is clear is that she served as a full-time nurse during 1917 and 1918, although the exact dates are not recorded, at the Wingfield Military Hospital, at Headington, Oxford.

As well as all of these fine individuals, there were many more, men and women, from other towns and villages up and down the country who came to the Channel Islands to work in the wartime hospitals.

As there were somewhere in the region of 1,600 individuals from Jersey who had enlisted with a VAD Section during the First World War, it has not been possible to include them all in this book.

CHAPTER SEVEN

War Memorials

Writing about war memorials can be a difficult process because there was no set criteria that necessarily catered for all of those who should rightfully have their names included. Most of these memorials originated in the early 1920s as a way of commemorating the names of the men from a village or town who had been killed in action, died of wounds, illness, accident or disease, whilst in the service of their king and country during the First World War. Some of the memorials also have the names of civilians included on them, who were killed as a result of enemy action on the home front.

The Channel Islands is a good example of just how difficult it can be to have a comprehensive list of those individuals who should rightly have their names recorded and commemorated as a mark of respect by their community.

Some men served with units from the Channel Islands, whilst others chose, or were otherwise selected, to serve with other British or Dominion forces. It also has to be remembered that at the outbreak of the war, there were a large number of Frenchmen living on the islands, particularly Jersey, who left to go and fight for their country.

In 1914 the French Army was made up of two elements, the Metropolitan Army, which consisted of professional officers and soldiers, a conscripted force that was stationed in France. The other was the Colonial Army, which consisted of volunteers from France along with volunteers and conscripts who lived in other countries and islands that formed part of the French Empire.

Conscription, which had been in place in France, long before it had in the United Kingdom, required French men, whether they lived in France or throughout the French Empire, and who were between 20 and 48 years of age, to make themselves available for military service. As such, men became liable for conscription once they had reached 19 years of age.

According to the Commonwealth War Graves Commission website, there were a total of 591 men from the island of Guernsey, who were either killed or died, as a result of their involvement in the First World War. Sadly, there are just too many to mention individually.

Instead, here is a list of those men who were serving with local Guernsey units at the time of their death. According to the CWGC website, there were a total of 359, whilst Wikipedia quotes 327, and ancestry.co.uk, quotes the total as being 328 men who were either killed or died whilst serving with the Royal Guernsey Light Infantry during the war. There were a further 667 men from the regiment who were wounded, along with another 255 who were captured and taken as prisoners of war by the Germans.

The list of those men from the regiment who died during the course of the war is compiled here in alphabetical order.

1. Private (845) Harold George **Allcock**
2. Private (1310) Thomas Simon **Allen**
3. Private (1844) William Thomas **Angling**
4. Second Lieutenant Frank William **Arnold**
5. Private (859) Raymond John **Arthur**
6. Private (528) Charles Owen **Ashelford**
7. Private (1765) James Henry William **Atkins**
8. Private (1766) Arthur Thomas **Ayling**
9. Company Serjeant Major (576) Fritz M.A. **Bachmann**
10. Private (406) Walter James **Bailey**
11. Private (1328) Hedley **Baker**
12. Private (1748) Lewis **Baker**
13. Private (637) Thomas Richard **Batise**
14. Private (1311) William **Benwell**
15. Private (365) Albert Edward **Berryman**
16. Private (1811) James William **Bevan**
17. Lance Corporal (1029) Ezra **Bichard**
18. Private (18) Edwin Walter **Bishop**
19. Private (1355) Henry Ogier **Bisson**
20. Private (1803) Oswald Henry **Bisson**
21. Lieutenant Frank Burrell **Blanford**
22. Private (1356) John **Blampied**
23. Corporal (773) Clifford de Garis **Blondel**
24. Private (373) Ivor Thomas **Boalch**
25. Captain Alfred Frank Cyril **Borrett**
26. Private (2531) Charles John **Bott**
27. Private (2268) Michael **Bowen**
28. Private (20) George A. **Bougourd**
29. Private (1544) William Henry **Bougourd**
30. Private (814) Henry James **Boulain**
31. Lance Corporal (772) Wilfred **Boulain**
32. Private (22) John **Bourgaize**
33. Private (1448) John **Bourgaize**
34. Private (1735) Thomas Henry **Bradley**
35. Private (1444) Wilfred Ernest **Brak**
36. Private (511) Louis Emile **Bray**
37. Lance Corporal (884) Douglas **Brehaut**
38. Private (1504) Freddy **Brehaut**
39. Private (971) Frederick **Brehaut**
40. Private (1728) Clifford James **Brimmage**
41. Private (860) Archibald **Brouard**
42. Corporal (774) John **Brouard**

43. Corporal (382) Peter Cecil **Brouard**
44. Private (1565) Percy James **Brouard**
45. Private (557) Thomas Alfred **Brown**
46. Private (102) George Farling **Burley**
47. Private (1619) George Henry **Burley**
48. Private (1336) Reginald Arthur **Burnell**
49. Private (784) Alfred William Louis **Caiphas**
50. Private (7661) Helier **Carre**
51. Private (507) James Stephen **Carre**
52. Private (133) Thomas **Carre**
53. Private (1419) Walter **Carre**
54. Private (1909) George David **Carter**
55. Private (1492) Peter J. **Cauvain**
56. Private (419) Thomas Charles **Chandler**
57. Private (1409) Arthur James **Chapman**
58. Private (1758) Harold Thomas **Chester**
59. Private (1906) John George **Chubb**
60. Private (194) Albert Edward **Clarke**
61. Lance Corporal (558) George Edwin **Clarke**
62. Private (306) Harold Sidney **Cleal**
63. Private (1339) Horace Charles **Cochrane**
64. Private (1904) Alexander **Collier**
65. Lance Corporal (2533) William **Cook**
66. Private (427) Harry **Coquelin**
67. Private (1869) Cecil **Corbin**
68. Private (89) George Edmund **Cornelius**
69. Private (939) Robert S. **Cornelius**
70. Private (143) Edward **Crocker**
71. Corporal (242) Michael James **Curtin**
72. Lance Corporal (217) Robert John **Curtis**
73. Lieutenant F.A.P. **D'Auvergne**
74. Major Archibald Henry Pingston **Davey**
75. Cadet (2224) C. **David**
76. Lance Corporal (958) William Henry **Davidson**
77. Private (1203) Alfred Thomas **Davis**
78. Private (1548) Francis Henry **De Carteret**
79. Private (1469) Stephen **De Carteret**
80. Private (1549) Andrew **De Jausserand**
81. Private (816) Henry Thomas **De Jersey**
82. Private (474) John **De Jersey**
83. Private (477) Peter **De Jersey**
84. Private (389) Alfred **De La Mare**
85. Private (1515) Bertie **De La Mare**
86. Private (1880) Edmond James **De La Mare**
87. Private (1516) Walter **De La Mare**
88. Private (2535) Percy James **De La Mothe**
89. Lance Corporal (357) Leon George **De La Porte**
90. Private (1479) Frederick Peter **Desperques**

91. Private (786) Albert John **Despointes**
92. Private (193) Francis Charles **Dienys**
93. Private (1060) Ernest **Domaille**
94. Private (887) Arthur James **Dorey**
95. Lance Corporal (1123) James Arthur **Down**
96. Private (377) Louis **Drouet**
97. Private (1798) John William **Duffey**
98. Private (244) John **Duquemin**
99. Private (820) Reginald **Duquemin**
100. Lance Corporal (1525) Stanley Martin **Duquemin**
101. Private (85) Wilfred **Duquemin**
102. Private (1802) Lawrence Wilfred **Duval**
103. Private (1288) Walter **Dyke**
104. Private (1840) Joseph Henry Thomas **Eaton**
105. Private (371) Ernest **Eborall**
106. Private (1684) Henry Adolphus **Eborall**
107. Lance Corporal (2537) Edward **Edmonds**
108. Private (1412) Wilfred George **Edmonds**
109. Private (270) John **Edmonds**
110. Serjeant (2514) Clifford **Elsbury**
111. Private (415) Alexandre Lock **Endraudee**
112. Private (904) Edwin Despres **Falla**
113. Private (1536) Walter James **Falla**
114. Private (1017) William James **Falla**
115. Private (1886) William **Fallaise**
116. Serjeant (152) Edwin James **Ferbrache**
117. Private (1390) Thomas William **Ferbrache**
118. Private (1243) Wilfred George **Ferguson**
119. Private (1925) Frederick Hugh **Fifield**
120. Private (1018) Alfred Edward **Foss**
121. Private (1219) Edward James **Frampton**
122. Private (1927) George William **Frost**
123. Private (2124) Ralph **Fryer**
124. Private (704) Adolphus **Gallienne**
125. Private (1665) Archibald **Gallienne**
126. Private (1585) Harold Thomas **Gallienne**
127. Private (1151) John **Gallienne**
128. Private (1097) Thomas John **Gallienne**
129. Private (1036) Walter Alfred **Gallienne**
130. Private (994) William Herbert **Gardner**
131. Private (1414) Basil Thomas **Gaudion**
132. Lance Corporal (1012) Thomas **Gavey**
133. Private (183) John Stanley **Gibson**
134. Private (906) Edward B. **Girard**
135. Private (1199) Martin Frederick **Godfrey**
136. Private (1361) Harry **Green**
137. Private (1648) Edward James **Guilbert**

138. Private (195) Frederick **Guilbert**
139. Private (864) Charles William **Guille**
140. Private (1225) James **Guille**
141. Private (1884) James **Guille**
142. Private (308) John Thomas **Guille**
143. Private (470) Philip **Guille**
144. Private (1529) Francis William **Guillou**
145. Serjeant (865) W.S. **Guppy**
146. Private (1237) Charles Winskill **Hall**
147. Second Lieutenant Robert Sydney **Hamel**
148. Private (2218) Alexander Leon **Hamon**
149. Private (1218) Nicholas Alfred **Hamon**
150. Private (396) Frances Percival **Harding**
151. Private (439) John **Help**
152. Private (1942) Albert Edward **Hipworth**
153. Private (826) Charles Richard **Hodder**
154. Private (1623) Albert Christopher **Horrell**
155. Serjeant (161) Eric Alfred **Hotton**
156. Private (437) Edwin William **Hough**
157. Corporal (196) Cecil Charles **Hubert**
158. Private (2156) Charles **Ingham**
159. Private (1019) Clifford James **Ingrouille**
160. Private (1790) Ernest **Jagger**
161. Lance Corporal (1307) A. **Jago**
162. Serjeant (586) Harry Leonard **James**
163. Private (138) Stephen John **Jegu**
164. Private (776) Alfred **Jehan**
165. Private (1474) Amos **Jehan**
166. Private (272) John **Jehan**
167. Private (2542) Marshal De Jersey **Jehan**
168. Private (1945) Walter John **Jenkins**
169. Private (929) Harry **Johns**
170. Captain Herbert **Johns**
171. Private (1860) John **Jones**
172. Private (273) Ernest John **Lacey**
173. Private (1387) Harry James **Laine**
174. Private (1038) George Henry **Langlois**
175. Lance Corporal (766) Harry **Langlois**
176. Private (623) Alfred **Lasauce**
177. Lance Corporal (717) Herbert Robert House **Lawrance**
178. Private (978) Thomas Samuel John **Lawrence**
179. Private (1693) Fred John **Laurier**
180. Private (86) Frederick James **Le Cheminant**
181. Private (631) Edwin **Le Cras**
182. Private (930) Alfred Ernest **Le Gallez**
183. Lance Corporal (1382) T.H. **Le Gallez**
184. Lance Corporal (559) Ernest Peter **Le Galloudec**
185. Private (906) E.B. **Girard**
186. Private (768) Jack **Legg**
187. Private (849) Thomas William **Legg**
188. Private (1079) Clarence Henry **Le Huray**
189. Serjeant (2519) Edward Cyril **Le Huray**

190. Private (210) Harold **Le Huray**
191. Private (251) Henry Edward **Le Huray**
192. Private (63) Francis Charles **Le Lacheur**
193. Private (912) Frank Aslett **Le Maitre**
194. Private (1247) Philip Paul **Le Moignan**
195. Private (176) Frederick **Le Moigne**
196. Private (2593) P.G. **Le Moigne**
197. Private (448) James **Le Noury**
198. Private (1251) Douglas John **Le Page**
199. Private (881) John **Le Page**
200. Private (1278) Peter Paul **Le Page**
201. Private (591) Richard **Le Page**
202. Lance Corporal (223) Herbert John **Le Poidevin**
203. Private (213) Wallace Henry **Le Poidevin**
204. Corporal (288) Wilfred Henry **Le Poidevin**
205. Private (2188) Albert John **Le Provost**
206. Private (880) Alfred **Le Provost**
207. Private (167) John **Le Provost**
208. Lance Serjeant (12) Francis Henry **Le Quelenec**
209. Private (1250) George **Le Sauvage**
210. Private (751) Sidney **Le Tissier**
211. Private (1377) Ernest Thomas **Le Tocq**
212. Private (1483) William **Lihon**
213. Private (1106) John Edward **Loveridge**
214. Lance Corporal (1494) George Tardif **Luscombe**
215. Lieutenant James Stewart **Lynch**
216. Serjeant (830) George Robert **Mahy**
217. Private (998) Henry Charles **Mahy**
218. Private (1304) Thomas John **Mahy**
219. Private (832) William **Mahy**
220. Private (1064) Cecil Walter **Mann**
221. Private (2027) Mansell A. **Mansell**
222. Private (709) John Henry **Marquand**
223. Private (1103) Charles Alfred **Marquis**
224. Private (594) John **Marquis**
225. Private (1650) Ernest **Martel**
226. Private (1470) Peter **Martin**
227. Private (1799) Herbert Livingstone **Marsh**
228. Private (1421) Francis Vaughan **Matthews**
229. Second Lieutenant Gerald **Mauger**
230. Private (214) Thomas **Mauger**
231. Private (517) Edward Joseph **Meagher**
232. Private (454) Charles **Mechem**
233. Private (1238) Harry James **Mechem**
234. Private (481) Aristied **Meheut**
235. Private (1217) Thomas L. **Millard**
236. Serjeant (2509) John **Miller**
237. Private (451) Frederick **Mitchell**
238. Corporal (797) Frederick **Mollet**
239. Private (1065) William **Mollett**

240. Private (2237) Victor Lucien George **Monvoisin**
241. Private (91) Charles Herbert **Moon**
242. Private (1747) George Henry **Mudd**
243. Private (471) Bernard **Mudge**
244. Corporal (672) Albert William Edward **Neville**
245. Private (282) Henry Richard **Nicholson**
246. Private (1167) Douglas **Nicolle**
247. Private (2050) John Ernest **Nicolle**
248. Private (1578) Alfred Thomas **Noel**
249. Private (999) Thomas Walter **Norman**
250. Private (1485) Walter John **Norman**
251. Private (982) Harry Sohier **Noyan**
252. Private (1191) Frank **Ogier**
253. Private (1697) John Albert **Ogier**
254. Private (387) Reuben John **Ogier**v
255. Private (853) Wilfred **Ogier**
256. Private (413) William **Ogier**
257. Private (548) William **Ogier**
258. Private (874) H. **Osborne**
259. Private (613) Harry **Ozanne**
260. Corporal (221) John **Ozanne**
261. Corporal (553) Peter John **Ozanne**
262. Private (1397) Thomas John **Ozanne**
263. Lance Corporal (850) Reginald John **Palmer**
264. Private (1596) Charles Nicholas **Pattimore**
265. Private (49) Leon **Perrodou**
266. Private (800) Henry George **Phillips**
267. Private (208) Frank **Pidgeon**
268. Private (104) John **Pidgeon**
269. Private (1874) Samuel Abel **Pike**
270. Lance Corporal (322) Alfred Henry **Pipet**
271. Private (1967) Robert **Plowright**
272. Private (1213) David **Powell**
273. Lance Corporal (1837) Clifford Victor Matthews **Powers**
274. Private (482) Henry Leon **Prevel**
275. Private (70) Alfred J. **Priaulx**
276. Private (411) Cecil **Priaulx**
277. Private (854) William **Priaulx**
278. Lance Corporal (1212) Roger **Price**
279. Lance Serjeant (12) Francis Henry **Quelence**
280. Private (742) Osmond John **Queripel**
281. Private (803) Wilfred John **Queripel**
282. Private (1461) Frederick William **Read**
283. Second Lieutenant Stanley Alfred **Rihoy**
284. Private (1205) Alfred **Robert**
285. Private (1534) Edward Slater **Robert**
286. Private (172) Henry **Robert**
287. Private (294) John Henry **Robert**
288. Private (460) Albert James **Roberts**
289. Private (688) Clifford Percy **Roberts**
290. Private (618) George Francis **Roberts**

291. Corporal (3541) G. **Roberts**
292. Private (1000) Henry William **Roberts**
293. Private (882) Stephen **Roberts**
294. Private (72) William Albert **Roberts**
295. Private (2121) William Le B **Robilliard**
296. Corporal (339) Charles **Robins**
297. Private (1196) Frederick John **Rolls**
298. Lance Corporal (2555) A.E. **Rosamond**
299. Private (687) George Albert **Rose**
300. Private (118) Thomas William **Ruse**
301. Lance Corporal (117) Frederick Charles **Russell**
302. Private 145 Albert John **Salmon**
303. Private (2516) George **Salmon**
304. Private (3788) Walter John **Sands**
305. Private (983) Edmund **Sarre**
306. Private (894) Nicholas **Sarre**
307. Private (679) Peter **Sarre**
308. Private (936) Wilfred **Sarre**
309. Private (2558) Alfred John **Seibre**
310. Private (1146) William John **Sebire**
311. Private (1510) Albert James **Simon**
312. Private (565) John **Slimm**
313. Private (290) Albert **Smith**
314. Private (946) Clifford Swaffield **Smith**
315. Private (2559) Herbert **Solly**
316. Private (1491) Frederick James **Sprackling**
317. Private (566) Charles Frank **Square**
318. Private (678) Roland **Stagg**
319. Second Lieutenant George **Stranger**
320. Captain Harry Easterbrook Knollys **Stranger**
321. Lance Corporal (724) Alfred Edward **Tapp**
322. Private (1292) Edward Leon **Tardivel**
323. Private (1986) Fred **Taylor**
324. Private (1852) Edward Herbert **Theobald**
325. Private (1989) Cyril Roy **Thompson**
326. Private (1441) Thomas William **Thoumine**
327. Lieutenant Harold Augustus Rupert **Tooley**
328. Private (1632) John Henry **Torode**
329. Private (1558) Wilfred Daniel **Torode**
330. Private (1091) William **Torode**
331. Private (1028) James **Tostevin**
332. Private (2513) Sydney **Tostevin**
333. Private (353) Walter **Tostevin**
334. Private (2109) Wilfred **Tostevin**
335. Lance Corporal (897) Henry **Varnham**
336. Private (1994) Alfred **Walker**
337. Private (1426) Reginald **Wallbridge**
338. Private (8) William **Wallbridge**
339. Private (770) Francis James **Walsh**.
340. Private (1159) Joseph George **Warren**
341. Private (1995) Bernard Arthur **Wass**
342. Private (352) Henry **Watson**

343. Private (957) Reginald Sidney **White**

344. Private (723) Thomas **Williams**

345. Lance Corporal (2324) George **Wilson**

346. Private (1817) Sidney Cyril **Winn**

347. Private (1725) Cecil James **Zabiela**.

To the families of loved ones whose names are not included in the above list, my apologies. This is simply an oversight on my part and no slight is intended or should be assumed by any such omission.

The following six men were all officers in the 1st Battalion, Royal Guernsey Light Infantry and were captured by the Germans and held as prisoners of war, before being repatriated after the end of the war.

Lieutenant A.V. **Andrews** of the 1st Battalion, Royal Guernsey Light Infantry, who was attached to The Buffs, was taken a prisoner by the Germans, after having been reported missing on 30 November 1917. He was repatriated on 3 December 1918.

Lieutenant J.C.O. **Beuttler** of the 1st Battalion, Royal Guernsey, Royal Guernsey Light Infantry. He was officially reported as missing in action on 30 November 1917, before it was discovered that he had been captured and taken prisoner by the Germans. He was repatriated on 14 December 1918.

Lieutenant G.K.F. **Borrett** of the 1st Battalion, Royal Guernsey Light Infantry, was captured and taken prisoner by the Germans on 30 November 1917 and was released on 14 December 1918.

Lieutenant F.A. **Hovil** of the 1st Battalion, Royal Guernsey Light Infantry, was captured and taken prisoner by the Germans on 12 April 1918, before being released and repatriated on 18 December 1918.

Lieutenant I.F. **MacAlpine** of the 1st Battalion, Royal Guernsey Light Infantry, was taken prisoner by the Germans on 12 April 1918 and repatriated on 14 January 1919.

Second Lieutenant P. **Stranger** of the 1st Battalion, Royal Guernsey Light Infantry, was taken prisoner by the Germans on 12 April 1918 and being repatriated on 18 December 1918.

Second Lieutenant James Stewart **Lynch**, 1st Battalion, Royal Guernsey Light Infantry, late of the Liverpool Regiment, was wounded and missing, presumed killed 30 November 1917.

Included in the De Ruvigny's UK Roll of Honour, which covers the period of the First World War, was an entry for Company Sergeant Major (576) Friedrich Marcus August **Bachmann**, 1st Battalion, Royal Guernsey Light Infantry. He was born in Guernsey on 1 April 1888, and he worked as an engraver of metals. He joined the Guernsey Militia on 1 January 1914, and enlisted in the 1st Battalion, Royal Guernsey Light Infantry in April 1916, with which he served as part of the British Expeditionary Force in France, first arriving there on 25 September 1917. He was killed in action on 1 December 1917 at the Battle of Cambrai. He left behind a wife, Doris, whom he had married on 16 March 1915 in York, and their daughter, also Doris, who was only ten months old at the time of his death.

His commanding officer, Lieutenant Colonel Hart Synnot, recommended him for the Military Medal for the conspicuous bravery which he displayed at Cambrai.

A search of the Commonwealth War Graves Commission website, with 'Guernsey' in the 'Additional Information' field shows 591 names of men who were killed or died as a result of their involvement in the First World War and who had some connection with Guernsey.

To highlight just how abstract it can be to determine whether someone warrants being included as a casualty of a particular town, take the case of Reginald John Petty **Aldridge**. He was born in Poole, Dorset in 1879. On 5 May 1908, he married Mabel Dulcibelia Noble in London, and some time after their wedding they went to live at, Sausmarez Place, Les Gravees, Guernsey.

Between 1905 and 1908, by which time Reginald was already serving in the military, he was attached to the West African Regiment. Between 1908 to 1910 or 1911, he was the Adjutant for the 2nd Battalion, Royal Guernsey Light Infantry, but the 1911 Census, taken at midnight on 31 March 1911, shows him at that time, as serving with the Royal Sussex Regiment.

With the outbreak of the war, Reginald was deployed to France as part of the British Expeditionary Force, and was serving with C Company, 2nd Battalion, Royal Sussex Regiment. He was killed in action at Troyon on 7 October 1918 and is buried at the Vendresse British Cemetery, in the Aisne region of France.

Alderney

The following list includes the names of those men who are recorded on the Commonwealth War Graves Commission website as being from Alderney, who were either killed in action or died during the First World War.

Private (1310) Thomas Simon **Allen** of the 1st (Service) Battalion, Royal Guernsey Light Infantry, who died on 3 January 1918, and is buried at the Ste Marie Cemetery, at Le Havre. He was 37 years of age and a married man who lived in High Street, Alderney.

Gunner (334350) Arthur James **Angel** (21) served with the 43rd Howitzer Battery, 8th Army Brigade, Canadian Field Artillery. He died of his wounds on 22 October 1918, just twenty days from the signing of the Armistice. He is buried at the St Sever Cemetery Extension at Rouen in the Seine-Maritime region of France. Although he was born in Alderney in 1897, his parents were living in Detroit, Michigan, USA, at the time of Arthur's death.

Midshipman John **Barber** (19) was a member of the Royal Naval Reserve, serving on board HMS *Ebro*, an armed merchant cruiser, when he was killed in action on 6 March 1917 (It would appear this date is actually 21 March 1917), whilst acting as an armed guard on a Norwegian steamship. The ship's log for 6 March 1917 mentions the following in relation to John Barber's death.

> *7.10am: Stopped and boarded Norwegian ship 'Majade', Lat 61 31 N, Long 11 10 W, ordered to Kirkwall with armed guard, Mr Barber RNR in charge. Boarding Officer S H Smiles, Lieutenant RNR.*

A subsequent wireless message was recorded as follows:

> *Ebro, armed merchant cruiser, 21 March 1917, north of British Isles – members of her armed guard were on board Naiade or Najade, when the barque was sunk by U.59 off Fair Isle. All four of the armed guard were lost.*

The deaths of all four men, including John Barber, were confirmed on the Naval Casualty List for 21 March 1917.

Whilst John was born at Holyhead, his parents, Lieutenant Daniel Barber, also of the Royal Navy, and Mrs Barber, lived at 'Woodlands', Alderney. John Barber is commemorated on the Chatham Naval Memorial.

Second Lieutenant Montagu Middleton **Barney** of the 253rd Company, Royal Engineers, was killed in action on 27 April 1916 when he was 26 years of age. He was a married man who lived with his wife at The Rectory, Alderney, but his parents lived in Pacific Grove, California, USA. He was buried at the Vermelles British Cemetery in the Pas de Calais.

Battery Serjeant Major (39365) H. **Bridle** of the 126th Siege Battery, Royal Garrison Artillery, died on 5 July 1917 aged 23. He is buried at the Vlamertinghe New Military Cemetery in Belgium. He was a married man who before his enlistment had lived with his wife, Mabel May Bridle at Hunt Farm, Alderney, although he was born at St Peter Port, Guernsey.

Serjeant (91267) William George **Christie** of the 391st Battery, 172nd Brigade, Royal Field Artillery, was 28 years old when he died on 10 April 1918. He was buried at the Ramleh War Cemetery in Israel. He was a married man, who before enlisting, had lived with his wife, Emily Helena Christie, in Braye Road, Alderney.

Gunner (192274) John **Duplain** of the 208th Siege Battery, Royal Garrison Artillery, died on 9 April 1918, and is buried in the Sailly-sur-la-Lys Churchyard in the Pas de Calais. His parents, Peter and Mary Duplain, lived at Simon Street, Alderney.

Gunner (91352) A. **Hammond** of D Battery, 155th Army Brigade, Royal Field Artillery, died on 26 October 1917 and is buried at the Buffs

Road Cemetery in the West-Vlaanderen region of Belgium. His father, Mr W. Hammond, lived in the High Street, Alderney.

Gunner (192279) Charles Harold **Hammond** of the 226th Siege Battery, Royal Garrison Artillery, was killed in action on 13 August 1918. He is buried at the Gonnehem British Cemetery, which is situated in the Pas de Calais. His parents lived in High Street, Alderney.

Stoker 2nd Class (K/21441) John Batiste Charles **Le Milliere** of the Royal Navy, was killed on 26 November 1914, when the vessel he was serving on, HMS *Bulwark,* blew up and sank whilst at anchor off Sheerness, Kent, due to an internal explosion. He has no known grave, but his name is commemorated on the Portsmouth Naval Memorial, in Hampshire. His parents lived at St Martin, Alderney.

Second Lieutenant Robert William **McLernon** Royal Field Artillery. He died on 8 May 1915, aged 23, and is buried at the Larch Wood (Railway Cutting) Cemetery, in the West-Vlaanderen region of Belgium. His parents, Robert and Harriet McLernon, lived at Oliver Street, Alderney.

Engine Room Artificer 4th Class M/7080 Thomas Philip **Mitchell**, serving aboard HMS *Columbine* died on 24 January 1921. This is an interesting inclusion, for several reasons. Firstly, because deaths attributable to the First World War, usually only covered the period up until to and including 1920. Secondly, because HMS *Columbine*, which had been a training vessel for the Royal Navy Reserve since 1901, was sold for scrap to the Forth Ship Breaking Company, on 4 May 1920. Thirdly, because the next HMS *Columbine*, a Flower-class corvette, wasn't launched until 1940. Thomas's mother, Laura Mitchell, lived at Portland House, Alderney.

Driver (91296) Desire **Pasquier** of the 172nd Brigade, Royal Field Artillery, died on 19 December 1918 when he was 22 years of age, and is buried at the Kantara War Memorial Cemetery, Egypt. His mother, Augustine Mocquet, lived at The Brecque, Alderney.

Gunner (269104) Norman Wilfred **Sharp** of the 3rd Battery, C Reserve Brigade, Royal Field Artillery, died on 21 February 1919 when he was only 18 years of age. His parents, Archibald and Minnie Sharp, lived at Manez, Alderney.

The fact that he is buried at the Aldershot Military Cemetery, suggests that he could have been treated at the nearby Cambridge Military Hospital. This was the first hospital in the British Empire, where plastic surgery was carried out on badly disfigured British and Allied troops. The hospital, which took its first patients on 18 July 1879, remained as a military hospital until 1996. Although now derelict, it still stands and is a listed building.

Gunner 192300 H.J. **Squires** of the 2nd/1st S.A.R.B Royal Garrison Artillery, died of his wounds on 24 March 1919, aged 20, some seventeen months after the end of the war, as a result of gas inhalation on the Western Front. He is buried at the Bear Road Cemetery, Brighton City. His parents, Richard and Elizabeth Squires, lived at Lower High Street, Alderney.

Benjamin Henry **Walden** was a fireman in the Mercantile Marine and a crew member of the SS *Dalegarth* when he died on 18 April 1918, the result of being torpedoed by two German submarines. The *Dalegarth* was a defensively armed British merchant vessel, en route from Tréport, France to Barry Roads, when she was attacked and torpedoed by German submarines *UB-86* and *UB-73*, when she was approximately 12 miles south-west of Hartland Point, North Devon.

Benjamin was one of the five crew men who were killed as a result of the attack. Of the others who were killed, Symon **Houlen**, also a fireman, who lived at Delancy Hill, St Sampson, Guernsey, was born in Alderney.

It is interesting to note that although born in Alderney, his name didn't come up when I searched the Commonwealth War Graves Commission website for men from there who died in the First World War. A good example of the difficulty of compiling accurate lists. It also throws up the question as to which war memorial a man's name would be added to, when he was born in one location but was living elsewhere at the beginning of the First World War. Both men are commemorated on the Tower Hill Memorial to merchant seamen.

Leading Seaman (203769) George Edward **White** was 31 years old and serving on board HMS *Cressy* when he was killed in action on 22 September 1914, when the *Cressy* was sunk by a torpedo fired by the German submarine, *U-9*. In the same action HMS *Aboukir* and HMS *Hogue* were also torpedoed and sunk by *U-9*. In total 62 officers and 1,397 enlisted men were lost. Of these 560 were from the crew of HMS *Cressy*.

George White, who had also served in the 2nd Boer War of 1899–1902, has no known grave, but his name is commemorated on the Chatham Naval Memorial. His parents, Henry and Sarah White, lived on Alderney.

Returning to the names of the 591 men with Guernsey connections. For some reason this does not include the name of a single man who served with the Royal Guernsey Light Infantry. Adding the name of the regiment in the same 'Additional Information' box still came up with nothing. I then removed the regimental name from that box and entered it in to the box marked 'Regiment,' and this time it came up with the names of 359 men who were killed or died during the First World War.

Below are the names recorded on the Commonwealth War Graves website, of the 591 men from Guernsey or with Guernsey connections who were killed or died during the First World War, but who did not serve with the Royal Guernsey Light Infantry.

1.   Private (42212) George **Clemence**, The Queen's (Royal West Surrey Regiment)
2.   Sailor J. **Jameson**, Mercantile Marine
3.   Able Seaman W. **Marks,** Mercantile Marine

4. Able Seaman Peter John **Girard**, Mercantile Marine
5. Private (21915) Thomas **Walton**, Royal Irish Fusiliers
6. Gunner (108314) Stanley Charles **Collins**, Royal Horse Artillery
7. Gunner (89156) Thomas Charles **Waterman**, Royal Field Artillery
8. Driver (89207) Stanley John **Madell**, Royal Field Artillery
9. Corporal (324464) Albert James **Rabey,** Royal Engineers
10. Gunner (89185) Henry Rupert **Rabey**, Royal Field Artillery
11. Private (2266) Frank **Stranger,** Australian Infantry
12. Second Lieutenant Ernest James **Blight**, Northumberland Fusiliers
13. Serjeant (25927) Thomas James **Solway**, Royal Garrison Artillery
14. Private (12373) Albert John **Hicks**, Lancashire Fusiliers
15. Private (2364) Herbert Doyle **Madell**, Australian Infantry
16. Private (21891) F. **Queripel,** Royal Irish Fusiliers
17. Private (3213) Eugene **Flatres**, Royal Irish Regiment
18. Rifleman (373280) Clifford John **Elliot**, London Regiment
19. Private (S/8083) H. **Niles**, Army Ordnance Corps
20. Private (3184) William Charles **Cornelius**, Royal Irish Regiment
21. Private (163227) William Harold **Knight**, Canadian Infantry
22. Corporal (M2/119138) John Thomas **Seedhouse**, Army Service Corps
23. Rifleman (6221) C.H. **Harrison**, Rifle Brigade
24. Private (985) Richard Lewis **Smith,** Royal Warwickshire Regiment
25. Able Seaman (216453) George **Marsh,** Royal Navy
26. Private (22076) Edward **Laine**, Royal Irish Fusiliers
27. Private (9371) Frank **Rowswell**, Dorsetshire Regiment
28. Private (3513823) G.W.J. **Trainel**, Manchester Regiment
29. Private (11176) Charles John **Smith**, The King's (Liverpool Regiment)
30. Lieutenant Kenneth Sven **Blad**, Royal Engineers
31. Private (5457) Peter **Rowland**, Royal Irish Regiment
32. Lance Corporal M. **Ord,** Durham Light Infantry
33. Artificer (176620) Charles Henry **Bean,** Royal Navy
34. Driver (91287) Cecil John **Falla**, Royal Field Artillery
35. Able Seaman Ormond **Stevens,** Mercantile Marine
36. Private (34526) Harold Leon **Green,** Royal Warwickshire Regiment
37. Lance Corporal (9032) J.W.E. **Chant**, Border Regiment
38. Lance Corporal (18356) William **Jehan**, Wiltshire Regiment
39. Able Seaman Ormond **Stevens**, Mercantile Marine
40. Captain Heneage Greville **Finch**, Irish Guards
41. Private (6228) Clifford James **Marquis**, Wiltshire Regiment
42. Fireman Desire Leon Edouard **Richer**, Mercantile Marine
43. Private (S/20041) W.A. **Budden**, Argyll & Sutherland Highlanders
44. Major Wilfred Thomas **De Lacey**, Royal Marine Light Infantry

45. Sapper (324584) John William **Rihoy**, Royal Engineers
46. Able Seaman (SS/1351) Edmund John **Le Page**, Royal Navy
47. Private (5745) John Stewart **McDougall**, Somerset Light Infantry.
48. Sapper (WR/28603) T. **Tostevin**, Royal Engineers
49. Gunner (90948) Charles Thomas **Wallbridge** Royal Field Artillery
50. Private (3/8812) Samuel A. **Toms**, Dorsetshire Regiment
51. Private (3490) Arthur **Williamson**, Royal Irish Rifles
52. Private (408141) J.G.W. **Le Page**, Canadian Infantry
53. Major George W. **Le Page**, Royal Irish Regiment
54. Private (3268) W.J. **Le Page**, Royal Irish Regiment
55. Captain Francis George Ross **Mockler**, Royal Irish Regiment
56. Private (3293) Harold **Mudge**, Royal Irish Regiment
57. Private (3456) James E. **Batiste**, Royal Irish Regiment
58. Rifleman (3598) Osmond **Collenette**, Rifle Brigade
59. Private (21817) Nicholas David **Dorey**, Royal Irish Fusiliers
60. Sapper (WR/28460) Alfred John **Falla**, Royal Engineers
61. Private (21826) E.D. **Falla**, Royal Irish Fusiliers
62. Private (3205) Edgar **Falla**, Royal Irish Regiment
63. Second Lieutenant Patrick George Rawlings **Storer**, Royal Field Artillery
64. Serjeant (14789) John **Chandler**, Royal Garrison Artillery
65. Private (13260) F. **Bynan**, Yorkshire Regiment
66. Gunner (91389) Cecil W.J. **Marquand**, Royal Field Artillery
67. Private (54479) Ralph **Ozard**, West Yorkshire Regiment
68. Private (11670) J. **Ingrouille**, North Staffordshire Regiment
69. Gunner (7248) John **McGarry**, Royal Garrison Artillery
70. Private (A/20514) William Charles **Frampton**, Canadian Infantry
71. Corporal (27611) Charles **Coyde**, Canadian Infantry
72. Rifleman (3702) Ernest Stanley **Card**, London Regiment
73. Private (6/3223) A.A. **Gillman**, Royal Irish Regiment
74. Gunner (192331) Walter Henry **Hill**, Royal Garrison Artillery
75. Lance Corporal (21818) Cecil Frank **De La Rue**, Royal Irish Rifles
76. Lance Corporal (3649) Albert Percy **Mallett**, Australian Army Medical Corps.
77. Serjeant (22054) E.L. **Nicholson**, Royal Irish Fusiliers
78. Company Serjeant Major (5610) Frederick **Workman**, Worcester Regiment
79. Private (73504) Sidney Charles **Brehaut**, Machine Gun Corps
80. Private (775461) Charles William **Crewe**, Canadian Infantry
81. Private (6616) Charles David **Churchill**, Royal Irish Regiment
82. Corporal (89239) William Henry **Herring**, Royal Field Artillery
83. Private (32478) Edgar Harold **Renison**, The Loyal North Lancashire Regiment.

84. Private (5074) William Herbert **Davey**, Australian Infantry
85. Second Lieutenant C. **Robin**, Royal Field Artillery
86. Company Serjeant Major (66518) Charles Henry **Chayter**, Royal Garrison Artillery
87. Lance Corporal (13550) Cecil Reuben Charles **Bichard**, Wiltshire Regiment
88. Leading Boatman (188020) Charles Francis Slade **Moorman**, Royal Navy
89. Rifleman (6667) Wilfred **Case**, London Regiment
90. Private (3455) Frank Rowland **Ayres**, Royal Irish Regiment
91. Private (21841) Theobald A. **Hooper**, Royal Irish Fusiliers
92. Sapper (314285) Owen Redvers **Foster**, Royal Engineers
93. Boy 2nd Class (J/92330) Walter Richard **Sparkes**, Royal Navy
94. Able Seaman James **Harry**, Mercantile Marine
95. Stoker 1st Class (K/20426) Alfred John George **Solley**, Royal Navy
96. Lieutenant Colonel Charles Edward **Lloyd**, Royal Irish Regiment
97. Private (4834) Patrick John **Ryan**, Royal Irish Regiment
98. Corporal (8877) William Edward **Walsh**, Welsh Regiment
99. Private (19249) G. **Mudge**, Wiltshire Regiment
100. Private (21868) W. **Mudge**, Royal Irish Fusiliers
101. Lance Corporal (18466) Albert Victor **Marsh**, Wiltshire Regiment
102. Private (50546) Raymond **Baudains**, North Staffordshire Regiment
103. Leading Seaman (London Z/2118) Frank D. **Wild**, Royal Naval Volunteer Reserve
104. Second Lieutenant Jack Maynard **Harding**, Queen's Own (Royal West Kent Regiment)
105. Gunner (89321) A. **Bichard**, Royal Field Artillery
106. Corporal (112208) Francis Henry **Allen**, Royal Engineers
107. Corporal (10/2617) W.J. **Gill**, New Zealand Infantry
108. Serjeant (62495) Irvin **Hullah**, Royal Field Artillery
109. Private (402356) John Edward **Meagher**, Canadian Infantry
110. Lance Corporal (R/23439) Michael **Meagher**, King's Royal Rifle Corps.
111. Private (200766) William Edward **Meagher**, Royal Warwickshire Regiment
112. Private (21821) A. **Farley**, Royal Irish Fusiliers
113. Private (22081) John **Le Cras**, Royal Irish Fusiliers
114. Private (23258) P.E. **Rabet**, Royal Irish Fusiliers
115. Stoker 2nd Class (K/22014) Thomas **Long**, Royal Navy
116. Able Seaman Thomas John **Willcock**, Mercantile Marine
117. Apprentice Eric Ryder Emly **Monsell**, Mercantile Marine
118. Serjeant (7961) James William **Drinkwater**, Gordon Highlanders.
119. Chief Armourer (165336) Francis Herbert **Reynolds**, Royal Navy

120. Private (9620) George **Cradwell**, East Lancashire Regiment
121. Signalman (236825) Cecil Albert **Taylor**, Royal Navy
122. Private (21790) August Daniel **Barrasin**, Royal Irish Fusiliers
123. Corporal (418034) Harold James **Ward**, Canadian Infantry
124. Private (3175) Hilary John **Carre**, Royal Irish Regiment
125. Private (3204) T. **Ferbrache**, Royal Irish Regiment
126. Private (21782) Frank **Gale**, Royal Irish Fusiliers
127. Private (21835) Leon Maximillien **Guerin**, Royal Irish Fusiliers
128. Sapper (324569) Henry Charles William **Osborne**, Royal Engineers
129. Bombardier (71784) Adolphus **Dodd**, Royal Field Artillery
130. Driver (T4/125415) George **Dodd**, Army Service Corps
131. Second Lieutenant Eric D'Auvergne **Collings**, The Queen's (Royal West Surrey Regiment
132. Lance Corporal (32874) George Langdale **Sackett**, East Yorkshire Regiment
133. Gunner (16098) Joseph Louis **Pagnier**, Royal Field Artillery
134. Sapper (61965) Albert **Renouf**, Royal Engineers
135. Gunner (89167) B. **Strappini**, Royal Field Artillery
136. Private (8515) Harold Thomas **Mauger**, King's Shropshire Light Infantry
137. Leading Seaman (229615) Wilfred Severin **Bullimore**, Royal Navy
138. Private (19588) Cornelius William **Rose**, Wiltshire Regiment
139. Corporal (21895) Harry **Rose**, Royal Irish Fusiliers
140. Private (3284) Nicholas **Martel**, Royal Irish Regiment
141. Gunner (91285) Rodney Frederick **Amos**, Royal Field Artillery
142. Private (935) George Edward **Male**, Manchester Regiment
143. Driver (179153) Bernard Milton **Jory**, Royal Field Artillery
144. Second Lieutenant Edwin Charles **Green**, North Staffordshire Regiment
145. Gunner (91218) S.S. **Green**, Royal Field Artillery
146. Private (27922) M.T. **Lynch**, Canadian Infantry
147. Second Lieutenant Eric D'Auvergne **Collings**, The Queen's (Royal West Surrey Regiment)
148. Lance Corporal (3321) Cecil Clifford **Queripel**, Royal Irish Rifles
149. Gunner (89225) Henri Auguste **Le Morzedec**, Royal Field Artillery
150. Private (23395) Frederick Charles **Phillpot**, Royal Irish Fusiliers
151. Gunner (90947) Clarence E. **Tostevin**, Royal Field Artillery
152. Lance Corporal (15529) Robert Stanley **Cooper**, Dorsetshire Regiment
153. Private (22080) Ernest **Le Sauvage**, Royal Irish Fusiliers
154. Chief Armourer (165336) Francis Herbert **Reynolds**, Royal Navy

155. Sapper (500540) Willie **Hotton**, Canadian Engineers
156. Private (689) Thomas **O'Hanlon**, Manchester Regiment
157. Private (9027) John **Rae**, Scots Guards
158. Rifleman (7490) Samuel Charles **Rae**, King's Royal Rifle Corps
159. Private (32680) Harold Frank **Pearse**, Hampshire Regiment
160. Private (304) John Wilfred **Wallbridge** Princess Patricia's Canadian Light Infantry
161. Private (27766) William Albert **Warren**, Canadian Infantry
162. Private (21841) Theobald A. **Hooper**, Royal Irish Fusiliers
163. Private (10313) Henry Levy **Noel**, Devonshire Regiment
164. Private (775461) Charles William **Crew**, Canadian Infantry
165. Private (31358) Maurice **Pond**, Devonshire Regiment
166. Private (23395) Frederick Charles **Phillpot**, Royal Irish Fusiliers
167. Private (3513518) Ethelbert Edgar **Mahy**, Manchester Regiment
168. Private (2005783) Wilfred Sidney **Hicks**, Canadian Infantry
169. Second Lieutenant George **Metcalfe**, Royal Scots
170. Corporal (89301) Thomas **De La Mare**, Royal Field Artillery
171. Corporal (43693) Walter John **Phillips**, Norfolk Regiment
172. Private (3197) H.C. **Domaille**, Royal Irish Regiment
173. Corporal (242440) Arthur Joseph **Willnow** The King's (Liverpool Regiment)
174. Private (9938) Victor **Matthews**, Border Regiment
175. Sapper (182263) Cecil Frederick **Chappell**, Royal Engineers
176. Petty Officer 2nd Class (155727) Stanley Marwood **Wiles**, Royal Navy
177. Pioneer (324529) T.H. **Kimber**, Royal Engineers
178. Private (43719) John Isaac **Malorey**, Royal Irish Fusiliers
179. Private (43719) Edward Hartley **Rumens**, Royal Army Medical Corps
180. Private (4343) G.E. **Bullock**, Royal Irish Regiment
181. Bombardier (31424) A. **Byde**, Royal Garrison Artillery
182. Private (92890) Lloyd Le Messurier **Agnew**, Tank Corps
183. Private (43658) W.J. **Potter**, Royal Inniskilling Fusiliers
184. Private (7026) Constant **Le Maitre**, Royal Irish Regiment
185. Private (12828) Herbert Charles **Bullock**, Queen's Own (Royal West Kent Regiment)
186. Private (3773) John Francis Marie **Guerin**, Australian Infantry
187. Private (6405) Edward **Coonan**, Royal Irish Regiment
188. Private (33358) Frank Dallas **Johns**, Oxfordshire & Buckinghamshire Light Infantry
189. Lieutenant Ranulf S. **De Saumarez-Brock**, Royal Field Artillery
190. Private (44142) John Willie **Davey**, Northumberland Fusiliers
191. Gunner (192109) Wilfred Cecil **Burton**, Royal Garrison Artillery

192. Stoker 1st Class (SS/109980) James William **Jackson**, Royal Navy
193. Private (2581) Edward Frank Joseph **Barrette**, Australian Infantry
194. Corporal (8890) Andrew **Martin**, Manchester Regiment
195. Private (3273) Wilfred Charles **Le Ruez**, Royal Irish Regiment
196. Serjeant (12482) Leonard **Toogood**, Royal Garrison Artillery
197. Private (3828) John Basil Thomas **Wimms**, Oxfordshire & Buckinghamshire Light Infantry
198. Lieutenant Averell **Lecky**, Leinster Regiment
199. Private (7006) Thomas **O'Meara**, Royal Irish Regiment
200. Private (9299) William James **Ballem**, Oxfordshire & Buckinghamshire Light Infantry
201. Private (22072) John F. **Hamon**, Royal Irish Fusiliers
202. Private (3196) George **Dimmer**, Royal Irish Regiment
203. Lance Corporal (3259) Cyril E.T. **Le Lievre**, Royal Irish Regiment
204. Lance Corporal (3244) Albert Edward **Keyho**, Royal Irish Regiment
205. Private (3169) James **Brehaut**, Royal Irish Regiment
206. Corporal (2317) Richard John **Beazley**, London Regiment
207. Private (20967) Cecil **De Carteret**, Wiltshire Regiment
208. Corporal (G/273) Arthur Nicholas **De Ste Croix** Royal Sussex Regiment
209. Private (21222) William **Henshall**, Grenadier Guards
210. Corporal (13815) Arthur **Attewell**, Royal Fusiliers
211. Able Seaman (236035 Dev) Arthur John **Oblin**, Royal Navy
212. Private (14993) Stephen **Brown**, Royal Dublin Fusiliers
213. Private (42519) Charles William **Brown**, Royal Inniskilling Fusiliers
214. Serjeant (9268) Matthew Joseph **Shiels**, Royal Irish Rifles
215. Lance Corporal (L/9478) Gilbert John **Atwell**, Royal Fusiliers
216. Private (8978) William **Moylan**, Leicestershire Regiment
217. Private (20323) F.J. **Le Poidevin**, Wiltshire Regiment
218. Lance Corporal (23440) F.G. **Hamilton**, Manchester Regiment
219. Trooper (13/887) Stanley **Blackburn**, Auckland Mounted Rifles
220. Captain Leslie Lionel **Sarchet**, Hampshire Regiment
221. Major George **Tostevin**, Australian Machine Gun Corps
222. Private (9331) George Henry **Dyson**, Royal Welsh Fusiliers
223. Private (2465) Ernest James **Brouard** Royal Gloucestershire Hussars
224. Gunner (91982) Cecil **John**, Royal Field Artillery
225. Private (199163) John Harrison **Hill**, Canadian Infantry
226. Private (21907) Arthur Edward **Taylor**, Royal Irish Fusiliers
227. Lieutenant Frederick St John Ford North **Echlin**, Royal Flying Corps

228. Corporal (8/630) Percival Charles **Toms**, Otago Regiment, New Zealand
229. Private (3690) Wilfred **Gould**, Australian Infantry
230. Second Lieutenant Norman Ernest Albert **Hill**, West Yorkshire Regiment
231. Wheeler (89237) Arthur **Jenkins**, Royal Field Artillery
232. Corporal (WR/28617) George Edward **Walden**, Royal Engineers
233. Private (5444) George **Ogier**, Australian Infantry
234. Private (427133) Cyril Julius **Hugo**, Canadian Infantry
235. Private (3363) W.S.J. **Williams**, Royal Irish Regiment
236. Regimental Quartermaster Serjeant (6129) J. **Smith**, Manchester Regiment
237. Private (12312) Bertie Alexander **Pengelley**, Dorsetshire Regiment.
238. Able Seaman (Mersey Z/183) Bertram Washington **Girard**, Royal Naval Volunteer Reserve
239. Officer's Steward 2nd Class (L/3087) Herbert John **Bott**, Royal Navy
240. Officer's Steward 3rd Class (L/7395) George Auguste **Dumond**, Royal Navy
241. Second Mate Leonard Richard John **Topp**, Mercantile Marine
242. Second Mate James Frederick **Masterton**, Mercantile Marine
243. Fireman Henry James **Crabb**, Mercantile Marine
244. Stoker 1st Class (SS/115094) Philip **Poingdester**, Mercantile Marine
245. Stoker 1st Class (K/20787) Thomas Batiste **Caudeville**, Royal Navy
246. Leading Seaman (234437) Ernest **Robilliard**, Royal Navy
247. Artificer 1st Class Henry Rodolphe **Van Cooten**, Royal Navy
248. Private (17019) Albert Edward **Warne**, North Staffordshire Regiment
249. Private (5173999) Walter Henry **Marquis**, Gloucestershire Regiment
250. Private (491123) Henry Charles **Farr**, Canadian Infantry
251. Private (3201) James **Dumaresq**, Royal Irish Fusiliers
252. Private (690316) F.J. **Pulsford**, Canadian Infantry
253. Private (6662) R.C. **Vasseur**, Leicestershire Regiment
254. Lieutenant Cecil John **Fulton**, Royal Irish Fusiliers
255. Leading Seaman (211587) James **Brehaut**, Royal Navy
256. Blacksmith (3434000) Thomas Aubert **Duffey**, Royal Navy
257. Second Lieutenant Richard de Beauvoir **De Lisle**, 97th Deccan Indian Infantry
258. Lieutenant Cecil Francis **Crousaz**, South Staffordshire Regiment
259. Lance Corporal (10714) Frank Walter **Flambard**, Wiltshire Regiment

260. Lieutenant Colonel Laurence Balfour **Cloete**, 41st Indian Dogras
261. Private (203498) William **Lock**, Oxfordshire & Buckinghamshire Light Infantry
262. Lance Corporal (5434) Wilfred J. **Mitchell**, Royal Irish Regiment
263. Private (135738) Thomas William **Hockaday**, Canadian Infantry
264. Private (80086) Philip John **Hamon**, Canadian Infantry
265. Private (690395) Henry Victor **Downton**, Canadian Infantry
266. Gunner (89222) William Thomas **Le Noury** Royal Field Artillery
267. Corporal (6/3325) John Henry Louis **Richer**, Royal Irish Regiment
268. Serjeant (8351) Leon **Le Blond**, Hampshire Regiment
269. Sapper (13132) Henry James **Hayes**, Royal Engineers
270. Private (21990) William Cecil **Davey**, Otago Regiment
271. Serjeant (129109) Thomas William **Foster**, Royal Fusiliers
272. Battery Serjeant Major (39365) H. **Bridle**, Royal Garrison Artillery
273. Corporal (9018) J. **King**, Royal Garrison Artillery
274. Captain Francis William **Durand**, Royal Munster Fusiliers
275. Captain Guy Greville **Napier**, 35th Sikhs (Indian Army)
276. Private (33633) S.W. **Hainsworth**, Royal Berkshire Regiment
277. Private (9186) Edward James **Tobin**, Royal Irish Regiment
278. Chief Officer Henry Beecher **Hansen**, Mercantile Marine
279. Rifleman (302954) Henry **Mahy**, London Regiment
280. Corporal (49994) Arthur **Hurst**, Essex Regiment
281. Lance Corporal (845567) T.W. **Wright**, Canadian Railway Troops
282. Private (800116) Walter Edgar **Le Maitre**, Canadian Infantry
283. Private (2251018) Percy **Maindonald**, Canadian Forestry Corps
284. Chaplain the Rev. Wallace Mackenzie **Le Patourel**, Royal Navy
285. Boy (16765) Michael **Moylan**, Leicestershire Regiment
286. Chief Yeoman of Signals (7619) Thomas Joseph **Moylan**, Royal Australian Navy
287. Second Lieutenant Leofwin Collings Fellowes **Lukis**, Royal Flying Corps
288. Private (13452) G. **Yates**, Royal Flying Corps
289. Lieutenant D.J. **Beaumont**, Gloucestershire Regiment
290. Private (12/3798) Adolphe Stanley **Roger**, Auckland Regiment
291. 2nd Engineer George **McGovern**, Mercantile Marine
292. Lieutenant Commander Reginal Arthur **Lee**, Royal Navy
293. Private (1051256) T.E. **Phillips**, Canadian Infantry
294. Private (9800) J. **Palmer**, Yorkshire Regiment
295. Stoker 1st Class (SS/110150) John Edward **Fisher**, Royal Navy
296. Carpenter George William Henry **Parsons**, Mercantile Marine
297. Able Seaman John Charles **Platt**, Mercantile Marine
298. Chief Officer Thomas Edwin **Pleace**, Mercantile Marine
299. Able Seaman Albert Walter **Welsh**, Mercantile Marine

300. Boatswain Francis **Legg**, Mercantile Marine
301. Able Seaman Edward **Le Page**, Mercantile Marine
302. Trimmer Charles Robert Prioux **Manger**, Mercantile Marine
303. Fireman Symon **Houlen**, Mercantile Marine
304. Gunner (RMA/9544) Edward Eli **Sims**, Royal Marine Artillery
305. Serjeant (20324) John George **Oldbridge**, Royal Fusiliers
306. Second Lieutenant James Hansford **Wheadon**, Royal Garrison Artillery
307. Gunner (2710) Alfred Henry John **LeLievre**, Royal Garrison Artillery
308. Lieutenant Arthur Henry **Sillem**, North Staffordshire Regiment
309. Gunner (89325) Clifford Phillip **Baker**, Royal Field Artillery
310. Lance Corporal (23983) Sidney **Ward** Oxfordshire & Buckinghamshire Light Infantry
311. Serjeant (L/9039) Charles Edward **Knee**, Middlesex Regiment
312. Corporal (18297) Charles James **Smith**, Wiltshire Regiment
313. Private (27801) William George **Pike**, Somerset Light Infantry
314. Private (2184) Charles **Gilbert**, Australian Infantry
315. Private (10310) Edward William **Pippard**, Yorkshire Regiment
316. Private (100971) Douglas Cameron **Shute**, Canadian Infantry
317. Gunner (8) Alfred John **De Garis**, Royal Garrison Artillery
318. Private (29229) John Frederick **Milnes**, East Lancashire Regiment
319. Private (916908) F.W. **Hillier**, Canadian Infantry
320. Private (1536) Frank **Picot**, Australian Infantry
321. Rifleman (A/2773) Arthur James **Williams**, King's Royal Rifle Corps
322. Trooper (209) Samuel Frank **Edmunds**, East African Mounted Rifles
323. Lance Corporal (2355) Roland Walter **Mourant** London Regiment
324. Private (25241) Leonard Ernest **Le Laucheur**, Duke of Wellington's (West Riding Regiment)
325. Captain Edward Graeme **Ozanne**, Royal Fusiliers
326. Captain Reginald John Petty **Aldridge**, Royal Sussex Regiment

It's truly amazing when you take a closer look at that list of Guernsey men, who not only served during the course of the First World War, but served with the numerous fighting units from England, Canada, Scotland, Ireland, Wales, New Zealand, Australia, Indian and different African nations.

According to the list of Citations for the Distinguished Conduct Medal for the period 1914–1920, the following six men from Guernsey, were awarded this medal for acts of bravery during the First World War.

Serjeant (L12730) C. **Baudains** of the 5th Lancers (Royal Irish):

...showed great gallantry at Ghlin on 10th November 1918, when his troop was engaged in clearing up a group of houses occupied by enemy machine guns. He led half his troop round the flank under heavy trench-mortar fire and forced the enemy to withdraw. On the same day, he showed great coolness in moving led horses of the troop out of heavy shell fire.

Ghlin is a village near the Belgian town of Mons.

Serjeant (6/3130) D. **Bisset** of the Royal Irish Regiment was awarded his medal:

For conspicuous gallantry and devotion to duty during an attack. Though badly wounded at the start of the attack he refused to leave his guns, and by his splendid example led them through the heavy barrage to the final objective. His actions weakened the enemy's resistance and greatly assisted in the advance. He showed great fearlessness and determination.

Serjeant (9639) J.W. **Cronin** of the 1st Battalion, King's Own (Royal Lancaster Regiment) was awarded his medal:

For conspicuous gallantry and good leadership in an attack on the Drocourt-Queant line 2nd September 1918. When all the officers of his company had become casualties, he took command, reached the objective, organised the defence and outposts to the flanks, personally super-intending these operations under heavy shell and machine-gun fire. All his dispositions were excellent.

Battalion Serjeant Major (14499) W.M. **Flaherty** of the Royal Garrison Artillery:

On the 3rd April 1918, at Cachy, near Villers-Bretonneux, he did excellent work, and showed great courage and ability in very trying circumstances. The battery was heavily shelled during the day, and several casualties occurred to the personnel. Throughout the day he was always on the spot where assistance was most required, organising bearer parties and taking charge personally of a gun after its No.1 was severely wounded, and organising ammunition fatigues which he personally supervised. He has done consistently good work.

Serjeant (590) W.J. **Le Poidevin** of the Royal Guernsey Light Infantry:

For conspicuous gallantry and devotion to duty. He held a barricade against the enemy when all his men except one were casualties. When wounded in both legs he crawled back and collected a few men to hold the position. He set a magnificent example of courage.

Lance Corporal (723000) A.P.V.G. **March** of the London Regiment:

> *For conspicuous gallantry and devotion to duty. On his own initiative, he*
> *went forward on patrol to get in touch with the enemy. He came across*
> *a party led by an officer, and with the greatest coolness and presence of*
> *mind he feigned death until the party was within 30 yards, when he shot*
> *the officer and dispersed the remainder of the party. He searched the*
> *officer, although under heavy rifle and machine gun fire, and obtained*
> *from him most valuable maps and papers. His courage and devotion*
> *have at all times greatly inspired the men with him.*

Lance Corporal March already held the Military Medal for a previous act of
bravery at the time of receiving the DCM.

The following two men were not from the Channel Islands, but were
serving with the Royal Guernsey Light Infantry at the time of their awards.

Acting Serjeant 569 W.H. **Budden**:

> *For conspicuous gallantry and devotion to duty. He rushed at two of the*
> *enemy whom he saw on the top of the bank and found himself faced by*
> *four enemy machine-guns and their crews, one of which at once opened*
> *fire. He shot the gunner and three others, and, calling on the remainder*
> *to surrender, captured several prisoners. He went back for some bombers*
> *to attack the guns, but on returning found three of the guns with-drawn.*
> *He at once got the remaining gun into action against the retreating*
> *enemy and inflicted many casualties. He showed magnificent courage*
> *and determination.*

Serjeant 586 H.L. **James**:

> *For conspicuous gallantry and devotion to duty. This NCO was in*
> *charge of a Lewis-Gun team when the enemy delivered a heavy attack.*
> *He manoeuvred his team under severe fire to a good position whence he*
> *commanded their approach, and worked his guns with great gallantry*
> *and untiring energy, he inflicted such large casualties that he materially*
> *assisted in holding up the hostile advance.*

Distinguished Conduct Medals awarded to men from Jersey

The list of those men from Jersey who were also awarded the Distinguished
Conduct Medal, shows just three names.

Serjeant (35014) E. **Cauvain**, 130th Battery, Royal Field Artillery, 40th
Brigade:

> *During operations on 4th November 1918, near Ruesnes, he performed*
> *gallant work as No.1 of his gun under very heavy shelling. The cartridge*

dump of his gun was set on fire and it was owing to his efforts that it was put out. He was the only one of his detachment left after the first hour, but with assistance from another attachment, he finished the barrage.

Lance Corporal (29523) A.C. **Marett** of the Duke of Cornwall's Light Infantry:

For conspicuous gallantry and devotion to duty. When in charge of a Lewis gun he brought up his gun successfully under heavy fire to the final objective when half his team were wounded. On two occasions, he went forward under very heavy fire to a position from which he could command a bridge, and thus prevented the enemy from crossing. He took charge of a second gun which was brought up, and worked the two guns with only three men. He showed marked courage and devotion to duty throughout the operations.

Acting Serjeant (9264) A. **Wheatley** of the South Staffordshire Regiment:

For conspicuous gallantry and devotion to duty. He attacked and captured a machine gun before it could be brought in to action. He showed great energy in constructing a strong point on a threatened flank. He kept a Lewis gun in his post, and killed many of the enemy who exposed themselves.

The Commonwealth War Graves Commission website records the names of 817 men, with Jersey connections who were killed or died as a result of their involvement in the First World War. Once again, this does not include those who served with the Royal Guernsey Light Infantry, as the names of those individuals are included on a separate list.

1. Private (9764) Herbert John **Abbott**, Royal Army Medical Corps
2. Corporal (9118) Alfred Lewis Phillips **Abraham**, Hampshire Regiment
3. Private (245477) John William **Abrey**, London Regiment
4. Lieutenant Briggs Kilburn **Adams**, Royal Flying Corps
5. Private (68488) John Gerald **Addison**, Machine Gun Corps (Infantry)
6. Private (17457) John **Aitken**, Cameron Highlanders
7. Able Seaman (J/27242) L.G.A. **Albert**, Royal Navy
8. Petty Officer 1st Class Alfred **Alexander**, Royal Navy
9. Private (2748) Norman **Alexander**, Australian Machine Gun Corps
10. Private (393) J.E. **Alexandre**, Royal Jersey Militia
11. Serjeant (PS/130) John William **Alexandre**, Middlesex Regiment
12. Second Lieutenant Adolphe Barbie **Amy**, Royal Irish Rifles

13. Private (782195) P. **Amy**, Canadian Infantry
14. Shipwright 1st Class (342066) William Monamy **Amy**, Royal Navy
15. Private (31571) Daniel Francis **Amey**, Auckland Regiment
16. Sergeant (59010) Ernest Henry **Amourette**, Canadian Infantry
17. Lance Corporal (673) Leslie **Anderson**, Australian Infantry
18. Private (3498) Cyril Louis **Ansbacher**, Australian Infantry
19. Second Lieutenant Clarence Wasson **Appley**, Royal Air Force
20. Private (10077) Adolphus James **Aubert**, King's Own (Royal Lancaster Regiment)
21. Deck Hand (1362SD) Clifford **Aubin**, Royal Naval Reserve
22. Rifleman (4064) Arthur Herbert **Bailey**, Royal Irish Rifles
23. Private (17985) Stanley George **Bailey**, Machine Gun Corps
24. Private (1375) Archibald John **Baker**, Seaforth Highlanders
25. Captain Harry Charles **Baker**, Canadian Infantry
26. Lieutenant Frank Ephraim **Ball**, Royal Air Force
27. Private (889845) A.C. **Balleine**, Canadian Infantry
28. Captain Cuthbert Francis **Balleine**, Rifle Brigade
29. Rifleman (4066) Edward Clarence **Baillie**, Royal Irish Rifles
30. Private (9711) Louis Alfred **Balston**, East Surrey Regiment
31. Acting Bombardier (36369) A.P. **Bannier,** Royal Garrison Artillery
32. Lance Serjeant (S/6634) F.D. **Barnes** Rifle Brigade
33. Lance Corporal (8209) Walter Edward **Barnes**, Yorkshire Regiment
34. Private (9010) J. **Barry**, South Wales Borderers
35. Private (12564) Richard James **Bartlett** Essex Regiment
36. Able Seaman P. **Battrick**, Mercantile Marine
37. Company Sergeant Major (5824) Ernest Victor **Batty**, King's Own (Royal Lancaster Regiment)
38. Lance Corporal (G/19966) Albert **Baudains**, Middlesex Regiment
39. Private (39324) Fred **Baudains**, Hampshire Regiment
40. Private (998) George **Baudains**, Royal Jersey Militia
41. Lance Corporal (8187) Edmund **Baxter**, Border Regiment
42. Private (10822) Lester **Beardsley-Hanf**, Royal Irish Regiment
43. Private (240619) Edwin Forrest **Beaumont**, Canadian Infantry
44. Private (36964) E. **Bechemin**, Duke of Cornwall's Light Infantry
45. Private (18535) Ernest **Beer**, Royal Fusiliers
46. Private (3030410) Walter Luxton **Bencraft**, Canadian Infantry
47. Private (292448) Edward Bienaime **Bertram**, Canadian Infantry
48. Private (3/20602) G. **Bewhay**, Devonshire Regiment
49. Private (31165) George Henry **Bisson**, Dorsetshire Regiment
50. Lieutenant Philip **Bisson**, Royal Naval Reserve
51. Private (2030176) John **Bilton**, Canadian Infantry
52. Lieutenant R. St John **Blacker-Douglass**, Irish Guards
53. Private (30290) J. **Blampied**, Dorsetshire Regiment

54. Private (11427) John **Blampied**, Middlesex Regiment
55. Air Mechanic 2nd Class (30241) R.S. **Blight**, Royal Flying Corps
56. Private (9257) Jules **Blondel**, Dorsetshire Regiment
57. Private (3030643) R. **Bloor**, Canadian Infantry
58. Sapper (22436) Eugene **Bonnemer**, Royal Engineer
59. Sapper (357797) P.F. **Bonny**, Royal Engineers
60. Private (26214) John **Booley**, Norfolk Regiment
61. Gunner (65173) J.C.A **Boullier**, Royal Field Artillery
62. Private (39358) Thomas Patrick **Bourke**, Hampshire Regiment
63. Serjeant (WR/251147) Robert Stanley **Bourne**, Royal Engineers
64. Lieutenant Harold Bartlett **Bradley**, Royal Air Force
65. Captain Ernest Felix Victor **Briard**, Norfolk Regiment
66. Second Lieutenant John Fortescue **Briard**, 35th Sikhs (Indian)
67. Private (38665) R.H. **Brown**, Hampshire Regiment
68. Second Lieutenant Langford Kyffin **Browne**, Northumberland Fusiliers
69. Private (136584) Charles **Browning**, Machine Gun Corps
70. Gunner (339462) William Palliser **Bruford**, Canadian Field Artillery
71. Private (9433) Alfred Henry **Bryant**, Devonshire Regiment
72. Private (1725) Henry William **Bryant**, Australian Infantry
73. Driver (42982) Peter **Buckle**, Royal Field Artillery
74. Company Serjeant Major (6842) John James **Bull**, Leicestershire Regiment
75. Lance Corporal (L/12452) John Thomas **Bullock**, Middlesex Regiment
76. Lieutenant Frederick Max **Burger**, Canadian Infantry
77. Sapper (WR/251499) Henry Charles **Butterworth**, Royal Engineers
78. Private (35714) C.A. **Cabot**, Wiltshire Regiment
79. Private (70181) George Alfred **Cabot**, Royal Army Medical Corps
80. Private (28649) Peter Marie **Cadin**, Royal Garrison Artillery
81. Private (SE/32913) J. **Cannan**, Army Veterinary Corps
82. Private (241344) W. **Carrington**, Worcestershire Regiment
83. Serjeant (20217) Alfred Denzil **Carter**, Lincolnshire Regiment
84. Private (27197) A.H. **Carter**, Dorsetshire Regiment
85. Corporal (4090) Harold **Carver**, Royal Irish Rifles
86. Lieutenant James Crosbie **Caulfield**, Manchester Regiment
87. Corporal Henry James **Catelinet**, Dorsetshire Regiment.
88. Private (PO/19184) John Alfred **Catelinet**, Royal Marine Light Infantry
89. Serjeant (278353) W.E. **Catelinet**, Royal Engineers
90. First Engineer Henry **Cave**, Mercantile Marine
91. Third Engineer Wallace George **Caws**, Mercantile Marine

92. Gunner (30805) Albert Henry **Challoner**, Royal Garrison Artillery
93. Private (3082308) William **Chapman**, Canadian Infantry
94. Private (S/5789) S.T.R. **Chapple**, Army Ordnance Corps
95. Company Serjeant Major (6783) J. **Charles**, Devonshire Regiment
96. Private (38838) Wilfred Arthur **Ching**, Hampshire Regiment
97. Private (G/11272) George **Chevert**, Middlesex Regiment
98. Able Seaman Walter Francis Henry **Churchill**, Mercantile Marine
99. Second Lieutenant Frederick John Noel **Clarke**, Worcestershire Regiment
100. Private (40561) Waller Helier **Clark**, Hampshire Regiment
101. Lance Corporal (879) Albert Edward **Clayden**, Seaforth Highlanders
102. Serjeant (10365) George James **Clayden**, Seaforth Highlanders
103. Captain Allen Mackenzie **Cleghorn**, Canadian Army Medical Corps
104. Serjeant (405505) C. **Clow**, Canadian Infantry
105. Private (2562375) William John **Coates**, Canadian Infantry
106. Private (1156) Austin Clifford **Collis**, Australian Infantry
107. Private (6480) Clement Bernard **Connell**, Australian Infantry
108. Sergeant (210219) Louis William **Corris**, Canadian Infantry
109. Rifleman (S/17765) Thomas Henry **Cole**, Rifle Brigade
110. Private (567) James **Collins**, Newfoundland Regiment
111. Private (6410) John Francis **Collins**, Devonshire Regiment
112. Gunner (35091) Thomas Michael **Condon**, Royal Garrison Artillery
113. Able Seaman Thomas **Cooney**, Mercantile Marine
114. Steward Sidney Philip **Cooper**, Mercantile Marine
115. Private (31560) Peter Francis **Corniere**, Hampshire Regiment
116. Stoker 1st Class (K/20827) Henry Louis **Cotillard** Royal Navy
117. Gunner (2001064) Douglas Johnstone **Coulter**, Canadian Light Trench Mortar Battery
118. Private (42342) John Henry **Courcoux**, King's Own Yorkshire Light Infantry
119. Serjeant (8120) Robert Charles **Courcoux**, Yorkshire Regiment
120. Sapper (3263) Alfred Henry **Coutanche**, Royal Engineers
121. Leading Seaman (229936) Stanley Vernon **Coutanche**, Royal Navy
122. Private (2917) William Lawton **Coxon**, The King's (Liverpool Regiment)
123. Captain John Wilbur **Crane**, Canadian Infantry
124. Rifleman (9469) Joseph **Crenan**, Royal Irish Rifles
125. Fireman Charles William Victor **Crespin**, Mercantile Marine
126. Second Lieutenant Francis Ricardo **Cristiani**, Royal Air Force
127. Telegraphist (J/46514) C.P. **Crowley**, Royal Navy

128. Ordinary Telegraphist (J/25366) John Michael **Crowley**, Royal Navy
129. Gunner (183549) Herbert Henry **Cudlipp**, Royal Garrison Artillery
130. Private (8203) D. **Cummings**, Devonshire Regiment
131. Captain Stuart Le Geyt **Cutler**, Royal Flying Corps
132. Private (S/13746) A.F. **Dallain,** Gordon Highlanders
133. Private (62120) G. **Dance**, Machine Gun Corps (Infantry)
134. Corporal (7153) W.J. **Daunt**, Royal Irish Regiment
135. Lance Corporal (2751) James Thomas **Davis**, Gloucestershire Regiment
136. Rifleman (R/33164) Thomas Leopold **Davis**, King's Royal Rifle Corps
137. Serjeant Robert Edward **Davidson**, Canadian Infantry
138. Serjeant (491267) William **Dean**, Canadian Infantry
139. Petty Officer 1ˢᵗ Class John Alexander **De Caen**, Royal Navy
140. Private (30291) W.J. **De Carteret**, Dorsetshire Regiment
141. Private (10353) John **Deegan**, Coldstream Guards
142. Corporal (18608) Joshua Laverty **De Gruchy**, Canadian Infantry
143. Private (477) Peter **De Jersey**, Royal Guernsey Light Infantry
144. Rifleman (4099) Arthur **De La Lande**, Royal Irish Rifles
145. Private (3106579) August Arthur **Delien**, Canadian Infantry
146. Private (6228) Clarence John **De La Haye**, London Regiment
147. Private (28770) John **De La Haye**, Dorsetshire Regiment
148. Corporal (9535) Josue Blampied **De La Haye**, Hampshire Regiment
149. Corporal (8366) Henry Alfred **De Ste Croix**, Hampshire Regiment
150. Second Lieutenant Wilfred Hunngerford **De Ste Croix**, Army Service Corps
151. Rifleman (4097) C.J. **De Veulle**, Royal Irish Rifles
152. Serjeant (5528) Michael John **Devitt**, East Surrey Regiment
153. Sub-Lieutenant Eric Oloff **De Wet**, Royal Navy
154. Stoker 1ˢᵗ Class (K/33972) Thomas **Dickson**, Royal Navy
155. Douglas Gerard **Diplock**, Machine Gun Corps
156. Private (14130) S.G. **Dillon**, Royal Irish Fusiliers
157. Second Lieutenant Robert Shedden **Dobbie**, Argyll & Sutherland Highlanders
158. Private (29971) C. **Dorkins**, Hampshire Regiment
159. Gunner (150266) Elias George **Dorey**, Royal Garrison Artillery
160. Serjeant (19502) Harold **Dowbekin**, Cheshire Regiment
161. Sick Birth Attendant (351232) Walter Harold **Dreland**, Royal Navy
162. Officer's Steward 3ʳᵈ Class Emile George **Drieu**, Royal Navy
163. Blacksmith (302121) Otto **Drube**, Royal Navy
164. Seaman (2592A) Camille Alfred **Duchemin**, Royal Naval Reserve
165. Private (4922) Edward **Dudley**, Gloucestershire Regiment

166. Company Quartermaster Serjeant (921) A.C. **Du Feu**, King's Royal Rifle Corps
167. Private (110127) Edward Syvret **Du Feu**, 5th Canadian Mounted Rifles
168. Private (39342) Norman Philip **Du Feu**, Hampshire Regiment
169. Private (9945) Walter Ernest **Du Feu**, King's Own (Royal Lancaster Regiment)
170. Rifleman (R/5776) Charles **Du Heaume**, King's Royal Rifle Corps
171. Captain Herbert Thomas **Du Heaume**, Royal Army Medical Corps
172. Private (6773) Adolphus **Du Jardin**, Devonshire Regiment
173. Captain Julian Silver Strickland **Dunlop**, South Staffordshire Regiment
174. Officer's Steward 3rd Class (L/7395) George Auguste **Dumond**, Royal Navy
175. Private (19241) Henry Charles **Durnford**, Somerset Light Infantry
176. Corporal (42233) Joseph **Dutton**, East Yorkshire Regiment
177. Officer's Steward 2nd Class (L/2703) (PO) Archibald Frank **Duvey**, Royal Navy
178. Private (45629) Ernest **Eckersley**, Lancashire Fusiliers
179. Private (195070) Sidney John **Ecobichon**, Canadian Infantry
180. Rifleman (P/820) James Waters **Ellett**, Rifle Brigade
181. Lance Corporal (4464) Herbert Leslie **Elvin**, Australian Infantry
182. Serjeant (129398) Gordon Stewart **Ereaut**, Canadian Infantry
183. Captain Harold John **Ereaut**, East African Medical Service
184. Rifleman (553037) Herbert Parker **Ereaut**, London Regiment
185. Corporal (163320) A. **Erskine**, Canadian Infantry
186. Chief Petty Officer (PO/159345) Albert Percy **Evans**, Royal Navy
187. Able Seaman (167339) James **Evans**, Royal Navy
188. Serjeant (5234) Walter **Fairs**, East Surrey Regiment
189. Private (38801) John Cantell **Falle**, Hampshire Regiment
190. Captain Robert Sylvester John **Faulknor**, The Loyal North Lancaster Regiment
191. Private (3541) A. **Ferguson**, Highland Light Infantry
192. Corporal (8279) Joseph Thomas **Finch**, East Surrey Regiment
193. Private (1217) Henry Charles **Finnett**, London Regiment
194. Private (14285) Percy Edwin **Fisher**, Gloucestershire Regiment
195. Captain Wilfrid Allan **Fleming**, Royal Flying Corps
196. Private (63359) Arthur Lambert **Fletcher**, Canadian Infantry
197. Private (203967) Arthur **Fone**, London Regiment
198. Ordinary Seaman (J/45410) Maurice Walter **Foney**, Royal Navy
199. Gunner (31059) P.E.F. **Foney**, Royal Field Artillery
200. Gunner (83656) Charles Albert **Forbes**, Royal Field Artillery
201. Private (101252) Edward **Forgerson**, Canadian Infantry

202. Captain Thomas Brittain **Forwood**, King's Own (Royal Lancaster Regiment)
203. Private (026660) R.W. **Fosse**, Royal Army Ordnance Corps
204. Private (14265) Frederick **Foster**, Northamptonshire Regiment
205. Second Lieutenant Vincent Jerome **Flynn**, Royal Air Force
206. Private (275499) Richard **Freeman**, Essex Regiment
207. Private (9188) Alfred **Gagneur**, Devonshire Regiment
208. Private (5490) Bert **Gale**, Australian Infantry
209. Second Lieutenant Ralph Goulstone **Gale**, Royal Engineers
210. Corporal (18499) Alfred **Gallichan**, Canadian Army Service Corps
211. Private (PO/10475) A.J. **Gallichan**, Royal Marine Light Infantry
212. Private (43349) D.E. **Gallichan**, Dorsetshire Regiment
213. Second Lieutenant Frances Ernest **Gallichan**, North Staffordshire Regiment
214. Deck Hand W. **Gallichan**, Mercantile Marine
215. Private (39317) William John **Gallichan**, Hampshire Regiment
216. Corporal (8915) Ambrose Edward **Game**, East Surrey Regiment
217. Private (31496) Edward **Gant**, Royal Defence Corps
218. Gunner (300919) A.J. **Gavey**, Canadian Field Artillery
219. Private (9804) H. **Geary**, East Surrey Regiment
220. Petty Officer Stoker (312415) Raphael Auguste **Genee**, Royal Navy
221. Second Lieutenant William Ian **Gibb**, London Regiment
222. Sapper (2005817) Redmond Joseph **Gibbons**, Canadian Engineers
223. Private (39311) Hedley Roland **Gibbs**, Hampshire Regiment
224. Private (100211) John Charles **Gibsone**, Canadian Infantry
225. Lieutenant Colonel George Michael James **Giles**, Canadian Army Medical Corps
226. Private (3030541) Frank Russel **Givens**, Canadian Infantry
227. Sapper (189706) George Ambrose **Glendewar**, Royal Engineers
228. Stoker 1ˢᵗ Class (SS/100453) John **Godfree**, Royal Navy
229. Private (L/10333) Richard **Godfree**, Royal Sussex Regiment
230. Private (245557) William Percy **Goodbody**, London Regiment
231. Corporal (19124) Percy Frank **Goss**, Wiltshire Regiment
232. Serjeant (9652) F. **Goude**, Cameronians (Scottish Rifles)
233. Private (68562) Alfred Harry **Gould**, Royal Army Medical Corps
234. Officer's Steward 1ˢᵗ Class Harold Phillip Alexander **Gould**, Royal Navy
235. Stoker 1ˢᵗ Class (K/20381) S.R. **Graham**, Royal Navy
236. Private (431) Charles Philip De Carteret **Grandin**, Australian
237. Infantry
238. Private (035088) H.Y. **Graut**, Royal Army Ordnance Corps
239. Second Lieutenant Arthur Berteau **Grellier**, Lancashire Fusiliers
240. Private (6741) Harold Frederick **Green**, Australian Infantry

241. Private (2497440) Thomas James **Greenhalgh**, Canadian Infantry
242. Gunner (7) Francis **Greppo**, Australian Field Artillery
243. Private (386A) Arthur William **Griffin**, Australian Infantry
244. Private (129143) Lawrence Ambrose **Griffin**, Canadian Infantry
245. Private (TR/8/5383) R.G.P. **Griffin**, Training Reserve
246. Gunner (61344) H.W. **Griffiths**, Royal Garrison Artillery
247. Private (14732) Joseph **Griffiths**, Dorsetshire Regiment
248. Gunner (341205) Charles Thomas **Grigsby**, Canadian Field Artillery
249. Private (6327) William **Grogan**, The King's (Liverpool Regiment)
250. Private (12234) Joseph John **Groizard**, Welsh Regiment
251. Captain Frank Le Maistre **Gruchy**, Leicestershire Regiment
252. Private (G/19559) J.O. **Guildford**, Royal Sussex Regiment
253. Serjeant (G/11426) George P. **Gulley**, Middlesex Regiment
254. Second Lieutenant Walter Roderick Hamilton **Gunn**, London Regiment
255. Corporal (592972) A.E.E. **Guppy**, London Regiment
256. Rifleman (4110) Harold John **Gulliford**. Royal Irish Rifles
257. Corporal (9388) Harry Francis **Gully**, South Staffordshire Regiment
258. Private (40640) Leonard V. **Hack**, Bedfordshire Regiment
259. Serjeant (429) Charles James **Haines**, East Surrey Regiment
260. Ship's Cook Charles Henry **Hacking**, Mercantile Marine Reserve
261. Corporal (40777) James **Hacquoil**, Essex Regiment
262. Sergeant (7312) C.D. **Hale**, Devonshire Regiment
263. Private (1890) S.R. **Hall**, Lancashire Fusiliers
264. Serjeant (9797) J. **Hamlett**, South Staffordshire Regiment
265. Engineer Commander Hilgrove **Hammond**, Royal Navy
266. Second Mate Alfred de Cruchy **Hamon**, Mercantile Marine
267. Private (305326) F.J. **Hamon**, Tank Corps
268. Private (PLY/2564/S) Frank Marie **Hamon**, Royal Marine Light Infantry
269. Driver (19100) Winter Francis **Hamon**, Royal Engineers
270. Rifleman (860819) Albert Henry **Handford**, London Regiment
271. Private (9354) H.F.W. **Hannaford**, Dorsetshire Regiment
272. Private (2745) John Thomas Firm **Harper** 5th (Royal Irish) Lancers.
273. Lance Corporal (45616) Frederick Charles **Harris**, South Wales Borderers
274. Gunner (198878) Percy **Harris**, Royal Field Artillery
275. Lieutenant Wilfred Ernest **Harris**, Royal Field Artillery
276. Able Seaman Francois J. **Harzo**, Mercantile Marine
277. Able Seaman S. **Head**, Mercantile Marine Reserve

278. Armourer's Mate (346926) Edward William **Herbert**, Royal Navy
279. Rifleman (652517) Frederick James **Herbert**, London Regiment
280. Private (11887) John Emile **Herbert**, Yorkshire Regiment
281. Private (907887) Joseph **Hernot**, Canadian Infantry
282. Rifleman (4822) W. **Herve** Royal Irish Rifles
283. Private (3105157) Archibald **Higgens**, Canadian Infantry
284. Private (8226) Frederick **Hill**, Worcestershire Regiment
285. Lieutenant Robert Brinton **Hill**, Royal Air Force
286. Lieutenant Horace James **Hillman**, Royal Engineers
287. Private (5301) George **Hills**, London Regiment
288. Leading Telegraphist (J/8529) Bertie Charles **Hockey**, Royal Navy
289. Lance Corporal (50787) James Robert **Hogg**, East Yorkshire Regiment
290. Private (14086) Cyril Ralph **Holbourn**, Inns of Court Officer Training Corps
291. Armourer's Mate (346926) Edward William Herbert **Holland**, Royal Navy
292. Corporal (8011) Charles **Hollister**, East Surrey Regiment
293. Private (261720) William **Holroyd**, Royal Canadian Regiment
294. Private (43956) William Arthur **Honeycombe**, Hampshire Regiment
295. Lance Corporal (11052) Charles **Hope**, South African Infantry
296. Gunner (89053) Frederick **Hopkins**, Royal Field Artillery
297. Lance Corporal (47024) James Adolphus **Horman**, Royal Fusiliers
298. Private (125385) Alfred Edward **Hotton**, Machine Gun Corps (Infantry)
299. Private (41005) John William **Hotton**, Somerset Light Infantry
300. Private (241706) Edgar Thomas **Howard**, Somerset Light Infantry
301. Company Serjeant Major (9120) Alfred Arthur **Howe**, King's Own (Royal Lancaster Regiment)
302. Lance Corporal (43900) Thomas **Howe**, King's Own Yorkshire Light Infantry
303. Officer's Steward 3rd Class (L/5513) Arthur Bond **Hubert**, Royal Navy
304. Captain Donald Franklyn **Hubert**, Indian Army Reserve of Officers
305. Private (41589) Alfred F. **Humphreys**, Norfolk Regiment
306. Private (457879) James Morrison McKenzie **Hunter**, Canadian Infantry
307. Gunner (90825) Roy **Hurd**, Canadian Field Artillery
308. Private (189841) C.P. **Hutchings**, Labour Corps
309. Lance Corporal (57402) Samuel Herbert **Hutchings**, Machine Gun Corps (Infantry)
310. Lance Corporal (L/8504) John **Jackson**, East Surrey Regiment

311. Lance Corporal (704112) Norman **Jackson**, Canadian Infantry
312. Private (18721) Frederick Josue **Jarrett**, 19th (Queen Alexandra's Own Royal) Hussars
313. Corporal (476) Frank Charles **Jarvey**, Australian Infantry
314. Serjeant (7218) Albert Edward **Jarvis**, East Surrey Regiment
315. Able Seaman Henry Charles **Jasper**, Mercantile Marine
316. Private (2265405) Edward **Jauvin**, Princess Patricia's Canadian Light Infantry
317. Private (3798) Frederick Charles **Jenkins**, Australian Infantry
318. Sapper (36716) Wilfrid John **Jennings**, Royal Engineers
319. Gunner (150269) C.J. **Jerrard,** Royal Garrison Artillery
320. Gunner (300918) Wallace **Jeune**, Canadian Field Artillery
321. Private (G/6913) Arthur William **Jewell**, Royal Sussex Regiment
322. Gunner (6221) Charles John Louis **Jewell**, Royal Garrison Artillery
323. Private (1054751) Alfred Charles **Johnston**, Canadian Infantry
324. Private (9275) Donald Bruce **Johnstone**, East Surrey Regiment
325. Captain Francis Ormonde Holden **Jollie**, East Surrey Regiment
326. Rifleman (S/9464) Robert **Jones**, Rifle Brigade
327. Rifleman (8050) Bernard **Jordan**, Royal Irish Rifles
328. Petty Officer (160124) Philip John Marett **Jordan**, Royal Navy
329. Private 6536 Harold Wilfred **Jouguet**, Northamptonshire Regiment
330. Stoker 2nd Class K/21979 William Francis **Journeaux**, Royal Navy
331. Second Cook Martin Alexander Walter **Kadrewell**, Mercantile Marine
332. 2nd Corporal (17902) John Retallick **Kark**, Royal Engineers
333. Leading Seaman (217600) Archibald John **Keeping**, Royal Navy
334. Private (L/1411) W. **Keith**, 5th (Royal Irish) Lancers
335. Private (15948) Louis McKenzie **Kellet**, Royal Scots
336. Lance Corporal (868) Peter **Kelly**, Australian Infantry
337. Private (178) Thomas Joseph **Kelly**, Newfoundland Regiment
338. Serjeant (371452) G. **Kennedy**, London Regiment
339. Lance Corporal (19368) John Francis **Kerfant**, Middlesex Regiment
340. Captain Harry **King**, Worcestershire Regiment
341. Private (S/43385) John William **Kingsland**, Seaforth Highlanders
342. Private (G/67242) A.J. **Kirby**, London Regiment
343. Rifleman (6558) Thomas Francis **Kirwan**, Rifle Brigade
344. Gunner (348899) Austin Carlton **Kyle**, Canadian Field Artillery
345. Bombardier (169847) Arthur Raymond **Lainey**, Royal Garrison Artillery
346. Private (5739) John **Laird**, Australian Infantry
347. Bed Steward John Henry **Lampon**, Mercantile Marine
348. Private (225691) C. **Landells**, Fort Gary Horse

349. Captain Horace A. **Langford**, British Columbia Mounted Rifles
350. Private (458149) F.P. **Langlois**, Canadian Infantry
351. Private (474) Philip John **Langlois**, Royal Jersey Militia
352. Private (14379) A.J. **Laurens**, Royal Army Medical Corps
353. Air Mechanic 2nd Class Albert Joshua **Laurens**, Royal Flying Corps
354. Private (595) Samuel John **Laurens**, Royal Fusiliers
355. Private (36318) F. **Lawrence**, King's Own Yorkshire Light Infantry
356. Private (1478) Thomas A. **Lawther**, British Canadian Recruiting Mission
357. Private (8081) Arthur **Le Bas**, London Regiment
358. Private (39338) John Cyril **Le Blancq**, Hampshire Regiment
359. Private (29500) Auguste Louis **Le Boutillier**, Duke of Cornwall's Light Infantry
360. Private (7993) Phillip Louis **Le Boydre**, Australian Infantry
361. Gunner (53635) William John **Le Breton**, Royal Field Artillery
362. Sapper (317143) Harold Lawrence **Le Caudey**, Royal Engineers
363. Private (10339) R.J. **Le Cocq**, Welsh Regiment
364. Rifleman (45067) Adolphus **Le Cornu**, King's Royal Rifle Corps
365. Private (1054442) Philip Francis **Le Cornu**, Canadian Infantry
366. Lance Corporal (5534) Reginald Clifford **Le Cras**, Rifle Brigade
367. Serjeant (MS/079765) B.E. **Le Dain**, Royal Army Service Corps
368. Private (G/20767) Arthur M. **Le Feuvre**, Middlesex Regiment
369. Second Mate Edward Thomas **Le Feuvre**, Mercantile Marine
370. Private (31916) George Philip **Le Feuvre**, Wiltshire Regiment
371. Private (238037) John C. **Le Feuvre**, Gloucestershire Regiment
372. Lieutenant Walter Tom **Le Feuvre**, Royal Engineers
373. Lance Corporal (4158) William Frederick **Le Feuvre**, Royal Irish Rifles
374. Gunner (150271) James Edward **Le Francois**, Royal Garrison Artillery
375. Lieutenant Reginald Walter **Le Gallais**, Royal Flying Corps
376. Company Quartermaster Sergeant (23010) John **Le Huguet**, Welsh Regiment
377. Rifleman (R/14331) J.S. **Le Huquet**, King's Royal Rifle Corps
378. Able Seaman W. **Le Huquet**, Mercantile Marine
379. Able Seaman (R/1569) John Auguste **Le Lievre**, Royal Naval Volunteer Reserve
380. Driver (20922) W.G. **Le Lion**, Royal Engineers
381. Lance Corporal (29522) Henry William **Le Masurier**, Duke of Cornwall's Light Infantry
382. Private (9249) J.G.W. **Le Masurier**, Dorsetshire Regiment
383. Private (108134) Philip Edward **Mauger**, Machine Gun Corps (Infantry)

384. Corporal (8856) Walter Charles **Le Mercier**, Royal Engineers
385. Private (84030) J.L. **Le Miere**, Royal Fusiliers
386. Gunner (182521) De Lecq John Richard **Le Montais**, Royal Garrison Artillery
387. Serjeant (9521) Edward John **Murphy**, Royal Munster Fusiliers
388. Private (9077) William Herbert **Lennard**, Dorsetshire Regiment
389. Lance Corporal 10133 Basil **Lelliott**, King's Own (Royal Lancaster Regiment
390. Gunner (162627) G.R. **Le Quesne**, Royal Garrison Artillery
391. Private (38850) Philip Nelson **Le Quesne**, Hampshire Regiment
392. Corporal (S4/060175) C. **Le Sauvage**, Army Service Corps
393. Second Lieutenant Ernest Davies **Le Sauvage**, Royal Flying Corps
394. Private (536643) Hedley **Le Selleur**, Canadian Army Medical Corps
395. Petty Officer (73) P.C. **Le Sueur**, Royal Australian Bridging Train
396. Private (28783) Arthur **Lester**, Worcestershire Regiment
397. Private (G/33333) Henry George **Letto**, Middlesex Regiment
398. Private (10692) Ernest John **Le Vavasseur**, South African Infantry.
399. Private (21305) Leon **Le Venois**, Middlesex Regiment
400. Private (37946) Joseph **Lewis**, Suffolk Regiment
401. Private (2562329) Christian White **Lickley**, Canadian Infantry
402. Private (786)1 R. **Lindsay**, Highland light Infantry
403. Able Seaman (205253) Walter Henry **Lock**, Royal Navy
404. Corporal (4375) E.F. **Louis**, Royal Irish Rifles
405. Serjeant (TR3/12331) Arthur William **Lovesey**, Manchester Regiment
406. Third Engineer Thomas **Loy**, Mercantile Marine
407. Rifleman (12896) F.J. **Lucas**, King's Royal Rifle Corps
408. Private (12401) John **Lucas**, Dorsetshire Regiment
409. Able Seaman (177913) Alfred George **Ludby**, Royal Navy
410. Private (737183) Robert **Lunn**, Canadian Infantry
411. Private (12136) Edward **Lynch**, York and Lancaster Regiment
412. Private (430A) Alfred **Machin**, Australian Infantry
413. Private (478550) Charles John **Machon**, Royal Canadian Regiment
414. Private (30004) Edward David **Machon**, Hampshire Regiment
415. Private (7488) Arthur Jack **Mackay**, London Regiment
416. Private (S/22024) John Alexander Churchill **Maclachlan** Gordon Highlanders
417. Lance Corporal (17/214) William Graham **Macmaster**, Royal Irish Rifles
418. Private (26169) Archibald William **Maguire**, Wiltshire Regiment
419. Rifleman (4174) Arthur Joseph **Male**, Royal Irish Rifles
420. Midshipman Clement Stanley Bertram **Mallet**, Royal Naval Reserve

421. Captain P.F.H. **Mallett**, Gloucestershire Regiment
422. Private (2202) George Ernest **Manger**, East Surrey Regiment
423. Private (29481) Ernest Edmund **Marais**, Dorsetshire Regiment
424. Able Seaman (R/1565) William **Marais**, Royal Naval Volunteer Reserve
425. Labourer Edward Clarence **Marett**, Admiralty Civilian
426. Sapper (184372) G. Le Leivre **Marett**, Royal Engineers
427. Third Mate Lionel **Marett**, Mercantile Marine
428. Private (2728) Archibald Roy **Marlin**, Australian Infantry
429. Gunner (11024) Henry George Stevens **Marquis**, Royal Field Artillery
430. Private (13516) J.G. **Mason**, Yorkshire Regiment
431. Second Lieutenant H.E.A. **Marindin**, King's Shropshire Light Infantry
432. Trimmer (1055/ST) John **Martin**, Royal Naval Reserve
433. Shipwright 2nd Class (342455) Taussaint Marys **Marquer**, Royal Navy
434. Private (306867) Robert **Mathieson**, Tank Corps
435. Rifleman (9493) Reginald Arthur **Mauger**, Royal Irish Rifles
436. Donkeyman Walter George **Mauger**, Mercantile Marine
437. Lieutenant Alexander Logan Nathan **Maxwell-Moffat**, Dorsetshire Regiment
438. Sapper (96745) William **McBurnie**, Royal Engineers
439. Private (17353) J. **McGrath**, Royal Irish Fusiliers
440. Lance Corporal (9488) Neil Sinclair **McGregor**, Argyll and Sutherland Highlanders
441. Lance Corporal (T4/241805) James **McIntosh** Army Service Corps
442. Private (30007) Edward John **McLeod**, Hampshire Regiment
443. Private (3030185) John James **McManus**, Canadian Infantry
444. Lieutenant William Arthur **(McRae)**, 59th Scinde Rifles
445. Captain John Alwarth **Merewether**, Rifle Brigade
446. Private (10497) John Francis **Michel**, Yorkshire Regiment
447. Corporal (9468) Philip **(Michel)**, Devonshire Regiment
448. Private (T4/071875) Frederick George **Millar**, Army Service Corps
449. Private (227293) C.J. **Miller**, Royal Army Service Corps
450. Chief Steward Frederick Clifford **Miller**, Mercantile Marine
451. Private (2245632) Kenneth M. **Miller**, Canadian Forestry Corps
452. Gunner (66537) John Francis **Minier**, Royal Garrison Artillery
453. Driver (M/339367) George **Moignard**, Army Service Corps
454. Fireman & Trimmer Henry **Montrose**, Mercantile Marine
455. Private (850761) Robert Thomas **Moody**, Canadian Infantry
456. Rifleman (R/5859) Emile Henry **Morel**, King's Royal Rifle Corps

457. Private (445282) Robert **Morris**, Canadian Machine Gun Corps
458. Private (G/35503) Walter **Moss**, Royal Sussex Regiment
459. Private (202915) P. **Moulin**, Wiltshire Regiment
460. Midshipman Lionel Geoffrey Fergusson **Moultrie**, Royal Navy
461. Private (29515) Thomas George **Mourant**, Duke of Cornwall's Light Infantry
462. Lieutenant Charles Stanley **Mossop**, Royal Air Force
463. Leading Seaman (201282) William Philip **Moyse**, Royal Navy
464. Rifleman (591959) Mitchell Joseph **Mulholland**, London Regiment
465. Seaman Edwin **Munson**, Mercantile Marine
466. Private (3033185) David Patrick **Murphy**, Canadian Infantry
467. Second Lieutenant Walter Scott **Murray**, Royal Air Force
468. Third Officer John Godfrey **Muscott**, Mercantile Marine
469. Private (1367) Harold Charles **Mutton**, Royal Engineers
470. Lance Corporal (27548) G. **Myers**, The King's (Liverpool Regiment)
471. Serjeant (1330) Joseph **Newman**, Gloucestershire Regiment
472. Private (238127) Edward James **Nichols**, Middlesex Regiment
473. Private (21183) W.G. **Nicholls**, Hampshire Regiment
474. Lance Corporal (PO/2562(S)) Clarence Durrell **Nicolle**, Royal Marine Light Infantry
475. Lance Serjeant (132235) Reginald Sidney **Nicolle**, Canadian Infantry
476. Acting Bombardier (89193) Wilfred Hilary **Nicolle**, Royal Field Artillery
477. Private (43949) W. **Noel**, Hampshire Regiment
478. Major Anquetil Philip **Norman**, Canadian Infantry
479. Able Seaman (236035) (Dev) Arthur John **Oblin**, Royal Navy
480. Second Lieutenant Roderick Stratford **O'Connor** South Staffordshire Regiment
481. Rifleman (4233) Sidney John **Olivry**, Royal Irish Rifles
482. Private (8198) Michael **O'Mara**, Manchester Regiment
483. Private (7907) John Phillip **Ozard**, Gloucestershire Regiment
484. Private (275800) Henry Charles **Paisay**, Essex Regiment
485. Lieutenant Commander John Edward **Pallister**, Royal Naval Reserve
486. Private (58523) A. **Pallot**, Essex Regiment
487. Private (515335) Ernest Philip **Pallot**, London Regiment
488. Serjeant (18902) John William **Pawson**, The Loyal North Lancashire Regiment
489. Private (20637) John **Peel**, Border Regiment
490. Sergeant (144347) Dominic A. **Pelusio**, Canadian Infantry

491. Private (19939) Albert **Pennac**, Canadian Infantry
492. Corporal (4913) Toussaint Philip **Pennec**, Rifle Brigade
493. Private (TF/293272) Horace Edgar **Penney**, Middlesex Regiment
494. Private (29519) Sidney **Perchard**, Duke of Cornwall's Light Infantry
495. Gunner (77232) C.H. **Pettifer**, Royal Horse Artillery
496. Private (772165) Arthur Edward **Philpott**, Canadian Infantry
497. Rifleman (4184) George Charles **Picot**, Royal Irish Rifles
498. Private (M2/077000) W.F.G. **Pink**, Royal Army Service Corps
499. Serjeant (4234) Arthur John Francis **Pirouet**, Royal Irish Rifles
500. Private (514295) James **Pitman**, London Regiment
501. Private (48531) J.F. **Poignand**, Wiltshire Regiment
502. Stoker 1st Class (SS/115094) Philip **Poingdester**, Royal Navy
503. Bombardier (RMA/8476) Charles William **Poling**, Royal Marine Artillery
504. Private (31193) Herbert Winter **Potier**, Dorsetshire Regiment
505. Lieutenant Brian Baden **Powell**, 69th Punjabis Indian
506. Leading Stoker (209348) Arthur Charles **Pralle**, Royal Navy
507. Gunner (184240) W. **Preston**, Royal Field Artillery
508. Serjeant (37963) H.G. **Priestwood**, Royal Field Artillery
509. Corporal (6288) Alfred **Puttick**, 4th Dragoon Guards (Royal Irish)
510. Private (23747) Henry Ernest **Puttick**, Wiltshire Regiment
511. Corporal (9860) P.E. **Quesnel**, Devonshire Regiment
512. Sister E.B. **Radcliffe**, Queen Alexandra's Imperial Military Nursing Service
513. First Engineer Herbert Leonard **Raffray**, Mercantile Marine
514. Lieutenant James **Ramsey**, Royal Air Force
515. Second Lieutenant Mervyn Gregory **Randall**, North Staffordshire Regiment
516. Worker (20425) Nellie Florence Ruby **Rault**, Queen Mary's Army Auxiliary Corps
517. Serjeant (355546) R. **Read**, Royal Welsh Fusiliers
518. Lieutenant Walter Douglas **Read**, Canadian Infantry
519. Gunner (940704) A.W. **Reed**, Royal Field Artillery
520. Captain Fergus Hamilton **Reid**, Royal Garrison Artillery
521. Lieutenant James **Reid**, Royal Air Force
522. Private (18931) William George **Rendall**, Royal Marine Line Infantry
523. Lieutenant Edward **Renouf**, Canadian Infantry
524. Private (G/36) Frank George **Renouf**, The Buffs (East Kent Regiment)
525. Private (3616) Stanley John **Renouf**, Australian Pioneers
526. Serjeant (4187) Harold Robrough **Reynolds**, Royal Irish Rifles

527. Boy 1st Class (J/30222) John Arthur George **Rice**, Royal Navy
528. Lance Corporal (9232) Alfred Samuel **Richards**, Yorkshire Regiment
529. Private (30012) Harry George **Richards**, Hampshire Regiment
530. Private (29877) A.G. **Richomme**, Dorsetshire Regiment
531. Able Seaman (190277) Arthur Henry **Rickett**, Royal Navy
532. Rifleman (4361) William George **Risbridger**, Royal Irish Rifles
533. Private (3/8615) James Henry **Roach**, Bedfordshire Regiment
534. Private (43969) John **Roache**, Hampshire Regiment
535. Corporal (50423) Charles Thomas **Robert**, Royal Warwickshire Regiment
536. Private (53686) Frederick Charles **Roberts**, York and Lancaster Regiment
537. Captain Charles Harold **Robin**, Royal Jersey Militia
538. Sapper (304311) Albert Edward **Rodda**, Royal Engineers
539. Private (4194) A.L. **Rogers**, Royal Irish Rifles
540. Stoker 1st Class (SS/102970) Herbert Ernest **Rogers**, Royal Navy
541. Private (41392) Clement John **Rondel**, Hampshire Regiment
542. Captain Henry B. **Round**, Canadian Infantry
543. Private (715500) Robert **Routledge**, Royal Canadian Regiment
544. Private (9797) Arthur Thomas **Rumfitt**, Coldstream Guards
545. Second Engineer Arthur Ernest **Rumsey**, Mercantile Marine
546. Ship's Chief Cook (341501) Samuel Edward **Rumsey**, Royal Navy
547. Second Lieutenant Cubitt Noel **Rundle**, South Wales Borderers
548. Lieutenant Colonel Cubitt Sindall **Rundle**, Indian Medical Service
549. Private (100718) Marion Wright **Russ**, Canadian Infantry
550. Private (4877) Walter Roy **Rutherford**, Australian Infantry
551. Rifleman (5535) A.J. **Sadot**, Rifle Brigade
552. Private (148671) James Orde **Sandilands**, Canadian Infantry
553. Private (M/331830) Thomas Henry **Sandrey** Royal Army Service Corps
554. Lance Serjeant (PO/11383) Stanley Rowland **Saunders**, Royal Marine Light Infantry
555. Rifleman (4201) Christopher James Philip **Scoones**, Royal Irish Rifles
556. Lance Corporal (37334) Frederick **Sewell**, South Lancashire Regiment
557. Company Sergeant Major (5811) William **Sharp**, King's Own (Royal Lancaster Regiment)
558. Captain Walter Roy **Sheen**, Australian Infantry
559. Fireman Harry **Shinn**, Mercantile Marine
560. Private (2184) Arthur Selwyn **Shoobert**, Australian Pioneers
561. Second Mate Henry Francis **Simon**, Mercantile Marine

562. Private (22590) H.W. **Single**, Wiltshire Regiment
563. Private (29487) Walter Dale **Single**, Dorsetshire Regiment
564. Petty Officer 1st Class (155565) Alfred **Smith**, Royal Navy
565. Private (19) Arthur Leonard **Smith**, Australian Army Medical Corps
566. Rifleman (372066) (4496) Ernest Duhamel **Smith**, London Regiment
567. Private (630409) G.H. **Smith**, London Regiment
568. Private (841710) Herbert Wallace **Smith**, London Regiment
569. Private (842061) Robert Black **Smith**, Canadian Infantry
570. Sapper (1016) Stanley Lazelle **Smith**, Australian Engineers
571. Private (29470) Thomas Harold **Smith**, Somerset Light Infantry
572. Private (39310) Walter **Smith**, Hampshire Regiment
573. Private (S/28789) Chester Gordon **Snyder**, Seaforth Highlanders
574. Private (408719) Bernard **Sohier**, Canadian Infantry
575. Serjeant (9848) Henry Lyman **Sohier**, Devonshire Regiment
576. Private (225925) Frank **Squires**, Canadian Infantry
577. Lance Bombardier (226233) Everard Chandler **Stent**, Royal Field Artillery
578. Second Lieutenant Richard John **Stevenson**, Hampshire Regiment
579. Lieutenant John Houghton **Stewart**, Royal Inniskillin Fusiliers
580. Air Mechanic 2nd Class (80548) Francis Philip **Syvret**, RAF
581. Trumpeter (5372) C.H. **Tank**, 6th Dragoon Guards (Carabiniers)
582. Driver (T2/017888) A.G. **Taylor**, Royal Army Service Corps
583. Captain Coutart-de-Butts **Taylor**, Royal Irish Rifles
584. Gunner (124118) P.J. **Therin**, Royal Garrison Artillery
585. Private (16822) George William **Thomas**, Dorsetshire Regiment
586. Private (489834) Allan Wates **Thomson**, Princess Patricia's Canadian Light Infantry
587. Lieutenant Leslie Irvine Lumsden **Thornton**, Indian Army Reserve of Officers
588. Ordinary Seaman George Albert Emile **Tirel**, Mercantile Marine
589. Able Seaman (SS/5493) Alfred Peter **Tisson**, Royal Navy
590. Serjeant (10086) Frank **Tisson**, Royal Dublin Fusiliers
591. Cooks Mate 2nd Class (M/11551) Henry Walter **Tite**, Royal Navy
592. Private (57236) Thomas James Sills **Tite**, North Staffordshire Regiment
593. Lieutenant Arthur Woodland **Toms**, Devonshire Regiment
594. Second Lieutenant Kennedy St Clair Hamilton **Toovey**, King's Own (Royal Lancaster Regiment)
595. Private (3130346) Sydney Alfred **Touzel**, Canadian Infantry
596. Private (733928) Roscoe Vaughn **Trask**, Royal Canadian Regiment
597. Shipwright 1st Class (342322) John Victor **Tredant**, Royal Navy
598. Lieutenant Arthur **Tregaskis**, Welsh Regiment

599. Lieutenant Leonard **Tregaskis**, Welsh Regiment
600. Lance Corporal (27025) Peter Donald **Treussard**, South Staffordshire Regiment
601. Waiter Edgar Robert Henry **Troon**, Mercantile Marine
602. Private (83498) Reginald J. **Trustam**, Royal Army Medical Corps
603. Trooper (645) Richard Mallet **Underhill**, Australian Light Horse
604. Private (31509) Archibald **Ussher**, Royal Inniskilling Fusiliers
605. Lance Corporal (182) James **Ussher**, Royal Irish Rifles
606. Able Seaman Stanley **Vantier**, Mercantile Marine
607. Leading Seaman (J/10282) George Touzel **Vardon**, Royal Navy
608. Private (8484) Harold George **Vardon**, Hampshire Regiment
609. Private (2304404) Francois Auguste **Vasselin**, 4th Canadian Mounted Rifles Battalion
610. Private (183385) Peter Abraham **Vibert**, Canadian Infantry
611. Staff Serjeant (S/13056) Winter **Vibert**, Army Service Corps
612. Private (103038) Charles Francis **Viel**, Machine Gun Corps
613. Private (70014) Cyril Clifford Philip **Vigot**, Canadian Infantry
614. Petty Officer/Stoker Alfred John **Vigott**, Royal Navy
615. Private (79465) John **Wakeham**, Canadian Infantry
616. Chief Engine Room Artificer 1st Class (269226) Alfred Edward **Wakley**, Royal Navy
617. Second Mate Harold Eugene Montague **Walden**, Mercantile Marine.
618. Private (6346) Arthur Edward **Wallace**, Royal Fusiliers
619. Private (33162) Reginald Charles **Wallace**, Essex Regiment
620. Private (234934) Martin Tore **Wallberg**, Canadian Infantry
621. Private (10284) Andrew **Wardlow**, Irish Guards
622. Rifleman (371453) Adolphus Herbert **Warren**, London Regiment
623. Corporal (54318) Arthur Ernest **Warren**, Lancashire Fusiliers
624. Bombardier (47503) F.G. **Warren**, Royal Field Artillery
625. Ordinary Seaman (J/26887) Archibald Grant **Watts**, Royal Navy
626. Private (761065) Frederick **Watson**, Canadian Infantry
627. Steward Wallace Helier **Waugh**, Mercantile Marine
628. Private (47200) Thomas Edward **Weiss**, York and Lancaster Regiment
629. Private (3137) Joseph Leonard **Wells**, Australian Pioneers
630. Second Lieutenant (7884) C.F.A. **West**, East Surrey Regiment
631. Rifleman (45096) J. **White**, King's Royal Rifle Corps
632. Private (2075) Philip Harold **Whitley**, East Surrey Regiment
633. Lance Corporal (43879) Alfred Henry **Williams**, Royal Berkshire Regiment
634. Private (15388) David **Williams**, South Wales Borderers
635. Lieutenant Frank Hill **Williams**, Australian Infantry
636. Driver (428328) G.A. **Williams**, Royal Engineers

637. Private (29809) Charles Samuel **Wilson**, Machine Gun Corps
638. Private (436204) H. **Wilson**, Canadian Army Medical Corps
639. Second Lieutenant Newnham L. **Winstanley**, South Staffordshire Regiment
640. Private (2153) Samuel **Withy**, Australian Infantry
641. Corporal (4216) Albert **Woonton**, Royal Irish Rifles
642. Private (15573) William **Woonton**, Dorsetshire Regiment
643. Able Seaman (203886) Harry Thomas **Wright**, Royal Navy

Men of Sark who were killed or died in the First World War

1. Private (1328) Hedley **Baker**, Royal Guernsey Light Infantry
2. Private (21797) Fred **Battle**, Royal Irish Fusiliers
3. Private (7661) Helier **Carre**, Royal Guernsey Light Infantry
4. Private (507) James Stephen **Carre**, Royal Guernsey Light Infantry
5. Private (1895) Thomas **Carre**, Royal Guernsey Light Infantry
6. Private (3187) Henry James **De Carteret**, Royal Irish Regiment
7. Private (1467) Stephen **De Carteret** Royal, Guernsey Light Infantry
8. Fireman Alfred John **Denis**, Mercantile Marine
9. Able Seaman John **Drillot**, Mercantile Marine
10. Driver (91459) Reginald Brett **Falle**, Royal Field Artillery
11. Private (864) Charles William **Guille** Royal Guernsey Light Infantry
12. Private (1884) James **Guille**, Royal Guernsey Light Infantry
13. Private (1225) James **Guille**, Royal Guernsey Light Infantry
14. Private (308) John **Guille**, Royal Guernsey Light Infantry
15. Private (470) Philip James **Guille**, Pioneer Monmouth Regiment
16. Private (1218) Nicholas Alfred **Hamon**, Royal Guernsey Light Infantry
17. Private (1065) William **Mollet**, Royal Guernsey Light Infantry
18. Corporal (PS/2597) Roy Herrick **Toplis**, Middlesex Regiment

There were at least forty-two men from the island of Sark who went to fight in the First World War. Those named above were the ones who sadly never returned. Of those who did return, some had been wounded, whilst others had been captured and taken prisoner by the Germans. Some came back without any physical scars, but every one of them had their own personal memories, which for some were extremely traumatic, whilst for others, they coped, mainly in silence, choosing not to talk publicly about the horrors of what they had seen and the things they had to do, just to stay alive.

CHAPTER EIGHT

Those Who Died After The Armistice

The end of the war didn't see the deaths of young men with Channel Island connections come to an end. After the signing of the Armistice some thirty-eight men from Guernsey, five from Alderney, eighty-seven men from Jersey and one from Sark, lost their lives, either having succumbed to their wounds, illness or disease. Although they may have been mentioned elsewhere in this book, it seemed only right to mentioned them separately here, to highlight that the deaths of young men didn't cease immediately with the end of the war.

The only slightly confusing point is what criteria was used to decide who should be included as a casualty of war. The Armistice was signed on 11 November 1918 and the Treaty of Versailles that ratified it was signed on 28 June 1919, which meant that the war was officially over. However, it would take Germany until 3 October 2010, to finally pay off her financial penalty as agreed by the terms of the Treaty of Versailles.

Lieutenant Kenneth Sven **Blad** aged 20, who had served with the Royal Engineers, attached to the 4th Tank Brigade, Signals Tank Corps, died on Tuesday, 26 November 1918. His parents Valdermar and Annie Blad, lived at Dunley, Guernsey.

Major Wilfred Thomas De Lacey **Clark** served in the Royal Marine Light Infantry. He died on Monday, 24 February 1919, aged 34 years. He was a married man and lived with his wife, Kathleen, at 'Ashburton', Lower Rohasi, Guernsey, and is buried at St John's Churchyard, St Peter Port, Guernsey. His parents, the Reverend Henry and Ada Blanche Clark, also lived on the island.

Private (69700) George **Clemence**, of the Labour Corps, had previously served as a Private (42212) with The Queen's (Royal West Surrey Regiment). He died on Tuesday, 21 September 1920, aged 44, and is buried at Highgate Cemetery in North London. He was a native of Guernsey.

Cadet (2224) Charles **David**, aged 19, who served with the 2nd Battalion, Royal Guernsey Light Infantry, died of influenza on Friday, 6 December 1918, and was subsequently buried at the Foulon Cemetery, at St Peter Port, Guernsey. He lived with his parents, John and Annie Margaret David, at Chaumont, Rohais, Guernsey.

Sapper (324516)John Oliver **Duquemin** of the 245th (Guernsey) Army Troops Company Royal Engineers, died on Tuesday, 19 November 1918 and was buried at Berchem Communal Cemetery in Kluisbergen, in the Oost-Vlaanderen region of Belgium. He was a married man, who before the war had lived with his wife, Lizzie Duquemin, at Grandes Rocques, Catel, Guernsey. John's story is told in Chapter 5.

Sapper (314285) Owen Redvers **Foster** aged 18 served in the 2nd Field Company, Royal Engineers. He died on 5 September 1920 and was buried in the Alexandra (Chatby) Military and War Memorial Cemetery, in Egypt. Prior to enlisting in the Army, he had lived with his parents, William and Mary Foster, and his three siblings, at 'Ivy Dene', New Road, St Sampson, Guernsey.

Private (906) E.B. **Girard** aged 30, of the 1st Battalion, Royal Guernsey Light Infantry, died on Tuesday, 26 November 1918. He is buried at the Niederzwehren Cemetery at Kassel, in the Hessen region of Germany. Before the war he had lived his wife, Mary, at Sandy Hook, St Sampson's, Guernsey.

Private (2218) Alexander Leon **Hamon** of the 1st Battalion Royal Guernsey Light Infantry, died on Saturday, 16 November 1918, just five days after the signing of the Armistice. He was only 19 years old and is buried at the Etaples Military Cemetery, in the Pas de Calais region of France. His parents, Mathurin and Marie Hamon, were inhabitants of Guernsey.

Sapper (500540) Willie **Hotton,** aged 28, was serving in the Headquarters Signal Company, Canadian Engineers, when he died of an unspecified disease on Saturday, 16 November 1918. He was buried at the Terlincthun, British Cemetery, at Wimille, in the Pas de Calais. His parents, John and Amelia Hotton, lived at Camp Du Roi, Vale, Guernsey.

Private (251) Henry Edward **Le Huray,** aged 25, of the 2nd (Reserve) Battalion, Royal Guernsey Light Infantry, died of pneumonia, on 6 December 1918 and is buried at St Sampson Churchyard, Guernsey. He was a married man who lived with his wife, Emily, at Route Militaire, St Sampson's Guernsey.

Gunner (89225) Henri **Le Morzedec,** aged 24, of the 9th Divisional Ammunition Column, Royal Field Artillery, he died on Sunday, 26 June 1921 and was buried at the Vale Parochial Cemetery in Guernsey. Before enlisting in the Army, he lived with his parents Henri and Anna Marie Le Morzedec, who were both French subjects, in St Peter Port, Guernsey. The 1901 Channel Island Census recorded the family surname as, Lemerzodee.

Private (49) Albert John **Le Provost,** aged 19, of D Company, 2nd Battalion, Royal Guernsey Light Infantry, died of meningitis on Thursday, 21 November 1918. He was buried at the Vale Parochial Cemetery in Guernsey. Before enlisting in the Army, he was living with his parents, Thomas and Mary Le Provost, at La Haize, Vale, Guernsey.

Serjeant (9278) Frederick George **Le Provost,** aged 25, of D Company, 1st Battalion, Devonshire Regiment, died of pneumonia on 18 February 1919 and is buried at St Sampson Churchyard, Guernsey. His mother was Mrs Julie Le Quelenec, who lived at Banks, St Sampson,

Private (167) John **Le Provost** of the 2nd (Reserve) Battalion, Royal Guernsey Light Infantry, died on Thursday, 26 February 1920. He was the grandson of Mrs Marguerite Bourgaiz of Rocque Poisson, St Peter in the Wood, Guernsey, and was buried at the parochial cemetery at St Peter in the Wood.

Private (1650) Ernest **Martel,** aged 27, of the Royal Guernsey Light Infantry died on Sunday, 30 March 1919, and was buried in the Vale (Domaille) Church Cemetery, Guernsey. He was a married man who lived at Albert Cottages, Les Pequeries Vale, Guernsey, which was the same area of the island where his parents lived.

Private (49) Leon **Perrodou,** aged 19, was serving in the 1st Battalion, Royal Guernsey Light Infantry, when he died of pneumonia on Saturday, 12 July 1919. He is buried in St Sampson Churchyard, Guernsey. Prior to enlisting he had lived with his parents, Francoise and Jean Perrodou, and his four siblings, at Sandy Hook, L'Islet, Guernsey, although the 1911 Channel Islands Census, shows the family living at 5 Gregory's Cottages, James Street, St Helier, Jersey.

Sapper **Rihoy,** aged 41, of the 245th Army Troops Company, Royal Engineers, died on 19 November 1918. He was a married man who lived at Victoria Road, Guernsey. He is buried at the Berchem Communal Cemetery, Kluisbergen, in the Oost-Vlaanderen region of Belgium. John's story can be found in Chapter 5.

Sapper (324585) George Henry **Robert** of the 245th (Guernsey) Army Troop Company died on 19 November 1918. His story can also be found in Chapter 5.

Sapper (WR/28603) Thomas **Tostevin,** aged 30, of the Royal Engineers, died on Wednesday, 7 January 1920, and was buried at the Vale (Domaille) Church Cemetery, Guernsey. His widow, Blanche, lived at 16 Paris Street, St Peter Port, Guernsey.

Private 3513823 (89255) G.W.J. **Trainel,** aged 20, of the 2nd Battalion, Manchester Regiment died on Saturday, 24 July 1920. His name is commemorated on the Basra Memorial in Iraq. Where his actual grave is situated, and what he died of, is not known. His father lived at 3 Burnt Lane, Guernsey, and was still living there in July 1924 when his son's award of the General Service Medal 'Iraq' was sent to him as his next of kin.

Pioneer (324529) Thomas Henry **Kimber,** aged 33, of the 245th (Guernsey) Army Troops Company, Royal Engineers, died on Wednesday, 20 November 1918. His death was the result of accidental carbon monoxide poisoning brought about by inhaling charcoal fumes. He was buried at the Kortrijk (St Jan) Communal Cemetery, which is situated in the West-Vlaanderen region of Belgium. He was a married man whose wife, Beatrice, was living at 4 Charroterie, St Peter Port, Guernsey after the end of the first World War. The 1911 Census showed them as living at 6 Church Hill, St Peter Port, Guernsey, with their three children, Thomas, Doris and their two-day-old daughter who had not yet been christened. Thomas's occupation at the time was recorded as an auctioneer's assistant. Thomas had enlisted on 7 January 1917 in Guernsey when he was 31 years of age, by which time he and Beatrice had two more children. The full story concerning Thomas's death, is included in Chapter 5.

Private (1066221) Thomas James **Mahy**, aged 38, of the 4th Canadian Mounted Rifles Battalion, died of pneumonia on Wednesday, 21 January 1920. He was subsequently buried at the Owen Sound (Greenwood) Cemetery, in Ontario, Canada. His parents, James and Matilda Mahy, lived at 51 Victoria Road, Guernsey.

Able Seaman (J/30149) John **Cowley,** aged 21, who served on board HMS *Canterbury*, died on Tuesday, 4 May 1920. He was buried at the Haslar Royal Naval Cemetery, in Hampshire. His parents, John and Mary Cowley, lived at Brompton Place, Piette Road, Guernsey, with their four other children, Olive, Grace, Winifred, and Percival.

Yeoman of Signals Frank Goslin Fournea **Moles,** aged 28, died on Monday, 30 May 1921, whilst serving on HMS *Victory*. He was buried at the Haslar Royal Naval Cemetery in Hampshire. His parents, John and Susan Moles, lived in Guernsey.

Private (M2/074332) George A. **Bougourd,** aged 26, was serving in 37th Divison Motor Transport Company, Royal Army Service Corps, when he died on Thursday, 13 February 1919. He was buried at the Charleroi Communal Cemetery, which is situated in the Hainaut region of Belgium. His parents lived at Hermitage Lodge, Croutes, St Peter Port, Guernsey.

Private (3455) Frank Rowland **Ayres** of the 6th Battalion, Royal Irish Regiment, died on 13 May 1919. He was buried at the Foulon Cemetery, St Peter Port, Guernsey. His parents lived at Primrose Cottage, Victoria Avenue, Banques, Guernsey.

Private (3513518) Ethelbert Edgar **Mahy,** aged 24, of the 2nd Battalion, Manchester Regiment, was a holder of the Meritorious Service Medal. He died of meningitis on 10 May 1921. His name is commemorated on the Kirkee 1914–1918 Memorial in India. His parents, Nicholas and Mary Mahy, lived at 20 Vauvert, St Peter Port, Guernsey.

Corporal (WR/28617) George **Walden,** aged 52, of the 321st Quarry Company, Royal Engineers, died on Wednesday, 5 March 1919. He was buried in the St Sampson Churchyard, Guernsey. The family home, where he lived with his wife Fanny, was at 9 Victoria Avenue, Banks, Guernsey.

Walter Henry **Marquis** who served as Private (5173999) John Jack Henry Marquis, in the 1st Battalion, Gloucestershire Regiment, died on 25 April 1921 aged 20 years. He is buried at the Foulon Cemetery at St Peter

Port, Guernsey. His parents, John and Louisa Marquis, lived at St Peter Port, Guernsey.

Lieutenant Colonel Laurence Balfour **Cloete**, holder of the Military Cross, was 43 years of age and serving in the 41st Dogras, Indian Army, when he died on 25 January 1919. His name is commemorated at the Kirkee 1914-1918 Memorial in India. His parents, Lieutenant General Josias Gordon and Marion Cloete, lived at 'Olean', Les Gravees, Guernsey.

Chief Yeoman of Signals (7619) Thomas Joseph **Moylan,** aged 36, was serving on board HMAS *Australia* with the Royal Australian Navy when he died on Sunday, 16 February 1919. He was buried at the Foulon Cemetery at St Peter Port, Guernsey, the island on which he was born.

Sapper Alfred John **Falla,** aged 28, of the 321st Quarry Company, Royal Engineers, died on Sunday, 18 January 1920. He was buried at the Vale Parochial Cemetery, Guernsey. Prior to enlisting in the Army, he lived with his wife, Maybliss Linda Falla, at Monica, Vale Road, Guernsey.

Private (21990) William Cecil **Davey** aged 38, served in the Otago Regiment, New Zealand Expeditionary Force. He was born in Guernsey and had served with his regiment on the Western Front. He died on 4 August 1921 and is buried at the Anderson's Bay Cemetery, Dunedin, New Zealand.

Lieutenant D.J. **Beaumont,** aged 41, of D Company, 11th Battalion, the Gloucestershire Regiment, died of pneumonia on 24 November 1918. He was buried at the Brookwood Cemetery in Surrey. Before receiving his commission, he had lived with his wife, Sibyl Mary Collings Beaumont, at Brock Road, Guernsey.

Private (2251018) Percy **Maindonald,** aged 31, of the 57th Canadian Forestry Corps, died of pneumonia on 20 November 1918. He was buried at the Biganos Communal Cemetery, Gironde, France. His parents, Thomas and Louisa Maindonald, lived in Guernsey, although by then, Percy, a married man was living in Toronto, Canada.

Serjeant (129109) Thomas William **Foster,** aged 31, of the 45th Battalion, Royal Fusiliers, died on Tuesday, 6 July 1920. He was buried at the Grangegorman Military Cemetery in County Dublin, Ireland. Prior to enlisting he lived with his wife, Olive May Foster, at Oberlands Cottages, St Martin, Guernsey.

Private (33633) S.W. **Hainsworth,** aged 24, initially served in the 13th Battalion, Royal Berkshire Regiment, before transferring, still as a private (98002), to the 942nd Artisan Works Company, Labour Corps, where he died on Friday, 3 January 1919. He was buried at the Dunkirk Town Cemetery in France. His parents, Samuel and Edith Hainsworth, lived at 2 Union Street, Guernsey, and his wife, Lily May Hainsworth, lived in Bournemouth. She had the following inscription added to his grave stone: *'Tis God who has taken my dear husband away from trouble, sickness and pain.*

Gunner (RMA/9544) Edward Eli **Sims,** aged 37, was serving in the Royal Marine Artillery on board SS *Konarky* when he died on 1 December 1918, when his ship was in collision with the Cunard liner *Orduna* off Queenstown. Edward was one of three casualties. His name is commemorated on the Portsmouth Naval Memorial, in Hampshire. His parents, Andrew and Caroline Sims, lived at L'Islet, Guernsey, although at the time of his death, Edward was married and living in Farnham, Surrey with his wife, Edith.

A total of sixty-five men from the island of Jersey died after the signing of the Armistice.

Serjeant (278353) Walter Ernest **Catelinet,** aged 26, was serving in the London Electrical Engineers, Royal Engineers when he died in an accident on Friday, 30 May 1919. He was buried at the Almorah Cemetery, St Helier, Jersey. Before enlisting in the Army, he lived with his wife, Gertrude, at 172 Windsor Road St Helier, Jersey.

Private 026660 Reginald W.S. **Fosse,** aged 23, of the 59th Company, Royal Army Ordnance Corps died on Sunday, 2 February 1919. He was buried at the Dunkirk Town Cemetery in the Nord region of France. His father lived at 40 Poonah Road Jersey.

Private 026660 D.E. **Gallichan,** aged 19 and a native of Jersey, was serving in the Dorsetshire Regiment when he died on 2 July 1919. He was buried at the Londonderry City Cemetery.

Private (PO/10475) Alfred J. **Gallichan,** aged 34, of the Royal Marine Light Infantry, was serving on HMS *Agincourt*, when he died of pneumonia on 28 February 1919. He was buried at the Kingston Cemetery in Portsmouth. He was a married man and before the war he had lived with his wife, Clara Labey Gallichan, at Eastcott, La Rocque, Grouville, Jersey, the town in which he was born.

Sapper (304311) Albert Edward **Rodda,** aged 29, of the 575th Works Company, Royal Engineers died on Monday, 6 January 1919. He was buried at the Dunkirk Town Cemetery, in the Nord region of France. Prior to the war he had lived with his wife, Mary Jane Rodda, at 5 Ann Street, St Helier, Jersey.

Private (85) Alexander Bertram **Cain** of the Garrison Battalion, Royal Jersey Militia died on Saturday, 31 May 1919. He was buried at the La Croix Cemetery, Grouville, Jersey. His wife, Hilda Rose Cain, lived at Fort D'Auvergne, Havre-des-Pas, Jersey. He had enlisted on 12 March 1917 and on 6 May 1919, he was medically discharged from the Army as no longer physically fit enough for wartime military service; just twenty-five days later he was dead.

Private (EMT/46512) J.F. **Nicolle** was serving in the Heavy Transport Section, Royal Army Service Corps, when he died on 13 September 1919. He was buried at the Almorah Cemetery at St Helier. He was a married man who lived at 48 Kensington Place, St Helier, Jersey.

Almorah Cemetery, Jersey.

Driver (T2/017888) A.G. **Taylor,** aged 39, of the Royal Army Service Corps, died on Tuesday, 9 September 1919. He is buried at the Almorah Cemetery in St Helier, Jersey. His family home, where he lived with his wife, was at 19 Cannon Street, St Helier, Jersey.

Driver (20922) Walter G. **Le Lion,** aged 29, of the 75th Field Company, Royal Engineers died on 23 November 1918, and was buried at the Mont-à-L'Abbé New Cemetery, St Helier. He was one of thirteen children, and one of his brothers also died during the war. Stoker 1st Class (K22356) Philip Frances **Le Lion,** aged 24, died of pneumonia just five days after Walter, on 28 November 1918, and is buried at the Royal Naval Cemetery, at Haslar, Gosport. Another brother, Leading Stoker (K21945) Frank John **Le Lion,** also served in the Royal Navy for 12 years between 17 February 1914 and 2 September 1926. Their father Eugene, lived at 7 Pomona Road, St Helier, Jersey.

Private (11405) John Francis **Turner,** aged 20, was serving in the Royal Army Medical Corps when he died of meningitis on Monday, 23 June 1919. He was buried at the St Ouen's Churchyard, Jersey. Before enlisting he lived with his parents, Francis and Eugenie Turner, at L'Etacq, St Ouen's Jersey.

Stoker 1st Class (K/20381) Samuel R. **Graham,** aged 23, was serving on HMS *Woolwich* when he died on Sunday, 1 December 1918. He was buried at Trinity Churchyard, Jersey.

His father, Samuel James Graham, lived at 34 Hill Street, St Helier, Jersey. He had served as a private, corporal and serjeant in the 3rd Battalion,

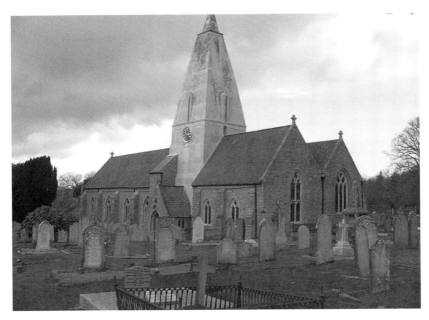

Trinity Churchyard, Jersey.

South Lancashire Regiment, between 23 August 1889 and 16 February 1907. He was promoted to the rank of serjeant on 25 April 1898, but on 1 June 1901, was reduced to the rank of private for a military offence of 'conduct to the prejudice of good order'. Having served for 18 years, he left the Army on 16 February 1907, discharged at the end of his term of engagement with the colours.

Midshipman Lionel Geoffrey Fergusson **Moultrie,** aged 17, was serving on HMS *Valiant*, when he died on Wednesday, 23 April 1919. He was buried at the Brookwood Cemetery in Surrey. Before enlisting he lived with his parents, James and Ethel Moultrie, at Springfield House, St Helier, Jersey.

Gunner (183549) Herbert Henry **Cudlipp,** aged 28, of the 38th Siege Battery, Royal Garrison Artillery, died on Wednesday, 4 June 1919. He is buried at the Macpela Cemetery, Jersey. Herbert was one of ten children born to, John and Louisa Cudlipp, and the middle of three sons, who lived at Mont-à-L'Abbé, Jersey.

Private (M/3331830) Thomas Henry **Sandrey,** aged 23, of the Royal Army Service Corps, was attached to the 5th Corps, Heavy Artillery Siege Park, at the time of his death on 5 December 1918. He was buried at the Caudry British Cemetery, in the Nord region of France. His parents, Joseph and Sarah Sandrey, lived in Jersey.

Captain Philip F.H. **Mallett,** aged 33, of the 1st Battalion, Gloucestershire Regiment, died just one day after the signing of the Armistice, on 12 November 1918. During his wartime service, he was twice awarded the Military Cross and twice mentioned in despatches for his bravery. He is buried at the St Sever Cemetery Extension, Rouen, in the Seine-Maritime region of France. His parents, Philip and Emma Mallett, lived at 12 Windsor Road, St Helier, Jersey. According to the 1911 Census, he was living at 56 Quarrington Road, Horfield, Bristol, with his wife, Elizabeth, and their six-month-old daughter, Doris. Philip was then recorded as being a serjeant in the Gloucestershire Regiment.

Gunner (150271) James Edward **Le Francois,** aged 30, was serving in the 396th Siege Battery, Royal Garrison Artillery, when he died on Tuesday, 26 November 1918. He is buried in the Kirechkoi-Hortakoi Cemetery in Greece. His parents lived at 38 Ann Street, St Helier, Jersey.

Corporal (18499) Alfred **Gallichan,** aged 22, of the 1st Field Butchery Unit, Canadian Army Service, died on Friday, 14 March 1919. He is buried at the St Mary Churchyard, Bramshott, Hampshire. His parents, Henry and Mary Gallichan, had lived in St Helier, Jersey.

Ordinary Seaman (J/91014) Hedley Augustus **Morcel,** aged 19, was serving on board HM Drifter *Catspaw*, when he died on Wednesday, 31 December 1919. The ship's crew of fourteen died when the vessel was lost in rough seas off the Swedish coast. It was part of the Baltic 1st (Light Cruiser) Squadron. He is buried at the Kviberg Cemetery, Sweden, along with the rest of the crew. His parents, Auguste and Emily Morcel, lived at Les Fougeres, St John's, Jersey.

Private (18931) William George **Rendall,** aged 21, of the 6th Battalion, Royal Marine Light Infantry died of his wounds on Wednesday, 27 August 1919. His name is commemorated on the Archangel Memorial, which is situated in the Russian Federation. His father, Percy Rendell, lived at Ocean View, First Tower, St Helier, Jersey.

Sapper (357797) Pierre F. **Bonny,** aged 23, of the 4th Field Survey Company, Royal Engineers, died on Wednesday, 27 November 1918. He was buried at the St Andre Communal Cemetery, which is situated in the Nord Region of France. His father lived near La Foret, St Mary, Jersey.

Private (PO/1918A) John Alfred **Catelinet,** aged 20, of the 3rd Royal Marine Battalion, Royal Marine Light Infantry, died of pneumonia whilst at sea, on Wednesday, 4 December 1918. He is buried at the East Mudros Military Cemetery in Greece. His parents, James and Annie Catelinet, lived at 1 D'Auvergne Cottages, Aquilla Road St Helier, Jersey.

Sapper (142509) Richard John **Fazackerley,** aged 23, of the Lines of Communication Signal Company, Royal Engineers died of influenza on Sunday, 8 December 1918. He is buried in the Upanga Road Cemetery in Dar Es Salaam, Tanzania. His parents, Richard and Clara Fazackerley, lived in St Helier, Jersey.

Joiner 4th Class (M/18574) Fred McLean **Guillard,** aged 20, was serving on board HMS *Penarth*, when he was killed as a result of a mine explosion on Tuesday, 4 February 1919. HMS *Penarth* was engaged in clearing mines from the waters of the North Sea, off the Yorkshire coast, when it struck one of the very mines. This resulted in two officers and thirty-five of the crew being killed; only seven of the crew survived. As the ship was sinking, one of *Penarth's* officers, Lieutenant David Wainwright, went below decks to search for a wounded member of the crew. For his actions he was awarded the prestigious Albert Medal for Lifesaving. Ironically, twenty years later in March 1939, David Wainwright, drowned whilst on a mine-sweeping course at Portland. Fred Guillard has no known grave, but his name is commemorated on the Portsmouth Naval Memorial. His father lived at Anchor Lodge, St Clement, Jersey.

Able Seaman (J/27242) Lancelot George Arthur **Albert,** aged 21, was serving on board HMS *Victory*, a shore-based training facility, when he died on Wednesday, 6 August 1919. He was buried at the Hasler Royal Naval Cemetery in Hampshire. The 1911 Channel Islands Census shows Lancelot as a 12-year-old Boarder at the House for Boys, in Gorey, Jersey. His father, Lancelot George Albert, lived at 30 Canon Street, St Helier, Jersey. He had also lived at 1 Clifton Place, Ann Street, St Helier, Jersey.

Officers Steward 3rd Class (L/7071) Emile George **Drieu, aged** 25, died of pneumonia on Tuesday, 18 February 1919 whilst serving on board, HMS *Minotaur*. He was buried at the Haslar Royal Naval Cemetery, Hampshire. His parents, Alfred and Eugene Drieu, lived at 3 Rosebank, St Saviour Road, St Helier, Jersey.

Sapper (516313) Leonard **Marks,** aged 22, was serving in the Cable Section of the Royal Engineers when he died on 3 January 1919. He was buried at the Batumi British Military Cemetery in Georgia, as well as being commemorated on the Haider Pasha Memorial, in Constantinople, today's Istanbul. His father, Michael Marks, lived at China Quarry, St Lawrence, Jersey.

Private (48531) John Francis **Poignand,** aged 33, of the 3rd Battalion, Wiltshire Regiment, died on Tuesday, 26 November 1918. He was buried in the St Peter and St Paul Churchyard, Aylesford, Kent. Before enlisting in the Army, he was a farmer and lived with his wife, Lydia, in Newmarket, St Peter Port, Guernsey. They had previously lived at Windsor House, St Lawrence, Jersey.

Private (035088) H.Y. **Graut,** aged 28, was stationed at the Calais Depot, Royal Army Ordnance Corps, when he died on Saturday, 8 February 1919. He was buried at the Les Baraques Military Cemetery, Sangatte, which in the Pas de Calais region of France. His widow lived at 10 Chevalier Road, St Helier, Jersey.

Sister Ethel Blundell **Radcliffe** was serving in the Queen's Imperial Military Nursing Service, when she died of broncho-pneumonia after having

St Martin Churchyard, Jersey.

contracted flu, on 10 March 1919. She was buried at Les Baraques Military Cemetery, Sangatte, in the Pas de Calais region of France. It appears that a possible birth date for her is 28 December 1873 in Barrackpore, Bengal, India. Her sister, Mrs Haig, lived at Fair Oakes, Samares, Jersey.

Worker (20425) Nellie Florence Ruby **Rault,** aged 21, served with the Queen Mary's Army Auxiliary Corps, attached to the Royal Engineers at Haynes Park, when she died on Friday, 9 May 1919. She was buried in St Mary Churchyard, in Haynes, Bedfordshire. Her mother, Ann, lived at Gordon House, St Aubins Road, Jersey, had re-married and became Mrs Bewhay. Her husband was John Bewhay with whom she had three children.

Serjeant (M2/079765) Bertie Edward **Le Dain,** aged 38, was serving in the C Siege Park, Royal Army Service Corps, attached to the 3rd Corps Heavy Artillery, when he died of 'accidental injuries' on Friday, 20 December 1918. He was buried at the Halle Communal Cemetery, in the Vlaams-Brabant region of Belgium. He was a married man, who before he enlisted, lived with his wife Ellen, at 15 Clarendon Road, St Helier.

Gunner (184240) W. **Preston,** aged 20, of C Battery, 47th Brigade, Royal Field Artillery, died of septic poisoning on 21 May 1919. He is buried at the Cologne Southern Cemetery, in the Nordrhein-Westfalen region of Germany. His parents, Alfred and Elizabeth Preston, lived at 30 Belmont Road, St Helier, Jersey.

St Brelade Churchyard, Jersey.

Lieutenant Albert **Bendell** MBE, aged 54, was serving in the Royal Navy when he died on Monday, 26 April 1920. He is buried in St Martin Churchyard and Cemetery. Prior to the war he had lived with his wife, Amelia, at Ebenezer House, Trinity, Jersey.

Gunner (31095) Philip E.F. **Foney,** aged 29, of the 5th Reserve Brigade, Royal Field Artillery, died on Sunday, 11 January 1920. He was buried in the St Brelade Churchyard and Cemetery, Jersey. His parents, Philip and Mary Foney, lived at Mont Les Vaux, St Aubin, Jersey. They lost two other sons during the war. Francis John **Foney**, who was only just 18 and serving as an Ordinary Seaman on board HMS *Hampshire*, when the ship hit a mine off the Orkney Islands on 5 June 1916. Francis, along with 735 others, including Lord Kitchener, the Secretary of State for War, were lost with just twelve survivors. Another son, Maurice Walter **Foney**, was also a victim of the war. He 'died of disease' on 15 August 1917, whilst serving as an Ordinary Seaman on HMS *Victory*, and was buried at the Royal Naval Cemetery at Haslar, Gosport, Hampshire.

Lieutenant Brian Baden **Powell, aged** 20 was serving in the 1st Battalion, 69th Punjabis, Indian Army, when he died of pneumonia on 11 January 1920. His name is commemorated on the Delhi Memorial in India. His parents, William and Agnes Powell, lived at Villa Nuova, Beaumont, Jersey.

St Ouen's Church, Jersey.

Private (19939) Albert **Pennac,** aged 28, of the 10th Battalion, Canadian Infantry, died of influenza on 20 October 1919. He is buried at the Notre Dame Des Neiges Cemetery in Montreal, Canada. His parents, Jean and Louise Pennac lived in Jersey

Officer's Steward 1st Class (L/6443) Harold Phillip Alexander **Gould,** aged 23, died of phthisis on 23 February 1920 on board HMS *Caledon*, and was buried at the Royal Naval Cemetery at Haslar, Hampshire. Phthisis is more commonly known as pulmonary tuberculosis or consumption. His parents ran the Seaforth Hotel, at Havre de Pas, Jersey.

Officer's Steward 2nd Class (L/7203) Archibald Frank **Duvey,** aged 24, was serving on board HMS *Undine*, when he died on Thursday, 13 March 1919. He was buried at the Lyness Royal Naval Cemetery in Orkney, Scotland. His parents, Henry and Elvina Duvey, lived at Temple Crescent, 26 St Mark's Road, St Helier, Jersey.

Rifleman (860819) Albert Henry **Handford,** aged 25, was serving in the 33rd Battalion, London Regiment, which was only formed in June 1918 at Clacton-on-Sea, Essex, when he died on Friday, 10 December 1920. He is buried at the Mont-à-L'Abbé New Cemetery in St Helier, Jersey. He left a widow, Mabel Harriet Handford, who was living in St Helier.

Private (58523) A. **Pallot,** aged 25, of the 3rd Battalion, Essex Regiment, died on 14 February 1919. He was buried in the All Saints Churchyard,

Dovercourt, Essex. His parents, George and Elizabeth Pallot, lived at 61 Trinity Square, St Helier, Jersey.

Private (G/35503) Walter **Moss,** aged 31, of the 3rd Battalion, Sussex Regiment, died on 28 February 1919. He was buried at Earlsfield Cemetery, Wandsworth. He was a married man and before enlisting in the Army, had lived with his wife at 5 Waterloo Street, St Helier, Jersey.

Private (108134) Philip Edward **Mauger,** aged 26 was serving with the Machine Gun Corps (Infantry) when he died on Sunday, 2 March 1919. He was buried at St Ouen's Churchyard, Jersey. A married man, his widow, Florence, was living at La Fosse-au-Bois, St Ouen, Jersey, after the war.

Captain Henry B. **Round,** aged 59, of the 49th Battalion, Canadian Infantry 'died of sickness' on Friday, 1 July 1921. He is buried at the Edmonton Cemetery, Alberta, Canada. Although before the war he was living in Quesnel, Canada, his mother, Mary, was living at 48 Eagle Terrace, St Helier, Jersey.

Captain Horace A. **Langford,** aged 67, was serving with the British Columbia Mounted Rifles, when he died of an unspecified sickness on 27 May 1920. Although having been living in Vancouver, Canada before the war, his parents were living in Jersey. Horace was buried in the Mountain View Cemetery, Vancouver, British Columbia.

Second Lieutenant John Fortescue **Briard** of the 35th Sikhs, Indian Army, had been awarded the Indian General Service Medal for service in Afghanistan. He died on 15 October 1919 of sickness after he was wounded during fighting in the Khyber Pass. His name is commemorated on the Delhi Memorial, India. His mother lived at Bulwark House, St Aubin, Jersey.

Captain Coutart-de-Butts **Taylor** of the Royal Irish Rifles died on 24 December 1918 of wounds received during fighting at Mormal Woods on 4 November 1918. The last major British offensive of the First World War, the Battle of the Sambre began on 4 November 1918, when seventeen divisions of the British Army attacked German defensive positions that were spread out along a 40-mile front. The intention was to deliver the Germans a decisive blow, which would finally force their surrender and an end to the war. Taylor had previously served as Serjeant 59747 C. Collins in the 17th Battalion, Welsh Fusiliers. It was during this period of service that he was awarded a Military Medal. He was a married man. His wife, Lilian Florence Blunden Taylor, lived at Clifton, Jersey.

Driver (91296) Desire **Pasquier,** aged 22, of the 172nd Brigade, Royal Field Artillery, died on Thursday, 19 December 1918. He is buried at the Kantara War Memorial Cemetery in Egypt. His mother, Augustine Mocquet, lived at The Brecque, Alderney, Channel Islands.

Sapper (250202) Ernest R. **Squires,** aged 21, was serving in the Royal Engineers when he died on Thursday, 9 June 1921. He was buried in St Anne's Churchyard, Alderney.

Horace A Langford aged 65.

Gunner (192300) Harold J. **Squires,** aged 20 years of the 2nd/1st SARB, Royal Garrison Artillery died of his wounds (Gas) on 24 March 1919, and was buried at the Bear Road Cemetery, Brighton. His parents, Richard and Elizabeth Squires, lived at Lower High Street, Alderney, with their two younger children, and Richard earned a living as a worker at a local quarry. The 1911 Channel Islands Census showed the family as living at Rocquettes, Alderney.

Horace A Langford grave stone.

Gunner Norman Wilfred **Sharp,** aged 18, of 3rd Battery, C Reserve Brigade, Royal Field Artillery died on Friday, 21 February 1919. He is buried at the Aldershot Military Cemetery in Hampshire. Prior to enlisting he lived with his parents, Archibald and Minnie Sharp, of Manez, Alderney.

Engine Room Artificer, 4th Class Thomas Philip **Mitchell,** aged 22, served at HMS *Columbine*, which was a 1917 purpose-built torpedo boat destroyer depot, at Port Edgar, Queensferry. He died on Monday, 24 January 1921 and was buried at the Douglas Bank Cemetery in Dunfermline, Scotland. His mother, Laura Mitchell, lived at Portland House, Alderney.

Private (7661) Helier **Carre,** aged 18, of the Royal Guernsey Light Infantry, died of pneumonia and the flu at Fort George Military Hospital, on 13 November 1918, just two days after the signing of the Armistice. He is buried in the Churchyard of St Peter's Church on Sark. Prior to enlisting in the Army, he had been a fisherman and lived with his parents, Helier and Harriet Carre, at La Colinette, Sark.

Conclusion

With the war finally over and people trying to get back to some kind of normality, the postwar years in the Channel Islands were not straight forward. There was an enormous shift on the social ladder, with most people expecting a better world for themselves and their families. With the suffering and loss, there needed to be something tangible to show for their collective effort over the years of the war. If this wasn't to be the case, people would for ever more be asking what it had all been for.

As with all communities throughout Great Britain the signing of the Armistice and the joy of victory over Germany and her allies, was tinged with sadness as the cost in the loss of human life was taken in to account. Many men returned from the war totally different to how they had been when they left. Some had experienced horrible sights that would haunt them for the rest of their lives, things that they would never talk of ever again. Some had had to do terrible things just to survive, which for god-fearing men was difficult to live with. Some returned to find loved ones changed and relationships broken. Having returned home they wanted their jobs back, for some that wasn't to be, which was hard to take when all they had done was answer the call to arms and to fight for their country.

There were some who had to move away and start all over again, never to return to their beloved Channel Islands. For each man it was different, all had slightly different experiences, had to deal with things in their own way. There were those who turned to drink to blot out their memories, whilst others were aggressive and turned to violence as they struggled to come to terms with how it was they had survived whilst many of their friends had been killed.

Overall, I believe the Allied victory in the First World War was a price worth paying, but I never had to fight in it and both my grandfathers survived and made it home. For families who lost loved ones, and for wives in particular who lost husbands, sons, and in some cases, both, they might just have a slightly different take on the matter.

As for the book, I hope you have enjoyed my ramblings. I have tried to balance the story of the First World War so as to include all of the Channel Islands, although I appreciate there is bound to be information not included that some might feel should have been. In a book such as this where it attempts to incorporate information from such a wide spectrum, sometimes it is just as difficult to determine what should be left out as much as what one eventually decides to include. Either way, I hope it has shed some light on the Channel Islands at war.

Sources

Wikipedia
Victoria College, Jersey
www.britishnewspaperarchive.com
www.cwgc.com
www.ancestry.co.uk
www.wartimememoriesproject.com
www.penarthnews.wordpress.com
www.theislandwiki.org
www.1914-1918.invisionzone.com
www.naval-history.org
www.nationaltrust.org.uk
www.epsomandewellhistoryexplorer.org.uk
www.bbc.co.uk
www.thisismoney.co.uk
www.greatwarci.net
www.submerged.co.uk
www.thevintagenews.com
www.redcross.org.uk
www.firstworldwar.com

Index